THE
POLITICIANS:
1945-1960

THE
POLITICIANS:

1945-1960

BOOTH MOONEY

J. B. LIPPINCOTT COMPANY

Philadelphia and New York

This book is dedicated to
THE POLITICIANS
from county courthouse to White House, from statehouse to Capitol Hill, who talked and permitted me to listen, who performed while I watched; nearly all of whom I liked, many of whom I respected, and some of whom I deeply admired;

and to
BETTY, TED AND JOAN
who, not altogether sharing my feeling about politicians, were tolerant of my obsession.

AUTHOR'S NOTE

When I went to work in my teens as a reporter—in fact *the* reporter—for a small-town weekly newspaper in Texas, I quickly learned that the most likely source of news was the county courthouse. Accordingly I spent much time there, and even now, some thirty-five years later, I recall vividly the fascination exerted over me by the sayings and doings of the country-type politicians I encountered.

Since then I have seen many politicians in action on local, state and national levels. The fascination has persisted, which explains why this book came to be written.

The book itself represents an attempt to tell the story of the principal national political figures who shaped the course of the United States government in the years 1945–1960. This period, it seems to me, stands apart in American political history, beginning as it did with the death of the father of the New Deal and ending with the election as President of a man who, for a time at least, brought a new quality to the American government.

The politicians dealt with in these pages were human beings

as well as public figures. They were men who ate (often at the expense of others), drank (sometimes too much), played (less, perhaps, than most men), joked with one another in the peculiar language of their profession, told off-color stories, worried about the state of the nation and the fact that their jobs allowed them to spend too little time with their families, thought constantly (because they had to) about the next election; men who worked hard—not always with wisdom or in the right direction but most often honestly and to the utmost of their varying abilities; men humble and arrogant, vain and modest, crude and polished, worldly wise and provincial—men, in short, possessed of all the customary human self-contradictions but in magnified form because they *were* politicians and therefore to a degree histrionic by nature.

In seeking to broaden my knowledge of these men and the events with which they were concerned I consulted many sources, including those listed in the Bibliography. I talked with many old Washington hands, and I am deeply grateful to them for the candor with which they spoke; I respect their wish that they remain anonymous. During the last half of the period covered I was involved, at times intimately involved, with some aspects of the Washington political scene, and I have used my notes and memories of those years to aid me in the preparation of this narrative.

Since it *is* a narrative, which I can only hope, with whatever modesty an author is able to summon, will be of some value to future historians, I have forgone the use of footnotes and other scholarly appurtenances. However, the book is fact (with, admittedly, some opinion), not fiction, and must stand or fall on that basis.

BOOTH MOONEY

Washington, D.C.

CONTENTS

	Author's Note	vii
1945	Changing of the Guard	1
1946	Man of His Own, with His Own Problems	23
1947	Robert A. Taft's Year	41
1948	Harry Truman's Year—at Last	60
1949	A Mixed Bag	83
1950 -51	Everything Coming Loose	101
1952	The General's Year	128
1953	New Boys in Town	159
1954	Spring Forward, Fall Back	186
1955	Lyndon Johnson's Year	213
1956	Encore, More or Less	238
1957	Battles, Phony and Real	255
1958	Ike's Decline and Adams' Fall	278
1959	Some Sounds and Fury	298
1960	John F. Kennedy's Year	320
	Bibliography	353
	Index	359

THE
POLITICIANS:
1945-1960

1945

CHANGING OF THE GUARD

When news of President Franklin Delano Roosevelt's death in Warm Springs, Georgia, at age sixty-three from a cerebral hemorrhage was flashed to the world in the early evening of April 12, 1945, officers at the Rome, New York, Army Air Field were gathering at the well-appointed officers' club for the monthly "Wing Ding," a stag social affair ordained by the commanding officer of the base. The armies of the United States were at the gates of Berlin and her fleets off the shores of Japan's home islands. Note was not made of this fact by the base commanding officer, a Regular Army man by way of Virginia Military Institute, as he took the microphone of the clubhouse's communications system to announce, in fittingly solemn tones, the President's death. Shortly afterward, made candid by bourbon, the colonel was heard to tell a group of his officers, "By God, it'll be a relief not to have to call that son of a bitch my commander-in-chief." In the men's room of the club, a young first lieutenant angrily brushed tears from his eyes and muttered, "There'll never be another like him. Never!"

Throughout the United States and around the world, American servicemen, millions of whom could but dimly remember a time when Roosevelt was not President of the United States, received the news with shocked incredulity.

In Detroit, a dazed housewife told a newsman, "It doesn't seem possible. It seems to me that he will be back on the radio tomorrow, reassuring us that it was all a mistake."

In the city of Washington, in a cluttered office on the fifth floor of the Old House Office Building on Capitol Hill, a secretary said in anguish to her boss, an obscure young Texas congressman named Lyndon Johnson, "Who is there now? Who is there for the country?" "Why, honey," said the congressman, "there's Truman."

There *was* Truman: Harry S Truman of Missouri.

It might well have been someone else. Although Roosevelt had dominated the American political scene since his election in 1932, other ambitious politicians waited restlessly in the wings. Truman was vice-president of the United States only because at the 1944 Democratic national convention the forces of organized labor would not accept James F. Byrnes of South Carolina and southern Democrats refused to take Henry Wallace for a second term.

During most of the nation's history the vice-presidency had been held by hack politicians, a term that in April of 1945 seemed accurately to describe Harry S Truman.

Truman had been on the political scene in a small way since 1922 when, under the sponsorship of the powerful Missouri political machine headed by Tom Pendergast, he was elected county judge (an administrative rather than a judicial post) of the eastern district of Jackson County. When he ran for re-election two years later, he was defeated, but in 1926, again with machine support, he was elected chief county judge. He showed a natural aptitude for county-courthouse politics and might contentedly have spent the remainder of his life in that milieu if Pendergast had not decided in 1934 that his protégé should go to the United States Senate. The fifty-year-old Missourian found a happy home in Washington. Many of his fellow senators also were graduates of the courthouse school of politics. Truman hobnobbed with them in the cloakroom, voted loyally for the New Deal measures that continued to flow from the White House, and did nothing to make himself stand out from the crowd. He wanted to stay in the Senate. He had to fight hard for re-election. The backing of the Pendergast machine was not what it had been, its sachem having pleaded guilty to a charge of not paying income tax on a large bribe he had accepted from an insurance company. Despite Truman's New Deal voting record, Roosevelt favored his primary election opponent, Missouri Governor Lloyd Stark.

In the face of this bleak picture, Truman set out to win. He called for help. Several of his Senate friends journeyed to Missouri to speak on his behalf, among them Lewis Schwellenbach of Washington State, Sherman Minton of Indiana, and the ever-obliging Alben Barkley of Kentucky. Another senator, Burton K. Wheeler, the plain-spoken maverick from Montana, lined up the railroad brotherhoods for Truman. Among Missourians who rallied to his side in the name of personal friendship were John Snyder, a St. Louis banker, and Harry Vaughan, both of whom were Truman buddies in his National Guard outfit. Robert E. Hannegan, powerful Democratic leader in St. Louis, announced his support for Truman, the *quid pro quo* being Truman's backing of Hannegan's candidate for governor. All these men were to play important roles in Truman's future, and he in theirs.

Truman won, although just barely. Yet he returned to Washington at the beginning of the Seventy-seventh Congress with new zest for his job. This time he did not owe his election to the smooth workings of a political machine, though

3

he had the support of its fragments. His campaign had been organized, fought and won—with the help, he would have been the first to say, of faithful friends—by himself. He was his own man as the junior senator from Missouri and he gloried in the knowledge.

He became chairman of a special committee to investigate the national defense program, a watchdog panel that, according to Truman's estimate, saved the government $15 billion by keeping a sharp nonpartisan eye on the conduct of war production plants. This was a noteworthy achievement, but it hardly drew national attention. Only his congressional colleagues, a few men in the Roosevelt administration, and some Capitol Hill correspondents—in particular a studious, painstaking writer for United Press named George Reedy—knew how much his committee had done to keep defense contractors honest, or reasonably so.

Still, he was gaining some power within the Democratic party structure. He helped to get Bob Hannegan, his St. Louis backer, into the position of chairman of the Democratic National Committee. This was important. Hannegan, Committee Treasurer Ed Pauley, Bronx Democratic Boss Ed Flynn, and Edwin M. (Pa) Watson, Roosevelt's appointment secretary, were determined that Vice-President Henry Wallace should not be nominated for a second term. Wallace had a bad press, and they were convinced he would be a drag on the ticket when Roosevelt sought a fourth term. George Allen, the Mississippi Democrat and insurance-company executive who had come to Washington to make a career as much more than the court jester he seemed to Roosevelt, organized the group's efforts months before the national convention.

Roosevelt wanted Wallace, but not urgently. He indicated that either Truman or Supreme Court Justice William O. Douglas would be acceptable. Truman himself issued a statement before the convention that he did not want the vice-presidency. He had promised to nominate Byrnes, former senator and former Supreme Court Justice. But in the end his own name was placed in nomination. According to a later observation by Alben Barkley, who had hoped to be the second man on the ticket, "Mr. Truman's candidacy was virtually stage-managed from the convention platform by Chairman Hannegan."

During the less than three months that he served as vicepresident, Truman did not find himself in the inner circles of the Roosevelt administration. To the men around the President he was a nonentity, a machine politician from a Midwestern state. Roosevelt himself largely ignored him.

Significantly, no policy maker from the administration was present at the small, informal gathering in Speaker Sam Rayburn's private room in the basement of the House wing of the Capitol from which Truman was summoned to the White House late in the afternoon of April 12. Truman had darted over as the Senate adjourned for the day to have a drink with Rayburn and other kindred souls such as House Parliamentarian Lew Deschler, New York *Times* correspondent William S. White (like Rayburn, a Texan), and James M. Barnes, a former House member from Illinois. Their purpose was to enjoy an hour of conviviality and the political talk on which they thrived.

Before they could settle down, Truman was called by telephone to come immediately to the White House. He reached there about 5:45 P.M. and was told by Mrs. Roosevelt, "The President is dead."

After exchanging a few words with Mrs. Roosevelt, Truman telephoned his wife at their modest five-room apartment on Connecticut Avenue. She received in tears what he had to say, but she had composed herself by the time a car arrived to transport her and the Truman daughter, twenty-one-year-old Margaret, to the White House. There, in the green-walled

Cabinet room, at 7:09 P.M., Justice Harlan Stone administered the oath of office to Harry S Truman.

John Adams, the first vice-president, had described the job as "the most insignificant that ever invention of man contrived," but added: "I am vice-president. In this I am nothing but I may be everything."

Harry Truman suddenly had become everything. Full realization of the change came to him slowly.

* * *

The first official document Truman signed on his first full day as President was the proclamation of Roosevelt's death. The fact of death was evident, but the spirit of the late President continued to dominate the house at 1600 Pennsylvania Avenue where he had lived so long. Truman confessed that it gave him a strange feeling to sign his name as President. Others shared the feeling.

Two days after he assumed the nation's highest office Truman appointed his old banker friend, John Snyder, as Federal Loan Administrator to replace Fred M. Vinson, the former Kentucky senator who had become Director of War Mobilization. He telephoned Jesse Jones, the crusty, glacial-eyed Texan who had headed the Depression-born Reconstruction Finance Corporation, to tell him that "the President" had made the appointment. Jones at once asked, "Did he make that appointment before he died?" "No," Truman replied, "he made it just now."

Truman understood Jones's reaction. He himself had trouble remembering that *he* was the President. In his first address to Congress he started speaking without being formally presented, forgetting that protocol for such occasions demands that the presidential address be preceded by the Speaker of the House intoning, "The President of the United States." Rayburn, behind him on the rostrum, whispered, "Just a minute, Harry," and spoke the requisite words.

Later that day the new President wrote his mother and sister in Independence, Missouri—"Dear Mamma & Mary"—about his talk before Congress. "It seemed to go over all right from the ovation I received," he reported. "Things have gone so well that I am almost as scared as I was Thursday when Mrs. R. told me what had happened. Maybe it will come out all right." A few days later, in another letter, he informed them with a touch of awe: "It has been necessary to talk to all the people you read about—Byrnes, Hopkins, Baruch, Marshall, King, Leahy, and all the Cabinet collectively and one at a time."

In those early days of his presidency, Truman spoke frequently to friends about his "unfitness" and "inadequacy" for the job. Such comments inevitably got into the newspapers. Some of his friends thought he was speaking much too freely in a way that could only do him harm. Rayburn and Barkley, who had been on the Washington scene since 1913 when they both entered the House of Representatives, separately urged him to stop talking that way.

"Have confidence in yourself," Barkley advised. "If you don't, the people will lose confidence in you." Rayburn went to see his old friend ("because," he said, "I wanted to help the fellow") and expostulated with the President for his tendency to "shoot from the hip" in making statements without any thought for how they would look in print. Rayburn also told him, "Your biggest hazard is in this White House." Some of the people there, he said, "are going to try to do to you what they've tried to do to every President since I've been here." And the Speaker explained bluntly: "They're going to try to build a fence around you, and in building that fence around you they will be keeping the very people away from seeing you that you should see."

Truman was conscious of this danger. He knew also that some members both of the Cabinet and the White House staff he had inherited regarded him with caution and suspicion. To

Jonathan Daniels, the North Carolina newsman who was Roosevelt's press secretary when he died, Truman seemed on his first day in the President's office "almost sacrilegiously small." Of that "moment of actual succession," Daniels wrote later, "I remember that he swung around in the President's chair as if he were testing it, more uncertain than even I was about its size." As for the Cabinet and old New Dealers in general, most of them knew in their hearts that they were better qualified to be President than the nondescript little man from Missouri.

Nevertheless, although Truman continued to maintain his attitude of humility for some time, he was moving to assume the powers that belonged to the presidency, regardless of whether the man who held that office came to it by choice of the people or, as some of the Roosevelt administration hold-overs sneered, by accident.

On the evening he took the presidential oath of office, Truman called a meeting of the Cabinet to ask its members to stay with him. But he knew and members of the Cabinet understood that any President must eventually have advisers of his own choice.

The English term "cabinet" had been used in the United States government as early as 1793 to describe George Washington's principal officers as a body of advisers. Although no such body is authorized in the Federal Constitution, long before Truman's time the Cabinet had come to consist of the department secretaries appointed by the President, subject to confirmation by the Senate. Charles G. Dawes, Coolidge's vice-president, was fond of saying, "The members of the Cabinet are a President's natural enemies," and the truth of this could be especially marked if they had not been appointed by him. In their departments, the secretaries had authority. In the Cabinet, they were advisers. The President was free to accept or to reject their advice or, for that matter, to listen to it without committing himself. He was also free to ask whenever he wished for a Cabinet member's resignation. Truman was to request or demand several in due time. When he took office, he also asked the Roosevelt staff to stay. Some lingered on for a while, but the new President immediately started bringing in men of his own.

His National Guard and political friend, Harry Vaughan, was already on hand. He had been brought to Washington by Truman as an office assistant after his 1940 victory. When he became vice-president, Truman made Vaughan his military aide, thereby becoming the first vice-president to have such a functionary on his staff. They were pals. Now he moved his friend into the White House as military aide to the President.

Other Missourians were summoned to service. Charlie Ross, who had gone to school with Truman, left his post as Washington correspondent for the St. Louis *Post-Dispatch* to become press secretary. Commodore Jake Vardaman, former St. Louis banker, was named the President's naval aide. Matt Connelly, who had served on the investigating staff of Truman's Senate subcommittee, became appointments secretary; he, too, was from Missouri.

Not a Missourian, but very much in evidence around the White House, was the ebullient George Allen. This native Mississippian had come to Washington in 1929 after experience as a chamber of commerce employee in Indiana and Kentucky and as a hotel man in Chicago. Now, in 1945, he was a professional Democrat and a professional member of corporate boards of directors. A big burly man with a wide grin on his full face and a large hat cocked on the back of his head, Allen easily made people laugh but at the same time had a hard appreciation of political realities. Roosevelt had appointed him one of three District of Columbia commissioners, in which post, Allen later reported with gay insouciance, "I served with great distinction as one-third of a mayor of

Washington." Truman was to name him one of the five directors of the Reconstruction Finance Corporation. Meanwhile, as the new President took over the reins of office, Allen was in the White House early and late.

Eddie McKim, another National Guard buddy, came up from Missouri to become chief White House secretary, but quickly proved to be spectacularly unfitted for the job. In his first week he came upon a group of White House stenographers engaged in typing replies to the thousands of messages of sympathy that had been sent to Mrs. Roosevelt. "So this is 'My Day!'" cried McKim, referring to the former First Lady's newspaper column. "Mrs. Roosevelt is no longer riding the gravy train," he informed the startled typists, ordering them to stop their work. But it was resumed after Bess Truman heard about the incident and complained to her husband. McKim was soon removed from the White House to the safety of a berth with the Federal Loan Administration.

Truman was unvaryingly considerate of Mrs. Roosevelt. He told her to take all the time she needed about moving out of the White House. The Trumans left their Connecticut Avenue apartment to live in Blair House, across the street from the Executive Mansion, and stayed there for almost a month after Roosevelt's death. They took up residence in the White House the night before Germany surrendered to the Allies. Early on the day of victory Truman noted in a letter to his mother, "I am sixty-one this morning and I slept in the President's room in the White House last night."

As the war with Germany roared to an end, representatives of the United States and her Allies were meeting in San Francisco to hammer out the organization of the United Nations. This conference, planned before Roosevelt's death, opened April 25 and lasted for nine weeks.

Secretary of State Edward R. Stettinius, Jr., was chairman of the United States delegation, although he played no more than his usual figurehead role. Key members of the delegation were Senator Tom Connally of Texas, who in appearance and manner was the prototype of what a member of the United States Senate should be, and Senator Arthur Vandenberg of Michigan, who had been converted from isolationism to internationalism by the war and the pretty wife of a foreign diplomat who lived next door to the Vandenbergs in Washington. Connally and Vandenberg were, respectively, chairman and ranking minority member of the Senate Foreign Relations Committee.

Others on the delegation were Representative Sol Bloom of New York, chairman of the House Foreign Relations Committee, and Charles A. Eaton of New Jersey, ranking minority member; Harold E. Stassen, former governor of Minnesota, just back from Navy service in the Pacific, and Dean Virginia Gildersleeve of Barnard College. They had been appointed by Roosevelt. Truman saw no reason to change the membership.

These men and this woman, working with representatives of other nations, undertook the task of welding together an organization designed to insure lasting peace in the world. Their task was not easy.

Free-world illusions regarding the postwar intentions of Soviet Russia were largely gone. In the very month that the conference began, Averell Harriman, U.S. ambassador to Russia, cabled the State Department, "We must realize that the Soviet program is the establishment of totalitarianism, ending liberty and democracy as we know and respect it." Later in the month he came to Washington to report at greater length to the new President, emphasizing the expansionist spirit of the Soviet Union.

Yet it was necessary to work with Russia in creating the United Nations Organization. Truman, who kept in close touch with Connally and Vandenberg, urged that there be no yielding on major issues, but suggested compromise on minor points if necessary to prevent a deadlock.

In the end, compromises had to be made on some major issues as well as numerous lesser ones. Formulation of a perfect document would have been impossible, considering the intransigence of the Russian delegation and the gap that existed between communist ideology and the democratic system. The Charter that finally emerged after days and weeks of sometimes bitter wrangling was perhaps the best that could be hoped for.

Truman flew to San Francisco for the signing of the Charter by member nations late in June and addressed the final session of the conference. "Under this document," he said, "we have good reason to expect the framing of an international bill of rights. . . . With this Charter the world can begin to look forward to the time when all worthy human beings may be permitted to live decently as free people."

It was a brave hope. Variations on the theme were sounded as the Senate ratified the UN Charter on July 28 by a vote of 89 to 2.

As vice-president, Truman had known little if any more than the average newspaper reader about the United States' relations with her Allies in the war and plans for postwar policy. He had no idea what had gone on when Roosevelt, shortly after his fourth inauguration, met at Yalta in the Crimea with Winston Churchill and Joseph Stalin. He had not been told about the Manhattan Project for building the atomic bomb.

His ignorance was rapidly remedied during his first weeks in office. He studied State Department documents and was briefed constantly by experts in foreign policy. So he was not unprepared for a meeting in July at Potsdam with Stalin and Churchill to discuss a surrender ultimatum addressed to Japan and to seek adjustment of vexatious territorial problems already rising in Europe. On the eve of his departure from Washington he wrote "Mamma and Mary" in Independence, "I have a brief case all filled up with information on past conferences and suggestions on what I'm to do and say."

Truman's preoccupation with international events during this period did not keep him from making sweeping changes in his Cabinet. He had determined on some of these within hours after becoming President. Several Cabinet members told him they wanted to leave as soon as convenient for him. But others had no desire at all to depart.

The first change Truman decided on, although not the first to be announced, was the replacement of Stettinius as Secretary of State by James F. Byrnes. Even as he returned from Roosevelt's funeral service at Hyde Park, accompanied by Byrnes, he told the South Carolinian he wanted him for the post—but not until after the UN organization meeting in San Francisco. When George Allen went to San Francisco to make advance preparations for Truman's speech opening the conference, he was instructed to sound out Stettinius about resigning. Stettinius was not happy about the suggestion, but dutifully agreed to resign at the end of the San Francisco meeting.

Jimmy Byrnes, born on the wrong side of town in Charleston, South Carolina, learned politics as a court reporter. He served in the House of Representatives fourteen years, in the Senate ten years, and as Supreme Court Justice for sixteen months. He left the Court at Roosevelt's request to take up wartime duties as economic stabilizer and war mobilizer. Truman and Byrnes, whose courtly southern manner was the cloak for a sharp political mind and a marked regard for his own abilities, had been friends since 1940. Byrnes was instrumental in getting Bernard M. Baruch, the New York financier who had an elaborate summer home in South Carolina, interested in contributing to Truman's campaign fund in his hard primary fight that year. He regarded himself, and perhaps rightly so, as both Truman's benefactor and his mentor. He was never quite able to forget that except for the vagaries of a national political convention he, rather than Truman, would be occupying the White House. But he was a knowledgeable and able Secretary of State during a critical time.

Postmaster General Frank C. Walker told Truman he had wanted for some time to quit, and his resignation was accepted. Bob Hannegan, who had come from St. Louis to be Commissioner of Internal Revenue, was named to replace him —a political man for a traditionally political office.

Francis Biddle, Roosevelt's last Attorney General, received the news of his upcoming resignation in a telephone call from Steve Early, who had been a White House secretary under Roosevelt and was carrying on with Truman. Since Early made the call, Truman was provided with a technical excuse for denying—as he later did deny—that he had asked the Attorney General to resign. But Early's message was wholly explicit: Biddle's resignation was accepted as of "day after tomorrow."

Biddle, true Philadelphia lawyer that he was, protested. He said he had expected the message but thought the President should be courteous enough to make the request personally. Early, agreeing, arranged for him to come to the White House that day to present his resignation. After the forced amenities were over, Biddle ventured to ask the name of his successor. Truman replied that he planned to appoint Tom Clark, a Texas lawyer then serving as head of the Justice Department's criminal division. Biddle strongly disapproved and said so, but Truman made the appointment anyway.

No unpleasantness attended the leave-taking of Frances Perkins as Secretary of Labor and Claude R. Wickard as Secretary of Agriculture. Miss Perkins, the first woman to serve in any President's Cabinet, told Truman early that she felt

14

she must leave to take a long-needed rest. Wickard asked to be placed at the head of the Rural Electrification Administration, and Truman acceded to this request. Wickard was succeeded by Representative Clinton P. Anderson of New Mexico. The Labor post went to Lewis Schwellenbach, who had been appointed a federal judge in late 1940 after one term in the Senate.

The departure of Henry Morgenthau as Secretary of the Treasury was both abrupt and acrimonious. Morgenthau by no means restricted himself to the official duties of his position. He was the author of a fantastic plan to reduce postwar Germany to a pastoral state by wiping out all its industry. In the fall of 1944, Morgenthau attended a Quebec meeting of Roosevelt, Churchill and Mackenzie King to present his plan. He succeeded in gaining Roosevelt's approval, even though the State Department vigorously objected.

Truman soon let it be known that the Morgenthau Plan was in the discard. Morgenthau would not accept the decision. Shortly before the President went to Potsdam in July, the Treasury Secretary visited the White House to ask if he could attend the conference. Truman coldly said he was more needed in the United States than at Potsdam. Morgenthau persisted. He added that if the President would not permit him to go he would have to resign from the Cabinet.

"All right," Truman said, "if that's the way you feel, I'll accept your resignation right now."

Fred Vinson of Kentucky left his position as Director of War Mobilization and Reconversion to become Secretary of the Treasury. The choice was a good one. During long service in the House of Representatives, Vinson had been chairman of the tax subcommittee of the powerful Ways and Means Committee. He understood financial matters, including tax policy, and was an excellent administrator.

By the middle of July, only four Roosevelt appointees re-

15

mained in the Cabinet: Henry Wallace, Commerce; Harold L. Ickes, Interior; James V. Forrestal, Navy, and Henry L. Stimson, War. In that month another link with the past was severed when the ailing Harry Hopkins, faithful servant of Roosevelt and helpful in many ways to Truman, resigned.

Three months after the death of Roosevelt his administration also was dead.

Yet on the day Japan surrendered, after the atomic bombing of Hiroshima and Nagasaki, it was Harry Truman's thought to telephone Mrs. Roosevelt to say that at this time of triumph for the nation he wished it had been President Roosevelt, not himself, who gave the message of the war's end to the American people.

* * *

A week after Truman became President, Speaker Sam Rayburn took advantage of a blanket invitation to drop in at the White House whenever he wished. He came down from Capitol Hill bearing a note just received from his younger brother Dick, back in Fannin County, Texas. He wanted to show the short note to the President.

"Sensible men will not walk the streets again looking for bread for their families," Dick Rayburn had written. "Neither will veterans of World War II peddle apples. That is just what a certain group of people will try to bring this country back to. They are beginning to say 'we are going conservative' now. So to you and President Truman don't let the wolves run away again. If you do, God pity us."

Truman read the note and sat back holding it in his hand for a moment.

"What will I tell my brother?" Rayburn asked.

The President looked straight at the Speaker through the thick glasses that magnified his eyes. "Sam, you tell him not to worry," he said firmly. "Of course we've got to get this war over, but I will have a program ready. We're not going to go backward in this country."

Rayburn left the White House satisfied but not surprised. He was familiar with Truman's voting record in the Senate. The sixty-three-year-old Speaker had a strong vested interest in much of the important domestic legislation that had been enacted during Roosevelt's early years as President. At that time Rayburn was chairman of the powerful Interstate and Foreign Commerce Committee. He sponsored the Securities Act of 1933 and the railroad holding-company bill to correct some of the financial abuses that had brought on the depression. He pushed to passage measures creating the Securities and Exchange Commission to regulate the stock exchanges and the Federal Communications Commission to regulate the use of the air waves in the public interest. He fought hard and successfully for the Public Utility Holding Company Act in the face of a bitter and costly campaign against it. His sponsorship of such measures had made him Roosevelt's working partner in creating key portions of the New Deal.

Now, with Truman in the White House, Rayburn knew that many Americans, who remembered the gloomy and sometimes almost hopeless years of the Great Depression, shared the uneasy feeling expressed by his brother. Their uneasiness was deepened by the glad predictions of some newspaper columnists and editorial writers that a new era of conservatism in the federal government was at hand. Business tycoons chortled that organized labor would no longer ride high. Truman was not Roosevelt, they assured one another, and the New Deal that FDR himself had said must give way temporarily to Dr. Win the War would never return. Missouri friends of Truman spread the word that he was a "mid-

17

dle-of-the-road man" on political and economic issues except in matters involving party organization and patronage. They knew him less well than they thought.

Labor leaders were not overly concerned by the talk of Truman as a conservative. He had been nominated for vice-president because he was acceptable to labor as well as to the southern delegates at the 1944 Democratic convention. He was particularly strong with railroad union men. George Harrison, president of the Brotherhood of Railway Clerks, and David Robertson, who headed the Brotherhood of Locomotive Firemen and Enginemen, agreed that he was "the best friend labor ever had in the Senate."

Truman had started thinking about converting the economy back to a peacetime basis even before Rayburn came to him with the note from his brother. But international events moved too fast for him to plan a concrete program during his first few months in the presidency.

In July, coming back from the Potsdam Conference, he asked a traveling companion, Samuel I. Rosenman, Roosevelt's counsel and sometime speech writer who temporarily had stayed on in the White House, to start getting together material for a message to Congress on his domestic program. Then and there, Truman outlined the plans and policies he had in mind for future legislation.

As Rosenman took notes, he expressed surprise and pleasure at the nature of the President's planned program. He was among those who had been exercised about the widespread talk that the country would be "brought back to normal" under Truman's administration. But now it appeared that the President proposed to go forward with Roosevelt's own prewar concept of an "economic bill of rights" for Americans.

Truman, with a politician's sensitivity to the mood of the country, knew that an enormous restlessness was stirring among the people. Although the war with Japan was still to be ended, in Europe it was over and servicemen were beginning to come home. In July half a million of them were already back, with millions more to follow. They had to be absorbed into the work force.

Labor was eying this necessity with some mistrust. The question that agitated the thoughts of people in the war-production plants was whether there would be jobs enough for all when peace came. Their anxiety was expressed in a rising wave of strikes for such trivial reasons as late arrival of paychecks, prohibition of lunchtime checker games, and simply hot weather. The daily average of strikes was up from twenty before V-E Day to about forty, and rising, in aircraft-supply factories, slaughterhouses, synthetic-rubber plants, trucking firms—anywhere and everywhere.

Labor leaders warned that when the time came for shifting away from war production, jobless workers would be choosy; not just any old job would do. At a Los Angeles chamber of commerce meeting, CIO Boss Philip Connelly declaimed, inelegantly but forcefully, "Rosie the Riveter isn't going back to emptying slop jars."

Businessmen looked forward to getting free from production controls. Farmers, who had responded wholeheartedly to the necessity of boosting agricultural capacity during the war, worried about whether there would be postwar markets at fair prices for what they were capable of producing. Housewives dreamed wistfully of a future in which they would be able to go into the stores and buy as much beef and sugar as they wanted. Those of the populace who thought about such matters wondered if the country really had leadership beyond the military leadership provided by the generals and admirals. The man in the White House was still an unknown quantity to most Americans.

Truman hoped he could say something that would provide a focus to the national mood. He had planned to send his message to Congress soon after returning from Europe in July. The sudden end of the war with Japan caused a postponement. Near the end of August, however, he took up the matter again.

Rosenman provided him with a rough draft of the proposed message, and Truman worked over its revision for a week or more. He then called in several of his advisers and with them painstakingly went over the text point by point. Some of those he consulted, in particular the conservative banker John Snyder, considered many of its proposals far too liberal and urged that they be toned down or, in the case of several, eliminated altogether. Clark Clifford, a bright and persuasive young lawyer who had recently been brought into the White House via the Navy, joined Rosenman in urging retention of the message's twenty-one points as they were.

Truman listened to the various arguments advanced, but he had already made up his mind that there was little he wished to change. The message contained the essence of what eventually was to become known as his Fair Deal program. He sent it to Congress on September 6.

It was one of the longest messages from a President ever received by Congress, running to some sixteen thousand words. It immediately proved to be one of the most controversial.

In it, Truman stated that his administration would follow eight specific policies: Demobilize at the earliest possible time armed forces that were no longer needed; cancel and settle war contracts with dispatch; clear the war plants for early peacetime production; retain price and rent controls for the time being to prevent inflation; hold wages in line where increases would cause inflationary price rises; remove government controls wherever feasible in order to speed conversion and expansion of the economy; keep such controls as were necessary to prevent bottlenecks, shortages of material, and inflation; avoid rapid decreases in wage incomes or buying power.

The President proposed a long list of legislative measures to put these policies into effect. At a time when economists were almost unanimous in predicting widespread unemployment, he declared that every able-bodied American had a right to a job at fair pay and asked for passage of a "full employment act." He also wanted legislation to increase minimum wages and to extend unemployment compensation to workers not covered under the existing law.

There was something in the program for everybody: for farmers, an increase in agricultural crop supports; for urban dwellers and returning servicemen, private- and public-housing programs; for the aged, a national health program. Truman also asked for federal aid to education, increased social security payments, and power-development programs such as the Tennessee Valley Authority in a number of areas. And he proposed to make permanent the Fair Employment Practices Committee, designed to give job protection to minority workers, which had been set up during the war and was still in tenuous operation.

Harry Truman set great store by this message. To him, as he said, it symbolized the assumption of the presidency in his own right. "It was on this day and with this message," he wrote in his *Memoirs*, "that I first spelled out the details of the program of liberalism and progressivism which was to be the foundation of my administration."

Many regarded his proposals with less esteem than he did. The Truman message precipitated an immediate uproar in Congress and in the press. Old New Dealers were mostly surprised and gratified, although some groused among themselves that the new President did not and never would have the style of the old. Southern friends of Truman in the Senate drew back in consternation at his recommendation for a permanent Fair Employment Practices Committee. Joe Martin of Massachusetts, the Republican floor leader in the House of Representatives, gave his party's reaction: "Not even President Roosevelt ever asked as much in one sitting. The scenery is new and there is a little better decoration, and he does dish it out a little easier. But it is just a plain case of out-New Dealing the New Deal." Arthur Krock, respected and articulate chief of the New York *Times* bureau, wrote: "Congress accepts it as a fact that Mr. Truman has thrown in his lot with the spenders, the anti-economizers, the New Dealers, the organized labor pressure squads and the social-economists of whom Henry A. Wallace is the appointed spokesman."

And the stock market went up to the highest level it had reached in eight years.

Not much of what Truman asked for was given. The Seventy-ninth Congress did eventually pass a so-called full-employment bill, much amended and largely meaningless. After the adoption of one amendment pushed by the Republican stalwart in the Senate, Robert A. Taft, which declared that for any additional expenditures by the federal government after 1947 there must be new taxes to prevent any net increase in the national debt, Alben Barkley commented acidly that the bill "now guarantees everybody out of work the right to a job—if he can find one."

Most of Truman's requests were left for future action and as future political issues.

1946

MAN OF HIS OWN,
WITH HIS OWN PROBLEMS

Call Me Mister was a hit musical comedy on Broadway in 1946, and its title expressed precisely the heartfelt sentiments of the millions of American servicemen returning with eager anticipation to civilian life.

Nearly twelve million men—and women—were in uniform at the end of the war. Most of them wanted out, and as fast as possible. As soon as the fighting ended in Europe, pressure started on the government to "bring the boys home." Japan's surrender intensified the public clamor. The White House was inundated with urgent appeals from families of servicemen and petitions from various organizations. Telegrams and letters on behalf of individual members of the armed forces poured into congressional offices.

As the year began, the Army alone had discharged more than 4,750,000 men and women since the cessation of hostilities in Europe. The Navy, Marine Corps and Coast Guard had released an additional 1,750,000 personnel. Secretary of War Robert P. Patterson and Navy Secretary Forrestal were gravely concerned. They warned the President that rapid dismantling of the nation's war machine would weaken the strategic position of the United States in dealing with postwar tensions already evident throughout the world. Truman agreed with the service chiefs. The "getting out" program, he declare, had swung from demobilization to disintegration.

But the tide of public sentiment was too strong to be resisted. As spring came, demobilization of the civilian military forces was almost complete.

The veterans returned to a nation which had lost the last of its innocence at home and in its relationship to the rest of the world. The America of 1946 was a vastly different kind of country from the one that in the late 1930s had started getting ready for war after years of struggling through the Great Depression. The men so recently out of uniform were first bewildered, then often angered, by the changes.

The housing situation was catastrophic. Experts estimated that five million additional homes were needed at once. Not as many as a million had ever been built in one year before the war.

Jobs were another problem. Before the war ended, predictions had been freely made that in the early postwar period the number of unemployed persons in the nation might rise as high as eight million. At the beginning of 1946 the unemployment figure did stand at approximately two million. The law provided that an ex-serviceman who was employed when he entered service had a right to the same job on his return to civilian life. But a large number of young men had gone into service without ever having held a job. In other cases former jobs had simply vanished. Where they still existed, business managers could, if they wished, usually find ways to get around the law. Besides, a war-toughened sergeant, grown accustomed to barking commands, might not care to return to his former job as office boy.

Many of the ex-GIs opted out and applied for unemployment compensation. They were entitled to draw twenty dollars a week for a period of fifty-two weeks; they sardonically called themselves members of the "52-20 Club." They were waiting.

Former members of the armed forces were not alone in the necessity for making adjustments in this postwar period. Millions of men and women who stayed at home had known new experiences during the war and their lives would never be the same. Workers had moved about all over the country to take war-production jobs at higher wages than they could have dreamed of earlier. Labor had become much more highly organized. The size, power and influence of the federal government had increased immeasurably.

Some families were driven apart when the wartime jobs and the flow of easy money came to a halt. Women found housekeeping a dull and unrewarding chore after the excitement of jobs they had taken to "help win the war."

Nearly everything in American life was different from what it had been. The politicians had to become different, too, although some of them came to acceptance of this fact slowly and with reluctance.

* * *

Harry Truman started the first full year of military peace with an address, broadcast to the nation, declaring war on the Seventy-ninth Congress.

After spending Christmas in Independence, he returned to Washington and soon was aboard the presidential yacht, the *Williamsburg*, for a four-day cruise down the Potomac River and on Chesapeake Bay. His traveling companions were Sam Rosenman, George Allen, and his labor adviser, John Steelman. During the four days the group worked out the speech the President was to give early in January.

Its theme was disappointment and anger, engendered by

congressional inaction on Truman's legislation program and by organized labor's bitter criticism of a plan he had advanced for a cooling-off period in labor-management disputes which he hoped would end the serious wave of strikes and threatened strikes. In his address to the nation he urged enactment of laws to put this plan in effect, demanded passage by Congress of a "real" full-employment bill, and called again for a permanent Fair Employment Practices Committee. And he appealed to the American people to put pressure on Congress on behalf of his program.

Truman had some reason for thinking the people would respond. Despite his bad press, a public-opinion survey made by *Fortune* Magazine at the end of 1945 had come up with the finding that 75.6 per cent of those included in the poll approved of the President's handling of foreign affairs, 58.9 per cent of his approach to home problems, and 64.7 per cent of his relations with Congress.

Perhaps the people participating in the survey did not understand the questions. About a hundred approving telegrams drifted into the White House the next day, a sharp contrast with the thousand or more that had usually poured in after a fireside chat by Roosevelt. Moreover, the President's urgent request that the people write their congressman about his program was largely ignored. This fighting speech, on which he had banked so heavily, drew no more than a passing ripple of attention.

Congress was not impressed and in fact Truman was at a marked disadvantage in making war on that body. The Democrats had a majority there, to be sure, but many of them, along with all Republicans, already were regarding this as a caretaker administration. They were not frightened by Truman's threats. After all, it was just "old Harry" talking. He had been one of them not long before—not very high on the totem pole either—and, as they knowingly told one another, he liked to sound off.

Congress revealed its attitude by starting the session with a twenty-four-day filibuster in the Senate against an effort by New Mexico's Dennis Chavez to force a vote on establishing the Fair Employment Practices Committee on a permanent basis. This weary, futile beginning was symptomatic of the entire session. The word "Congress" derives from the Latin *congressus*, a coming or walking together. But members of this Congress did little walking together and, for the most part, they did not walk at all with the President of the United States.

Along with his troubles with Congress the President had to deal with vexing personnel problems. Many of the able men who had come to Washington before and during the war were leaving government service. Replacements came, but they were mostly a different breed: lame-duck politicians from the courthouses, country bankers, business failures, men on the make. Many offered as their sole qualification for jobs in the administration the fact that they had known Truman, or claimed to have known him, "in the old days."

While New Dealers and conservatives remained sharply divided over the President's policies and programs, they were together in their opposition to "government by crony." They complained that "the Missouri gang" was taking over the executive branch of the government, that a cult of mediocrity had come into existence. Walter Lippmann wrote oracularly in his influential newspaper column that the men closest to Truman "do not have enough brains, and have practically none of the wisdom which comes from experience and education, to help him be President of the United States."

Truman's personnel difficulties extended to some of his inherited Cabinet members. An abrasive controversy with one of these early in the year grew out of his nomination of Edwin W. Pauley, a rich California oil man, as undersecretary of the Navy. The nomination was the first step in a plan to get Pauley in a position to succeed Forrestal as Navy Secretary when the latter resigned, as he had been wanting to do ever since the end of the war.

Pauley had unquestionably proved his value to the Democratic party. As treasurer of the National Committee between 1942 and 1944, he raised enough money to convert a substantial deficit into a surplus. Later he was reparations commissioner with the status of ambassador. He and Truman had long been close.

When his nomination was announced, some Republican members of Congress let it be known that they would give the proposed appointment more than cursory attention. Truman was not worried. He depended comfortably on the Democratic majority in the Senate. The President was not greatly concerned even when his (and Roosevelt's) Secretary of the Interior, Harold Ickes, told him he had been asked to appear before the Senate Naval Affairs Committee in connection with the appointment.

Ickes, a man possessed of incorruptible honesty and an incorrigible conviction that he was unique in having more of that quality than anyone else, told the committee of a talk with Pauley on the train coming back from the Roosevelt funeral. The conversation had to do with raising money for the Democratic party. Ickes testified that Pauley assured him he could get hundreds of thousands of dollars in contributions from oil men if the government would drop a plan to bring suit to gain federal title to the rich oil deposits in the tidelands off California and the Gulf Coast.

Pauley appeared before the committee to give his own sworn testimony. Senator William Tobey of New Hampshire, who fancied himself as a relentless inquisitor and who looked like one, put a direct question to the witness: "Did you ever tell Mr. Ickes that the filing of the government suit would be a political mistake—get this carefully, please—and that if you could assure California oil men that the suit would not be filed, you could raise several hundred thousand dollars in campaign contributions?"

"I did not!" Pauley cried. "I did not!"

In the face of this heated denial, Ickes came back the next day to tell the committee, with professed embarrassment, that Pauley's statement was "not accurate." Norman Littell, a former assistant attorney general, also appeared before the committee to state that the Californian had talked to him about dropping the suit. Pauley, he testified, had said, "These men have contributed to the campaign and they expect something for their money."

Truman, predictably, stood behind Pauley. He made his position clear at a news conference, snapping that Ickes "might be mistaken." A few days later he received a long letter from Ickes complaining that Truman's statement amounted to a vote of no confidence in him and that he had no choice but to resign. "It was the kind of letter," Truman commented, "sent by a man who is sure he is going to have his way if he threatens to quit."

This was not, of course, an effective approach to the stubborn tenant of the White House. Truman shot Ickes a note accepting his resignation effective the following day, although his Secretary of the Interior had indicated that he was willing to stay on the job for another six weeks to clear up matters pending in his department.

Recriminations followed. Ickes went on the radio to say that he could not stay in Truman's Cabinet and keep his self-respect. Truman retorted that Ickes would not dare to impugn the integrity of the President. Ickes came back defiantly, "I would dare to impugn the integrity of the Presi-

29

dent on any occasion that my country's welfare demanded it."

Finally, nobody won. The incident created such an uproar in Congress and in the press that Truman, albeit reluctantly and at Pauley's request, withdrew the nomination.

Another member of the holdover Cabinet departed in the early fall. Henry Agard Wallace had served nearly eight years as Roosevelt's Secretary of Agriculture before he became vice-president. After the 1944 election Roosevelt, feeling he owed the man something, appointed him Secretary of Commerce. It was an absurd choice for a position which is designed to provide a link between the federal government and the business community. The dreamy, mystic Wallace was far from having the confidence of businessmen, who regarded him as an impractical and left-leaning exponent of the welfare state. Opposition to his nomination was so heavy that Vice-President Truman, presiding over the Senate, had to break a tie vote to bring about Wallace's confirmation.

Uncomfortable and dissatisfied in the Commerce slot, Wallace broke the monotony by attempting to get himself up as a maker of United States foreign policy. This was unfortunate. His views did not coincide with those being officially expressed at the time by Byrnes at a meeting of the Council of Foreign Ministers in Paris. Wallace was opposed to what he called Byrnes' "Get tough with Russia" policy, and he said so at length in a speech at a Madison Square Garden pro-Soviet rally in New York City.

He had told the President about the speech in advance. He explained, according to Truman, that he proposed to say the United States "ought to look at the world through American eyes rather than through the eyes of a pro-British or rabidly anti-Russian press." Truman did not read the speech, but when asked at a news conference a few hours before Wallace spoke if it had his approval, he replied that it did.

After the speech was delivered, the reporters came to the President again. One of them pointed out that midway through it Wallace had interpolated the statement "When President Truman read these words, he said they represented the policy of this administration."

"That is correct," Truman said.

"Does that apply for just that paragraph or to the whole speech?" the newsman persisted.

"I approved the whole speech," replied the President.

Another reporter asked, "Do you regard Wallace's speech as a departure from Byrnes' policy."

"I do not," Truman retorted.

It was a classic example of his tendency, so deplored by wise old Sam Rayburn, to "shoot from the hip." "You don't *have* to give a direct answer to any and every question those buzzards throw at you," the Speaker repeatedly urged. But it was a Truman characteristic to hate the idea of appearing at a loss in dealing with the press, so he often talked fast and tried to get out of trouble later.

That is what happened in this case. Byrnes frigidly sent word from Paris that Wallace's speech undercut his work there. If Wallace stayed in the Cabinet, he declared, he would get out. Wallace came back to Washington and issued a statement that he would continue to strive for peace in the way he thought right. But in a meeting with the President he promised not to speak again on the subject until the Paris conference was over. They agreed on a statement for him to give the press. When he met with reporters as he left the White House, Wallace added to the statement and, carried away by the self-righteousness of the crusading ideologue, indicated that he expected to continue as before.

Connally and Vandenberg, arbiters of foreign policy in the Senate, issued statements of their own. The former voiced support of the official U.S. foreign policy. Vandenberg caustically observed that he wanted to cooperate with the administration but could work with only one Secretary of State at a time. The President was left in a wholly untenable position vis-à-vis his Secretary of Commerce.

Eight days after the sensation-making speech in New York, Truman called Wallace to the White House and asked for his resignation. Wallace agreed, without rancor, and one more old New Dealer was out of the administration.

Byrnes himself was not to be around much longer. Through the year Truman came increasingly to feel that his Secretary of State regarded himself as something of an independent entrepreneur in making foreign policy. He considered that Byrnes gave up too easily on vital points of difference between the United States and the Soviet Union. He resented the issuance of State Department communiqués of which he had no prior knowledge. He spoke bluntly to Byrnes, and relations between the two men became strained. In the middle of the year the proud South Carolinian told the President that because of poor health he must plan to resign. His resignation was deferred, however, until January of 1947.

Truman had known for months who his new Secretary of State would be: General of the Army George C. Marshall, wartime Chief of Staff. The President thought that Marshall might well be the greatest living American.

As for Byrnes, he noted bitterly and somewhat unrealistically, "He failed miserably as Secretary of State, and ran out on me when I needed him worst."

The comings and goings of men to and from the administration attracted widespread attention in the press. Much of the comment was unfavorable. "One has the feeling," editorialized the New York *Post*, "that a poorer and poorer cast is dealing desperately with a bigger and bigger story. Hopkins dead, Ickes gone, and their replacements are men like Pauley and George E. Allen." This was hardly fair. Ickes was in fact replaced by Julius A. Krug, an engineer who had made a good record with the Tennessee Valley Authority. As for Harry Hopkins, Truman now had at hand a man who would be to him almost what Hopkins had been to Roosevelt.

This was Clark M. Clifford, a tall, good-looking, forty-year-old lawyer who had been brought to Washington by Jake Vardaman. The two had become acquainted through a common interest in the Symphony and the Opera Guild in St. Louis. While Truman had summoned a number of Missourians to the White House, he did not even know Clifford when he became assistant naval aide in 1945. Besides, the lawyer was a native of Kansas, not Missouri.

After Vardaman was named to the Federal Reserve Board, his assistant moved up to become the President's naval aide. Accustomed before the war to the exciting life of a successful trial lawyer, Clifford soon became bored with the undemanding nature of his new job. He started giving a helping hand to Sam Rosenman in the preparation of Truman's speeches and messages. When Rosenman left the White House staff in mid-1946, Clifford succeeded him as special counsel to the President.

Soon he was seeing Truman more often than anyone except the presidential secretaries. He wrote speeches, exerted strong influence in forming domestic policy, and as a kind of unofficial chief of staff helped bring order to the often sadly uncoordinated operations of the Truman administration. Personable, persuasive and untiring, he frequently offset much of the conservative pressure that was brought on the President.

Clifford helped draft administration strategy for meeting several serious labor situations that came up in 1946. The first speech he wrote for Truman was concerned with one of these.

Two railroad unions had rejected presidential fact-finding recommendations for settling a dispute over wages and work rules. Eighteen of the unions involved were willing to accept a proposed compromise settlement. Two unions refused. Old friends among the railroad brotherhood leaders denounced Truman. A strike was called, taking 300,000 union members off their jobs and affecting most major lines. Truman went on the air with a speech, largely composed by Clifford, to announce that unless operation of the railroads was resumed at once, he would call on the Army to assist the Office of Defense Transportation in getting trains moving again.

The next day the President appeared before a joint session of Congress with a message proposing to draft into the armed forces "all workers who are on strike against their government." His reasoning was that, if the government took over the carriers, the strike would be against the nation itself.

Even as he prepared to address Congress, negotiations between union leaders and representatives of the operators were going on at the Statler Hotel in downtown Washington. John Steelman was with them.

Truman had started speaking when Clifford, stationed in the Speaker's office adjoining the House chamber, received a telephone call from Steelman. After hearing his terse report, Clifford scribbled a note—"Mr. President, agreement signed, strike over"—and gave it to Les Biffle, Secretary of the Senate, for delivery to Truman.

The President announced to Congress that the strike had been settled. He still wanted the legislation he had proposed, but he did not get it. His bill passed the House, but was stopped dead in the Senate by Robert A. Taft, the Ohio senator who, some thought, was always against labor. "I am not willing," said Taft with his usual bluntness, "to vote for a measure which provides that the President may be a dictator. It offends not only the Constitution but every basic principle for which the American Republic was established." Taft's dry, matter-of-fact demeanor gave no indication of the pleasure he must have experienced at being able to uphold the Constitution and oppose Truman on a single issue.

Throughout the year John L. Lewis, boss of the United Mine Workers, had been smoldering and rumbling like a far-from-extinct volcano. More than once he erupted.

In the spring he threatened to call a strike unless mine operators set up a welfare fund for the 400,000 bituminous coal miners. The fund was to be established and maintained by the operators paying into it a royalty on coal tonnage mined. Lewis himself would be solely in charge of the fund, a proposal at which the mine owners boggled. Truman invited the tough, shaggy-browed union official to the White House and won from him an agreement that negotiations would be conducted without a strike. But a few days later Lewis changed his mind and called a strike.

Truman, coldly angry, decreed that Lewis should never again enter the White House as long as he was President; he would not deal with a man who broke his word. After seven weeks he ordered the Department of the Interior to take over operation of the soft-coal mines. This put Secretary Krug in the position of representing the administration in dealing with the union and the mine operators. He was able to negotiate a contract which provided for joint control of the welfare fund instead of permitting Lewis alone to control it.

This agreement did not hold for even six months. On November 1 Lewis announced that the contract was at an end, and he issued a call for a strike later that month. When the miners walked off their jobs, Attorney General Clark went to court to get an injunction against Lewis and the union to force cancellation of the strike. Lewis roared defiance, but he was quickly brought into federal court. He himself was fined $10,000 and the United Mine Workers were fined $3.5 million (later reduced to $700,000). The miners were ordered back. It was a notable victory for the doughty little fighter in the White House.

Truman never forgave Lewis. In 1950, when a Colorado

state senator wrote him proposing that the head of the United Mine Workers be named ambassador to Russia, Truman replied that he wouldn't appoint Lewis dogcatcher.

Clark Clifford said later that the successful showdown with the powerful Lewis marked the moment when Truman finally and irreversibly moved out from the shadow of Roosevelt. "There was a big difference in the Old Man from then on," Clifford observed. "He was his own man at last."

* * *

"Had enough?" was the wickedly effective slogan of the Republican party in the 1946 congressional campaign.

"Had enough? Vote Republican!"

This insidious appeal to the widespread feeling of discontent and frustration came in the face of rosy economic statistics. The heavy postwar unemployment so authoritatively predicted had not materialized. Instead, employment in the United States was at a record high; fifty million people, including ten million veterans, had jobs. Farm income, business profits and dollar volume of industrial production were all at new peaks. So were income payments to individuals at $167 billion a year, and so was consumer spending at $126 billion a year. With factory wheels spinning to turn out products mostly unobtainable during the war, people were able to get new cars (by turning in old cars for giveaway allowances or paying a bonus), washing machines, refrigerators, radios, electric irons, automobile tires.

But living costs zoomed and real wages were reduced to their lowest point since shortly after the war began. Between April 1945 and the fall of 1946 take-home pay dropped by 8.5 per cent. Inflationary pressures were growing heavier.

The greatest cause of unquiet was none of these. Real anger was aroused among the people by shortages and continued rationing in one form or another of essential food products.

Price controls and rationing had been turned off and on during the year, but as the November elections approached, they were very much on. In the spring Truman, acting against the advice of such astute politicians as Rayburn and Barkley, had vetoed as not strong enough a controls-extension bill passed by Congress. Controls were off during July and August. Then the President signed another bill—which he also regarded as inadequate—and prices were again regulated on meat and other products. But such controls were meaningless, the Republican campaigners pointed out, if the controlled products were not to be found in the market place.

Plenty of meat had been available in July and August, but now suddenly there was a drastic shortage. The opening up of a free market during those two months had resulted in overslaughtering of animals that normally would have been fed to greater weight. But housewives confronted by empty meat counters neither understood nor cared. Even Chicago, where 40,000 packing-house workers were idle, ran out of meat. For the average customer anywhere there was simply no meat to be had. Butchers were kings, doling out their restricted supplies to favored customers or conducting their own black markets. Sad jokes ran through the country about how far housewives were willing to go in currying favor with their butchers.

The situation was no laughing matter to the uneasy Democrats. John McCormack, House floor leader, was so pressed by his Massachusetts constituents that he issued a public demand for a sixty-day suspension of price ceilings. Rayburn gloomily told a friend, "This is going to be a damn beefsteak election." Newspaper editorialists bitterly criticized "the little man in the White House" for his stubbornness in insisting on continued controls.

As October wore on, Truman finally called together some of his most trusted advisers to discuss how to combat what he angrily called "this hysteria." It was a solemn meeting. Participating in it were Clark Clifford, Tom Clark, Bob Hannegan, OPA Boss Paul Porter, Undersecretary of State Will Clayton, Undersecretary of the Treasury Max Gardner, Robert Shields from the Agriculture Department, and Richard Fields from OPA. Such a group of men could be expected to disagree on many issues, but they were in full agreement that the Democratic party was in deep trouble. Most of them were convinced that price controls were the main cause.

Four days later the President made a nationwide radio broadcast to announce the lifting of controls on meat, food and feed products. Republican spokesmen sneered that Truman had changed his mind—again—as a political ploy, declared the move was long overdue, and placed responsibility for promptly soaring prices on the slowness of the administration in removing controls.

Along with everything else, there was trouble for the Democrats on the labor front. The American Federation of Labor in New York and Pennsylvania refused to give a blanket endorsement to either party. A similar line was taken by the United Mine Workers in West Virginia. Dan Tobin, head of the A.F. of L. Teamsters, straddled the same fence. The potent coalition of big labor, big city machines, little business, Southern conservatives and minority groups, which Franklin D. Roosevelt had fashioned and which four times had carried him and his party to victory at the polls, was in pronounced disarray.

In the November 5 election more voters went to the polls than in any nonpresidential-election year since 1938. Their verdict was overwhelmingly against the Democrats. Republicans took control of both houses of Congress for the first time in sixteen years.

Some of the Republican victories were especially significant. In New York State, Governor Thomas E. Dewey scored a resounding win, even taking New York City over his Democratic opponent, Senator James M. Meade; it was the first time a Republican had carried the city in a statewide election since the long ago year of 1928. In Massachusetts, young and handsome Henry Cabot Lodge, Jr., who had re-signed his Senate seat for active duty in the war, regained it by beating the incumbent, David Walsh, a veteran Democratic politician who had previously served several terms in the Senate. In California, another young man, an ex-naval officer named Richard Nixon, was elected to the House from Los Angeles over the liberal Jerry Voorhis, who was serving his fifth term.

In all, the Republicans scored a net gain of eleven seats in the Senate and fifty-four in the House of Representatives. The election outcome was an unmistakably clear answer to the jeering query "Had enough?"

Republican leaders began to lay plans for the 1948 presidential campaign, which they now felt comfortably certain of winning. Democrats who lost were inclined to place the blame on Truman and his policies. A Democratic freshman senator, J. William Fulbright of Arkansas, suggested publicly that Truman resign after appointing a Republican Secretary of State who, there being no incumbent vice-president, then would succeed to the presidency. That, said Fulbright, would hand over to the Republicans complete responsibility until the people had an opportunity to make a new choice in 1948. Colonel E. M. House had made a similar suggestion to Woodrow Wilson before the 1916 election. He said that if Wilson lost, which appeared probable, he might ask both his vice-president and secretary of state to resign, appoint his opponent, Charles Evans Hughes, secretary of state and then himself resign. "That," House told Wilson, "would be the patriotic thing to do."

Fulbright left patriotism out of his proposal, but the omission did not keep Truman from ejaculating that the Arkansas senator was "an overeducated Oxford S.O.B." The President had no far-fetched idea of resigning. If the people wanted him out of office, they would have a chance in two years to vote him out—and few political observers doubted that they would.

Senator Wayne Morse was one who expressed some doubt about it. Representative Carroll Reece of Tennessee was elected chairman of the Republican National Committee to structure the victory program for the next two years. Morse, at the time still nominally a Republican, thought the choice of Reece was probably the worst that could have been made. The tart-tongued Oregonian stated that if the program adopted by the committee was to constitute Republican policy during the ensuing two years, "the Republican National Committee will re-elect Harry Truman in spite of everything he is doing to defeat himself."

But hardly anybody ever listened to Morse.

1947

ROBERT A. TAFT'S YEAR

Members of the Republican majority in the Eightieth Congress were eager to get down to business as the first session was convened on January 3, 1947. Euphoric with victory, their leaders announced that they expected "to get things done, go home and give the people a breather." What they wanted to do in the main was to reverse the course the federal government had followed since 1933. Specifically, they proposed to reduce the national budget, cut taxes, revise the Wagner Labor Relations Act, and re-examine the reciprocal trade program. In addition, they planned to solve the excruciating housing problem and eliminate the shortages of goods, a subject on which they had played so heavily during the fall campaign.

In the Senate, Robert Alphonso Taft of Ohio took charge of this ambitious program.

The Republican senator, fifty-seven years old, was the leading conservative in Congress. Not up for re-election in 1946, he had nevertheless campaigned for the party, vigorously attacking the entire concept of Truman's Fair Deal. He was chairman of the Republican Policy Committee and of the Committee on Labor in the Senate. The first position gave him a leading role in laying down the party line and making committee assignments. The second enabled him to shape legislation to supplant the Wagner Act.

He would use both positions to try to attain two objectives about which he had strong personal sentiments: to restore the prestige and authority of Congress; to get himself elected President of the United States in 1948.

Taft was born to politics. As a boy he had lived in the White House during the presidency of his father, William Howard Taft—and had seen his father's aspiration to a second term blasted by the decampment of a renegade Republican named Theodore Roosevelt. After graduation from Yale, Robert Taft built a thriving law practice in Cincinnati. It was expected in Ohio that members of the Taft family would offer themselves for public office, and Bob Taft duly served in both branches of the state legislature and as speaker of the lower house. First elected to the United States Senate in 1938, he was a delegate to Republican national conventions in 1932, 1940 and 1944. In 1940 he made a premature bid for his party's presidential nomination. His wife Martha, watching him lose to the dark horse Wendell Willkie, commented to Joe Pew, Pennsylvania political powerhouse, "They say this is the first unbossed convention in the party's history. I hope it's the last." As she so often did, Martha Taft spoke her husband's sentiments. Taft, himself never "bossed" by anybody, accepted bossism as a fact of political life.

It was often said of this grave, studious and ambitious man that he possessed the best eighteenth-century mind in America. This was unjust. If he harked back to the days of the Founding Fathers, it was in his instinctive belief that nothing in the world was more important than the liberty of the individual American. Coupled with this belief was an unwavering conviction that only the Republican party—and only the Taft ideological branch of the party—could insure protection of liberty. To Taft these were not matters subject to debate; they were simply facts to be recognized.

Impatient with nonsense, he was not a man to suffer fools gladly and often he would not suffer them at all. But, as his fellow senators, both Republicans and Democrats, knew, he was by no means the cold, unapproachable person he was generally pictured as being. He had a dry, friendly wit, liked a moderate drink of Scotch in the company of friends, and enjoyed a special rapport with certain senior southern members of the Senate establishment.

Taft, always self-possessed, felt very sure of himself as the 1947 session began. All the high cards were his. If he played them right, he reasoned, the Republican presidential nomination could hardly be denied him in 1948. And since it was widely agreed that Truman had already been repudiated by the people, the prize would be a valuable one. Naturally, other ambitious men would reach for it, but Taft reckoned that he was in the most advantageous position to secure it.

So it seemed, and not to him alone, as the Republicans set out to dismantle as much of the New Deal as possible.

Taft himself would be in command of domestic legislation. Vandenberg, having ascended to the chairmanship of the Foreign Relations Committee, would guide foreign-affairs legislation. Wallace White of Maine, aptly described as "old, mild and anxious," was named majority floor leader; he took all his signals from Taft. Kenneth Wherry, a vehement anti-New Dealer from Nebraska who spoke long and often in the Senate, became party whip. The press sometimes referred to these men as the "Big Four," but there was at most a "Big Two," and so far as most of the Republican legislative program was concerned, it was dominated by a "Big One": Robert A. Taft.

On the other side of the Capitol, Joseph William Martin, Jr., of North Attleboro, Massachusetts, who had entered the U.S. House of Representatives in 1925, moved up from minority leader to Speaker. Martin's credentials as a conservative Republican were impeccable, even though his father had been a Grover Cleveland Democrat before deserting William Jennings Bryan on the gold issue. Nobody in the family ever went back to the Democrats. "The very air I breathed in North Attleboro was Republican," said Joe Martin. The little New Englander was held in high regard by his colleagues on both sides of the aisle. Turning the speakership over to Martin, Rayburn described him as "a friend of mankind, a man of unquestioned integrity, of demonstrated ability, with a great, fine heart."

Charles A. Halleck of Indiana, starting his seventh term in the House, was chosen floor leader. A tough-minded politician from a state where politics was a full-time game, Halleck once had been a Willkieite but had steadily become more conservative. He now was considered Tom Dewey's man in the House. His selection as majority leader was rather a snub to Taft, who had preferred a fellow Ohioan, Clarence Brown. But Taft made no overt objection.

These men, in Senate and House, embarked on a determined drive to kill what they could of the New Deal and to make certain that Harry Truman's hoped-for extension of it would never enjoy the breath of life.

Their chances for success appeared bright. Nor was the luster dimmed by Truman's State of the Union message, in which the President did little more than repeat demands for legislative measures which both he and Congress knew would not be enacted in that year. Republicans accused him of "intentional failure" to give Congress a comprehensive legislative program. Big Jim Farley, Roosevelt's personal political genius and Postmaster General until he broke with the President over the third-term issue, appeared on the radio program *Meet the Press* to say that Truman was dead political timber. In a presumed counterfoil to this kind of talk, White House aides arranged for Gene Tunney to visit the White House, and the former heavyweight boxing champion of the world came away from a talk with Truman to say, "I never saw a more solid citizen. His eye is clear and he's just as solid as a wall. His jaw is square and his stomach is as flat as an athlete's." But this amusing *non sequitur* did not frighten the Republicans.

* * *

One proposal in the State of the Union message was new. The President asked for a labor bill that would end jurisdictional strikes and secondary boycotts, strengthen the Department of Labor, and establish a commission to examine the labor-management relations problems in general.

A bill embodying these proposals would work no great hardship on labor and might calm the continued public outcry that something be done to curb what much of the populace had come to think of as its arrogant abuse of power. Truman hoped to meet that clamor without further alienating the leaders of organized labor. He might even get back in their good graces, which he needed to do.

Taft and his Republicans had no intention of letting the administration get by with a mild labor bill. The Ohio senator felt that this was the ordained year for bringing about total revision of a federal labor law which had been little changed for a dozen years. He considered that he was the man to do the revising.

The Wagner Act of 1935, named for Democratic Senator Robert F. Wagner of New York, was regarded by labor leaders as labor's Magna Charta. Passed in reaction to management's own arrogance in dealing with its workingmen during the Depression years, the Wagner Act erected strong guards around labor's right of collective bargaining. Its passage had brought valuable and continuing political dividends to the Democratic party.

But now conditions had changed. Prior to 1935 there had been an average of 753 strikes annually, involving 297,000 workers. In 1946 there were 4,985 strikes, involving 4,650,000 workers. Union membership had soared and union treasuries had benefited proportionately. Labor leaders began to display approximately the same tender solicitude for the public interest as that expressed by William H. Vanderbilt in his famous "public be damned" statement.

At the beginning of 1947 a new coal strike was in prospect. Labor contracts in steel and other basic industries were soon to expire. Union leaders were making it clear that they would demand substantial wage increases in new contracts, and the people were fretting about the high cost of everything. The atmosphere was favorable for a move toward the right in labor legislation.

Through hard study Taft had become an expert on the issues involved. He needed to have all the answers, for in his Labor Committee all of the Democrats were solidly on the side of organized labor and some of the Republicans were not in any way sympathetic toward Taft's determination to tear down a basic structure of the New Deal. Irving M. Ives of New York, for example, as a close associate of Dewey and a member of the "Eastern Establishment" which the Ohioan looked upon with suspicion, would hardly go along with a measure certain to be deeply offensive to labor. Morse of Oregon and George Aiken of Vermont, other Republican members of the committee, were more prolabor than not. On the whole, Taft faced a committee in which the majority was hostile to his objective. He realized the situation and was prepared to deal with it out of his own knowledge and his steadfastness of purpose.

For six weeks the Senate Labor Committee conducted hearings on Taft's bill, receiving a mass of evidence from employers, employees, union leaders and experts in labor relations. The union spokesmen opposed any change in the Wagner Act and angrily labeled the proposal before the committee a "slave-labor bill." Taft countered that the weight in collective bargaining was all on the side of labor except perhaps against the very largest business concerns. "In particular," he said, "I believe that in dealing with small business, with farmers and even with the workers themselves the labor-union leaders have acquired a power which today the people resent and which inevitably has been abused."

As he expected, many of the key provisions of his bill were eliminated in committee. With dogged persistence, he worked successfully to have them restored in the whole Senate.

Meanwhile, in the House of Representatives, Fred Hartley, Jr., a New Jersey Republican, sponsored a labor bill far more restrictive than Taft's. It included virtually everything that could be desired by the National Association of Manufacturers and the United States Chamber of Commerce. Hartley himself admitted that he was only nominally the author of the bill bearing his name. It was, he said, a leadership bill.

Taft was not at all pleased with it and before the matter was finished he had rewritten it. He wanted to be painstakingly fair. "Our aim," he said, "should be to reach the point where, when an employer meets with his employees, they have substantially equal bargaining power, so that neither side feels it can make an unreasonable demand and get away with it." He did not propose to give business management a lethal weapon to use against labor but to place restraints around the weapons labor had available to use against management and the public.

The Taft-Hartley bill, in its final form, banned the closed shop forbidding the hiring of non-union workers. Jurisdictional strikes and secondary boycotts were outlawed, as

Truman himself had asked. The measure provided that employers could sue unions for broken contracts or property damage suffered during strikes. Unions must make their financial affairs public. A sixty-day moratorium must precede any strike in an industry engaged in interstate commerce, and provision was made for an eighty-day injunction against strikes determined by the President to imperil the national health or safety. Contributions to political campaigns by unions were forbidden. Collection of union dues by employers was ended.

While such provisions obviously were looked upon with disfavor by the union leaders, the bill could hardly be said to place labor in the chains of slavery. The Senate approved it by a vote of 68 to 24. Passage in the House came by a vote of 308 to 107.

Now a bitter struggle began among Truman's closest advisers over the question of what action he should take. The majority of his Cabinet said he should sign it, and they were joined by Sam Rayburn. Hannegan and Schwellenbach favored a veto, but they were both unwell and fading from active influence in the administration. Clark Clifford, who had informally brought together a group of men to work unobtrusively to lead Truman away from the more conservative line that was continually urged upon him by other advisers, made veto of Taft-Hartley a priority project. Besides Cliford, this group included Oscar Ewing, director of the Federal Security Agency; Leon Keyserling, member of the Council of Economic Advisers; Girard Davidson, assistant Secretary of the Interior, and Charles S. Murphy, an administrative assistant to the President. Quietly and one at a time, they presented to Truman the reasons—compelling in their view—why he should veto a bill so overwhelmingly approved by Congress. Clifford prepared and placed before the President a comprehensive analysis of the measure to support his contention that, both for political gain and for the good of the country, the bill should be vetoed.

The battle to influence Truman's decision was not confined to administration circles.

Shouting "slave-labor bill" louder than ever, the American Federation of Labor poured an estimated million dollars into newspaper advertisements, radio programs and mass meetings to demand a veto. In Pennsylvania and Indiana, thousands of John L. Lewis's mine workers walked out in strikes protesting congressional passage of Taft-Hartley. From California, A.F. of L. and C.I.O. delegates moved on Washington in a "veto caravan" of one hundred automobiles. In New York City, Mayor William O'Dwyer, with an eye on the governorship, proclaimed a municipal "Veto Day," and at a Madison Square Garden rally C.I.O. President Philip Murray denounced Taft-Hartley as "dastardly," "dangerous provocation," and "a foul brew." "Our liberties are threatened by reactionary monopoly," the labor leader shouted, "driving us on the first long step toward domestic fascism."

The National Catholic Welfare Conference, with a membership made up of all Catholic bishops in the United States, condemned Taft-Hartley as playing into the hands of the Communists. Two former chairmen of the old War Labor Board, William H. Davis and George W. Taylor, said the law was unworkable. Mrs. Roosevelt in her newspaper column and Henry Wallace, who was assiduously courting labor and left-wing support for a third party with him as its presidential candidate, added their voices to the roaring chorus of denunciation.

On the other side, spokesmen for business, most of the press, and many leading members of the President's party called just as insistently, if less stridently, for Truman to sign the bill.

He vetoed it.

In his sharply worded veto message he attacked the bill's basic philosophy, calling it "a shocking piece of legislation" which was "bad for labor, bad for management and bad for the country." He went on the radio to defend his action before the nation. If the bill became law, he said, it would encourage "distrust, suspicion and arbitrary attitudes." And he predicted that the legislation would cause a substantial increase in strikes.

Taft, in a radio broadcast of his own, denied all these statements. In reply to many of Truman's charges, he said, flatly and without feeling the need for further explanation, "This is not so." Congress, he declared, had "simply tried to restore equality in collective bargaining and correct only those abuses which were clearly shown to exist." Taft thought his handiwork came about as close to perfection as was possible for any measure subject to the legislative process.

The President's veto was a direct flouting, and as deliberate as it was direct, not only of the Republican majority in Congress but of Democratic conservatives as well. It probably also flouted majority public sentiment. As William S. White wrote in his book *The Taft Story*, a brilliant appraisal of the Ohio senator, the Taft-Hartley bill "was the only major accomplishment, in the affirmative sense, that in all of Robert Taft's political life was genuinely popular." But Truman was looking beyond immediate popularity. He had sound political motives for vetoing the bill. His refusal to approve it would win back the support of labor leaders and their allies. The veto also, he and his advisers hoped, would cut the ground out from under Wallace's third-party movement. And while many voters would be outraged by the veto, most of them were people who likely would never have voted for Truman anyway.

The President expected that Congress would override,

which it promptly did by greater majorities in both houses than the bill had received on original passage.

Republicans—along with many Democrats—got the labor bill they wanted. Truman got the political issue he deemed essential.

The presidential campaign of 1948 had begun early.

Yet, on at least some occasions during this year, there was more than partisan politics in the air. Despite all the shrill outcries against the man in the White House, he defiantly and against odds carried the Republican-controlled Congress and the nation to accomplishments which would have a lasting effect on the world.

Early in the year Great Britain served notice that she could no longer continue economic and military aid to Greece, which, with Turkey, was threatened by Soviet Russia's demands for territorial expansion. Truman went before Congress to declare, "It must be the policy of the United States to support free people who are resisting attempted subjugation by armed minorities and by outside pressures." This Truman Doctrine was the basis for American help to Greece and Turkey in resisting Communist aggression. It was opposed by isolationists, pacifists, and Russophiles, but it prevailed.

The Marshall Plan to aid in the rehabilitation of the war-ruined Old World was drafted to deal with European reconstruction as a single problem. Named for Secretary of State Marshall, the plan committed the economic might of the United States to meeting that problem. When Congress was informed that $6.8 billion would be needed during the first fifteen months of the European Recovery Plan, Bob Taft expostulated, "People don't completely collapse. They go on living anyway." Richard B. Russell, the conservative and sagacious Georgia senator, suggested sarcastically that the United States would save money by admitting England, Scotland and Wales as states. "The King could run for the Senate," Russell added, "as could Winston Churchill."

The Marshall Plan split the Republicans in Congress. Vandenberg led the fight to appropriate the money requested by Truman. Wherry vociferously opposed the entire concept, and Taft sniped constantly at "giving away" billions of U.S. dollars to Europe. They, joined by some Democrats, whittled down the President's proposal, but Congress finally approved the European Recovery Plan.

Almost as controversial on the domestic front was the proposal to unify the armed forces of the United States. Truman had been working for such unification almost from the day he became President. Generally speaking, the plan was favored by the Army and opposed by the Navy. The admirals were especially passionate in their opposition to creation of a separate Air Force in the proposed new department. But a compromise was reached and the National Security Act of 1947 became law. Forrestal, who never had resigned as Navy Secretary, was named the first Secretary of Defense; that was part of the compromise.

For a divided government these were accomplishments of magnitude. Full understanding of their significance was obscured, however, by the incessant political controversy engendered not only by these issues but also by other issues and by diverse personalities. Nineteen forty-seven was a vintage year for off-season politicking.

* * *

When Congress recessed in late July, the campaign pattern so carefully constructed by Bob Taft during the past seven months was satisfactorily completed. Taft's hand, for or against, was on every major legislative measure considered. He could point to the Taft-Hartley Act as important legislation bearing his name. Throughout the session he had spoken his mind on every issue that came up. The Eightieth Congress was uniquely his, and he now went before the people to point with pride to its record.

First he journeyed home to Ohio. In an address before 2,000 Republicans in Columbus, he laid down the trail that he was to follow consistently in the months ahead, praising the work of the Republican Congress and raking the Democratic President fore and aft. In every crisis, he declared, Truman "has shown that he is still dominated by the principles of the C.I.O." He "clearly believes in the New Deal doctrine of spending, spending, spending." "He believes in taxing, taxing, taxing." "He insists upon a health plan which will socialize our entire medical profession." "He has violently opposed every effort to bring about tax reform." And so on.

After a vacation in Canada, Taft traveled westward to California, Oregon and Washington. He was accompanied by a large body of newsmen, many of whom, like Taft himself, believed they were in the company of the next President. Actually, these observers noted, in most of his talks the senator seemed to be selling his party more than himself. His was the party, he told western audiences, which could handle foreign affairs with first attention to the interests of the United States, reduce government controls, lower taxes, encourage business enterprise, deal fairly but firmly with labor, and administer national affairs on a sound basis. The Democratic party, on the other hand, was closely and irretrievably allied with labor and left-wing groups, had no sense of sureness in foreign affairs, encouraged inflation, suppressed individual initiative, and was given to bumbling administration of the government.

As usual, Taft was rational and unexcited. What he said about Democrats and Republicans was spoken in a reasoning, nonargumentative tone which assumed that, since his listeners were themselves reasonable people, they naturally agreed with his views. He was cheered by the favorable reception accorded him. At times, to be sure, his meetings were picketed by representatives of labor, but Taft told the news reporters that the picketing helped him with most of the people.

His innate suspicion of the press flared up after a news conference in Santa Cruz, California. He was asked what he thought could be done about the high prices of food. "Voluntary reduction of consumption is the first step," he answered. "We should eat less." He was not pleased when newspaper headlines labeled him "Eat Less Taft."

On the whole, however, he felt that this precampaign tour was a great success. Its effect was to re-enforce his conviction that the Republican nomination for President would come his way in 1948.

Other Republican hopefuls were busy. Governor Thomas E. Dewey, the party's 1944 nominee, left the security of his enclave in Albany and ventured out into the hot summer to talk with Republicans. In four weeks he traveled more than six thousand miles and conferred with Republican leaders in fifteen states. Dewey knew that in some quarters he was suspected of being too much the glib easterner and even of being soft on the New Deal. He was out to allay these suspicions. In Sapulpa, Oklahoma, his attractive wife's home town, he gave autographs to youngsters and was photographed in his shirt sleeves. He admired for the press a farmer's improvised hay-bale loader, saying it was just what he needed on his own farm near Pawling, New York. It was difficult for Dewey to be folksy, but he tried. More importantly, he bore in on Republican meetings with the theme that he was opposed to almost everything Truman stood for, that he strongly approved of the Taft-Hartley Act, that he was for a deep tax cut—in short, that he was the soundest Republican anyone could hope to find.

As he ended his tour, Dewey was optimistic. He believed

he had firmly nailed down 420 of the 547 delegates he would need to get the presidential nomination. He and his supporters hoped that before convention time his nomination would appear inevitable, making uncertain delegates anxious to get on the bandwagon.

Meanwhile, Harold Stassen was enjoying a vacation at the home of his parents in Minnesota. But the one-time boy-wonder governor, now turning bald at the age of forty, had been running for President ever since he left the Navy in November of 1945. He traveled through forty states and made innumerable speeches before men's service clubs, women's garden clubs, university commencement audiences, community forums, Republican clambakes. He went on a nine-week tour of Europe, meeting with heads of state in England, France and Czechoslovakia and interviewing Stalin in the Kremlin. Stassen had run for office five times, twice for county attorney and three times for governor of Minnesota, and had never lost an election. Although distrusted by the Old Guard Republicans because he had served as Willkie's floor manager at the 1940 convention, he expected to convince the mass of voters, and through them the politicians, that he deserved the presidency. He was not a man afflicted with self-doubt.

Other men dreamed wistfully of a deadlocked convention that would cause lightning to strike them. Governor Earl Warren of California had rejected Dewey's offer of the vice-presidential nomination in 1944 because he thought the higher place might come to him four years later. Vandenberg considered himself a distinct possibility if Taft and Dewey canceled each other out. General Douglas MacArthur, the new American Emperor of Japan, was willing to come home if the people called him. Joe Martin was mentioned by some as a possible dark horse, and he listened.

Professional politicians in both parties were keeping a wary eye on General of the Army Dwight David Eisenhower. Anti-Truman Democrats were hopeful that General Eisenhower could be induced to accept the Democratic presidential nomination. Republican party leaders were uncommunicatively afraid that their convention might be blitzed by an Eisenhower movement like the Willkie surge in 1940. The popular general's political leanings were unknown, perhaps at the time nonexistent. A Gallup poll asked the question "Is General Eisenhower a Republican or a Democrat?" Twenty-two per cent of those answering said he was a Republican; 20 per cent thought he was a Democrat, and 58 per cent said they didn't know.

Eisenhower himself had repeatedly denied that he had any interest in political office. As early as 1943 George Allen sent him a newspaper clipping which told of a resolution adopted by an American Legion post in New York boosting the general for President. Eisenhower replied, "Baloney! Why can't a simple soldier be left alone to carry out his orders?" At a 1945 homecoming celebration in Abilene, Kansas, where he grew up, he told reporters, "In the strongest possible language you can command you may say that I have no political ambitions at all." He had privately told Truman the same thing.

Still it was noted that his face with its appealing grin appeared in the press with increasing frequency. Eisenhower continued to say testily that of course he was not a candidate and would not become one. But he had his picture taken with a fish he caught and he held a news conference in Washington. The professionals remained lingeringly fearful of this popular hero.

Among the Democrats, Truman was being urged by many party leaders not to run for a term of his own. Their political judgment appeared to be strongly backed up by public sentiment. A poll showed only 32 per cent of the people approving his conduct of the presidency. The loud sports shirts he wore on periodic vacations in Key West, Florida, provoked widespread jeers. Funny and cruel quips about the President proliferated. "I'm just mild about Harry," people said. "To err is Truman," they chucklingly told one another. "Don't shoot the piano player, he's doing the best he can." And unkindest of all: "I wonder what Truman would do if he were alive."

Grimly setting his jaw, Truman rapped out his reply to suggestions that he stand aside: "I was not brought up to run from a fight."

On the basis of advice urged upon him by Clark Clifford, plus his own hardening conviction that Bob Taft and his Republicans would, if they had their way, carry the country back to the horse-and-buggy days, he determined to take the offensive. Clifford told him he must no longer appear before the country as "a man of the people trying to do his best" but as a forceful leader who knew what he was up to. The President's special counsel prepared a long memorandum which he did not claim was a blueprint for victory but which at least suggested possible ways to win the 1948 election.

"The Democratic party," wrote Clifford, realistic as always, "is an unhappy alliance of southern conservatives, western progressives, and big city labor. . . . The success or failure of the Democratic leadership can be precisely measured by its ability to lead enough members of these misfit groups to the polls." Thus a high priority should be given to an appeal to farmers. Thus the Taft-Hartley Act should be relentlessly attacked. Thus heavy emphasis should be given to civil rights to keep the Negro vote from going over to Wallace's third party. This program, certain to be denounced by southerners, still would not lose the South, Clifford thought; that section would remain safe for the Democrats.

"The blunt fact is," he added in his memorandum, "that the party has been so long in power that it is fat, tired, and even a bit senile." He suggested that the President should go among the people of the nation on the kind of "inspection tours" which Roosevelt had used so successfully.

Truman studied Clifford's counsel and found it good. His first step was to shake up the party organization. Out went Hannegan as chairman of the Democratic National Committee. In went J. Howard McGrath, an aggressive freshman senator from Rhode Island, three times governor of his state, a millionaire, a party worker since his college days who had held almost every job from bell ringer and ward heeler on up.

And the President, using the power of his office, called a special session of Congress in November.

The stated purpose was to implement the Marshall Plan and to attack inflation. A steely-eyed President delivered a political message which was received by the Congress with stunned incredulity. Truman demanded that the legislators restore consumer-credit controls, limit speculation on commodity prices to hold down the soaring price of grain, and give the President authority to control inventories and allocate such essentials as grain and steel. He wanted power to place ceilings on the price of goods affecting the cost of living, to ration such items as a preparedness measure, and to prevent increases in wages.

Only a few days earlier Truman had argued at a press conference that such controls were the methods of a police state, thereby causing visible pain to Clifford, who was present. But the man from Missouri was never bothered by such small inconsistencies. Nor was he bothered by Taft's statement after his message that the President's proposals were totalitarian in nature and, if enacted into law, would mean "the end of economic freedom."

As expected, the President got much less than he asked for, certainly no price and wage controls. With professed reluctance he signed a bill he scored as "pitifully inadequate" and stored away more ammunition for future attacks on the Eightieth Congress.

The stage was set for 1948 and the cast assembled, but the complete scenario was still to be written.

1948

HARRY TRUMAN'S YEAR—
AT LAST

It was the year that the New Look in women's dresses brought hemlines down below midcalf, the year that the vice-president of the Pittsburgh Planned Parenthood clinic gave birth to triplets, the year that the Anti-Saloon League of America changed its name to the Temperance League of America. It was the year of Communist takeover in Hungary and Czechoslovakia and of U.S. leadership in formation of the North Atlantic Treaty Organization. New York City began the year by digging out from under the biggest snowstorm in its history, outdoing the legendary blizzard of 1888. President Truman ordered the building of a back porch on the second floor of the White House and was severely called to task by the New York *Herald Tribune* for "meddling with a historic structure which the nation prefers as it is." Chiang Kai-shek fought a losing battle with Communist forces for control of the Chinese mainland. Governor Thomas E. Dewey submitted to the State Assembly the highest budget in the history of New York State and vetoed a bill which would have made it legal for men to patronize beauty shops. It was the year a staff member of the House Un-American Committee hinted darkly that Shirley Temple might have been taken in by the Communist conspiracy. The Cold War between the United States and the Soviet Union threatened to turn hot. The Russians blockaded land traffic between West Germany and the Allied sections of divided Berlin, but the United States and Great Britain successfully mounted a gigantic air lift for the delivery of food and supplies. Farm prices fell because of inadequate government storage facilities for a bumper grain crop. Sam Rayburn had to shoo away a pigeon from lighting on his head as he presided over the Democratic national convention.

An exceptional year in many respects, including the political.

* * *

Harold J. Laski, the British political scientist, wrote in one of his discussions of the American presidency, "An American presidential campaign is like nothing else in the world." All hands strove mightily in 1948 to prove the validity of this contention.

The Republicans early in the year abandoned their dream of making Dwight Eisenhower their presidential nominee. The general, who had become president of Columbia University, wrote a letter to a New Hampshire newspaper publisher saying firmly, "I could not accept the nomination even under the remote circumstance that it were tendered me." An organization called the Draft Eisenhower League had formed a number of state chapters, which were now disbanded. Talk increased about the possibility of a convention deadlock between Taft and Dewey, with Stassen regarded as the most likely beneficiary.

Anti-Truman Democrats, unlike the Republicans, did not give up on Eisenhower. Three separate groups wanted him, each for its own reasons: liberals who felt that Truman was not carrying forward New Deal policies with sufficient vigor; southern leaders who were up in arms over his civil-rights proposals; and just plain organization Democrats who were convinced that the party could not possibly win with Truman. All three groups saw Eisenhower as their great hope, perhaps their only hope. Since he had not voted in the past, he might as well be a Democrat as a Republican. Of his national popularity there could be no question.

Two Roosevelt sons, James and Elliott, along with Ickes, Senator Claude Pepper of Florida, and Minneapolis Mayor Hubert Humphrey, were prominent among the liberals who spoke of the necessity of drafting Eisenhower as the Democratic candidate. Americans for Democratic Action, a new organization with a shrill voice and little strength, discovered Eisenhower as the embodiment of liberal hopes and dreams. The ADAers were not comfortable with Truman; he was not intellectual enough. The Liberal party of New York, counted on by the Democrats for support in presidential-election years, first announced that it would stay with Truman but then decided the general would be better. John L. Lewis thundered that Truman "is a malignant, scheming sort of an individual who is dangerous not only to the United Mine Workers but dangerous to the United States of America."

The southerners admittedly did not know Eisenhower's views of civil rights, but they knew Truman's only too well. Again this year he had asked Congress to enact federal laws against lynching, the poll tax and discrimination in employment. Senator Jim Eastland of Mississippi cried, "This proves that organized mongrel minorities control the government." A representative from Georgia, Gene Cox, said on the floor of the House that the President's proposal "sounds like the program of the Communist party." The Southern Governors Conference warned, "The President must cease attacks on white supremacy or face full-fledged revolt in the South." In a Lincoln Day address before fellow Republicans, Senator Ken Wherry asked, "Where are the Jeffersonian Democrats today?" and gave his own answer: "They are just waiting to be asked to join us." Many Democrats agreed—unless they could get Eisenhower as their nominee. Senator Olin Johnston, white supremacist from South Carolina, who paid for a table for ten at the Democrats' Jefferson–Jackson Day dinner and ostentatiously left it unoccupied because, he explained, he was afraid his wife "would have to sit by a Nigra," visited Eisenhower and announced afterward that he was "the man of the hour" for the Democratic party.

Those still-faced men, the party bosses in metropolitan areas, were openly willing to throw Truman overboard. Jake Arvey in Chicago and New York Mayor William O'Dwyer stated that almost any other candidate would be preferable. Frank Hague, the noted Jersey City boss, and Connecticut State Democratic Chairman John M. Bailey wanted Eisenhower. Such pragmatists realized that the Democrats would have little chance of winning the presidency if they simply dumped Truman at this late hour. But with a popular figure like Eisenhower at the head of the ticket they could hope for local Democratic victories and therefore for their own retention of power. Truman, on the other hand, would almost surely drag them down with him.

The clamor of these diverse elements within the floundering party was not stilled when, on March 8, National Chairman McGrath came away from a meeting with Truman to announce, "The President has authorized me to say that, if nominated by the Democratic national convention, he will accept and run." The dissenters still looked longingly in Eisenhower's direction, although the general thought he had made his noncandidacy position clear. Almost on the eve of the convention Pepper, a leading force among the would-be drafters, came up with a desperate proposal that the Democrats name Eisenhower as a "national" candidate, leaving him free to pick his running mate and to write his own platform. From Columbia came the unequivocal statement: "No matter under what terms, conditions or premises a proposal might be couched, I would refuse to accept the nomination."

That settled that, finally. For the Democrats.

In the months before the July convention Truman gave no sign that he was dismayed by the widespread defections from his banner. He was campaigning in his own way not merely for the nomination, which he knew could not be refused him if he remained adamant in demanding it, but also for re-election.

He started out, in his State of the Union message, with an aggressive restatement of the policies he had previously placed before Congress. The press told him these policies were not looked upon with favor by most Americans. The public-opinion polls told him he could not be re-elected. Walter Lippmann told him and a waiting world of the perils of a situation in which "the affairs of the country are to be conducted by a President who has not only lost the support of his party but is not in control of his own administration." Ernest K. Lindley, Washington correspondent for *Newsweek*, advised in kindly fashion, "The most popular, and probably the best, service that Truman could render his party now is to step aside."

That was exactly what the embattled President had no intention of doing. He was not moved by what the press—"the kept press," as he was fond of characterizing it—said about him and his policies. He did conclude, however, that he must do something to overcome gloom and pessimism among Democrats. "I decided," he said later, "that I would go directly to the people in all parts of the country with a personal message from the President. . . . I wanted the people in out-of-the-way places to have a chance to see and hear the President face to face so that they could form their own opinions of me and my program on the basis of firsthand acquaintance rather than on the basis of polls and propaganda."

Fortunately for his resolve, in the spring an invitation was extended for him to accept an honorary degree from the University of California. This gave him an opportunity to go all the way across the continent on a "nonpolitical" trip, which meant the cost of the journey would be paid by the federal treasury and not by the impoverished Democratic National Committee. Even a special train was not too much for the President of the United States in traveling to accept a degree from a leading American university.

Leaving Congress to its fulminations, the President set off for the West Coast early in June. The train carried him across eighteen states and, going and coming, he delivered seventy-six speeches in cities, towns and villages. Planned stops for major addresses were made in five strategically located cities. Constantly along the way the President gave off-the-cuff talks from the rear platform of the train.

Whatever the occasion, he never neglected to deliver his "personal message," which usually went like this: "There is just one big issue. It is the special interests against the people, and the President, being elected by all the people, represents the people." As for the representatives of the special interests, they could be found—where else?—among the Republicans in the Eightieth Congress. Truman repeatedly paid his respects to that body. "You've got the worst Congress in the United States you've ever had," he told big and little audiences. "If you want to continue the policies of the Eightieth Congress, it'll be your funeral."

This avowedly nonpolitical journey was a preview of the technique Truman was to use in more overt campaign swings later in the year. He laid out the main issue, casting the Eightieth Congress in the role of villain. His simple, even simplistic, approach had an appeal of its own among people who felt vaguely that they were being put upon by forces they could not control. Truman learned on this trip that, regardless of the sneers of sophisticated newspaper columnists and eastern politicians, the people liked the way he talked, liked his forthright, no-nonsense style. "I had never lost the faith, as some of those around me seemed to," he reported, "and I found renewed encouragement and confidence in the response that came from the crowds that gathered at all the train stops on this first tour."

The Republicans naturally fumed about the "political campaign trip paid for by the taxpayers," but there was nothing they could do about it except issue indignant statements. Besides, the Grand Old Party was suffering inner frictions of its own during the first half of the year.

The quarrel between the midwest Old Guard and the eastern liberal wing of the party grew more bitter. Dewey's spokesmen, led by Herbert Brownell, exuded confidence, but the Taft forces had not yielded an inch. Stassen continued to believe that neither Dewey nor Taft would be able to get a majority at the convention, which would then have to turn to him. Vandenberg remained hopeful, although he made no active effort to line up delegate support; he was just available.

So, as he made clear in March, was General Douglas MacArthur, serving as proconsul in Japan. In Tokyo he released to newsmen a gem of MacArthuresque prose: "I would be recreant to all my concepts of good citizenship were I to shirk because of the hazards and responsibilities involved from accepting any public duty to which I might be called by the American people." No wild public acclaim greeted this, although the general's headquarters reported that he received many congratulatory messages and the New York *Times* commented, "There can be no doubt that his candidacy would command wide support in a national election." Jeering ex-servicemen started "Veterans Against MacArthur" clubs on college campuses and in a dozen large cities. Wisconsin Republicans, claiming him as a native son, entered MacArthur in their presidential primary. But the victor there was Stassen, who won nineteen delegates to eight for MacArthur, and that was the last of the general's effort.

The Wisconsin primary marked the beginning of a new kind of effort by Dewey. Startled by Stassen's showing, he abandoned his attitude of aloofness toward the primaries. He got out of Albany and headed for Nebraska, where a primary was scheduled a week after the one in Wisconsin. But Stassen had been exceedingly active in Nebraska. On election day he beat Dewey, and the Gallup poll promptly reported that he had forged ahead of the New York governor among the nation's Republicans. In Oregon, site of the next primary, polls showed Stassen well in the lead. By now frightened as well as startled, Dewey plunged into a hard-hitting campaign. For three weeks he barnstormed throughout the state, climaxing his drive with a radio debate with Stassen in which he came out the obvious winner. He also won the primary, which raised his standing throughout the nation at a crucial time.

As the Republican national convention opened in Philadelphia on June 21, Dewey, Taft and Stassen were seen as the principal contenders in one-two-three order. The odds were heavy that one of this trio would become the next President. In every national political convention someone is sure to offer an oratorical observation that the delegates have convened to nominate the next President of the United States. What was unique about this convention, as Joe Martin remarked, was that everyone there really believed the statement this time. Clare Booth Luce, wife of the editor of *Time* and a former congresswoman from Connecticut, expressed the prevailing sentiment when she said in a speech to the delegates: "Let us waste no time in measuring the unfortunate man in the White House against our specifications. Mr. Truman's time is short. His situation is hopeless. Frankly, he is a gone goose."

Nobody at the convention expressed disagreement with this biting verdict. The question was who would be chosen to pluck the gone goose's feathers.

Tom Dewey came to Philadelphia with a solid base of 350 delegate votes—but he needed a total of 548. Taft, Stassen and Vandenberg believed that a stop-Dewey movement could be successful; each thought he should head such a movement. While they and their emissaries bickered, Dewey men moved out among the uncommitted delegates with persuasion and promises. More than one stanch Republican thought he had been assured of the vice-presidential nomination if he carried his state delegation for Dewey.

These tactics paid off. On the first ballot Dewey had 434 votes, Taft 224, and Stassen 157. Several favorite sons garnered the rest, but their strength began to fall away on the second ballot. Dewey's lead increased on that ballot; he had 515 votes. A recess was called, giving Taft an opportunity to get in touch with Stassen and urge that he release his delegates to him. The eternally optimistic Minnesotan was not yet quite ready to surrender. He said he would not turn his supporters loose until the fourth ballot.

But there was not to be a fourth ballot, and Taft knew it. He conceded by giving his fellow senator from Ohio, John Bricker, a message to read to the convention before the roll call of states began for the third ballot. "Dewey is a great Republican," the gallant message said, "and he will make a great Republican President." Other candidates quickly withdrew, Dewey was unanimously nominated, and soon the candidate was in the convention hall to make his acceptance speech.

There remained the business of choosing a vice-presidential

nominee. Dewey met for several hours with Vandenberg and other advisers to draw up a list of possibilities and make a choice. Various names were suggested, and someone said, "What about Charlie?" "Charlie who?" asked Vandenberg. "Why, Charlie Halleck." "Oh, my God!" roared the Michigan senator, and no more was said about Charlie Halleck, although he bitterly maintained, then and thereafter, that Brownell had definitely promised him the nomination for vice-president. When he taxed Dewey with this promise, the candidate, his mustache neatly in place, shot him a cool glance. "Why, I never gave Brownell authority to speak for me," he said of the man who was known to be his alter ego.

The final list of vice-presidential possibilities contained three names: Bricker, Governor Dwight Green of Illinois, and Governor Earl Warren of California. Bricker had run with Dewey in 1944, and it would hardly do for the Republicans to present the same ticket this year, so he was ruled out. Green had incurred the enmity of Robert McCormick, publisher of the Chicago *Tribune*; he might be a liability in the territory where the "World's Greatest Newspaper" was influential. That left Warren, the man Dewey had wanted all along. His name on the ticket would assure the Republicans of California in the November election, and the warmth of his personality might be an effective counterbalance to Dewey's businesslike crispness.

So Dewey-Warren it was, and *Time* Magazine observed, "Barring a political miracle, it was the kind of ticket which could not fail to sweep the Republican party back into power." *Time* extolled Dewey as "a comeback man." He had run for governor of New York in 1938 and lost, then won the governorship in 1942 and 1946. He had tried vainly for the presidential nomination, then had won it in 1944. He had lost the election that year. Now the 1948 election was coming up and the sequence called for him to win. So reasoned *Time*, and most Republicans happily and many Democrats glumly agreed that this had to be Tom Dewey's year.

Under these circumstances the Democratic national convention, which got under way in the same Philadelphia hall on July 12, might well have been a dull, dispirited affair. But it turned out to be nothing of the sort.

Despite the last-minute efforts of disaffected liberals to get another candidate, there was no question about Harry Truman's nomination. The assembled Democrats accordingly had to seek other matters with which to divert themselves. They found one immediately in the keynote speech by Alben Barkley, eloquent orator from a thousand platforms.

The colorful Kentuckian, now seventy years of age, was known and loved by Democrats throughout the nation. In national politics since 1932, he had been a delegate to every Democratic national convention since 1920 and in 1944 had nominated Roosevelt for his fourth term. At every convention since 1928 he had been mentioned as a possible candidate for vice-president. He was "Mr. Democrat."

Barkley was greeted with hearty applause when he rose to address the convention, and when he finished, he was given a roaring spontaneous demonstration that lasted more than half an hour. The old Democrat had brought the convention to life with his proud account of sixteen years of Democratic administration of the federal government and his fiery call for the Democrats to "lead the children of man into a free world and a free life."

Barkley's speech not only made him the hero of the convention, it made him the vice-presidential nominee as well. Back in Washington, Truman had been trying to get Justice Douglas to accept the nomination for second place but was turned down. The President therefore was in a receptive frame of mind when Les Biffle and Barkley, ecstatic over the reception accorded the keynote speech, telephoned him from Philadelphia to ask if he would have any objection to Barkley as the vice-presidential nominee. "Why didn't you tell me you wanted to be vice-president?" Truman asked, not without disingenuousness. "It's all right with me." It was all right with the convention delegates, too.

No such unanimity greeted the submission of the civil-rights plank formulated by the platform committee. Presented to the convention by Senator Francis Myers of Pennsylvania, the plank was the usual bland pronouncement—a sop to the northern and eastern liberals but not calculated to cause grievous offense to southerners. There was a general endorsement of full extension of civil rights and a call on Congress to assure them within "constitutional limits." Southerners routinely offered an amendment to reassert the principle of State rights, and it was routinely defeated.

Then the liberals, disappointed and sore over their inability to nominate somebody besides Truman or to get a vice-presidential candidate of their choosing, offered their own civil-rights plank. It craftily began, "We highly commend President Harry Truman for his courageous stand on the issue of civil rights," and proceeded to list key legislative items the President had in vain urged on Congress. This minority plank was presented by Hubert Humphrey, darling of the ADA and candidate for the Senate from Minnesota. "The time has come," Humphrey exhorted the delegates, "to walk out of the shadow of states' rights into the sunlight of human rights." He made a stirring appeal, and after abrasive debate the plank was adopted on a roll-call vote. Thirty-five delegates from Mississippi and Alabama stalked out of the convention hall and did not return.

Rayburn, serving as permanent chairman, had a hard time maintaining order. The convention hall was hot and uncomfortable, and many of the delegates were angry much of the time. One light note was struck when a group of crusading ladies came by prearrangement to the platform and released a flock of symbolic doves of peace—in actuality, pigeons. The hall was ablaze with lights, blinding the birds. They fluttered aimlessly about, crashing into standards and drawing roars of laughter from the bored delegates. Rayburn was not amused. His face grew red with anger as he pounded his gavel on the lectern and shouted for order, all the while fending off with one wildly flapping hand a pigeon that threatened to light on top of his onion-bald head. When one did come to rest on the lectern, he savagely knocked it away. Sam Rayburn striking a pigeon!

After Truman arrived in Philadelphia, he remained in seclusion, according to custom, until the time came for his acceptance speech. During the fight on the civil-rights plank he waited in a small room below the convention hall. With that controversy out of the way, the roll of the states was called to nominate a candidate for President. Southern delegates who had not walked out gave their votes to Russell of Georgia, but he received only 263. Truman got 947½, and at nearly two o'clock in the morning, McGrath went downstairs to see if he wanted to accept the nomination immediately or wait until the next day.

Truman did not want to wait. Wearing a glisteningly white suit and with a broad smile on his face, he strode cockily into the hot auditorium. From the platform he beamed down at the delegates as they roared a welcome. As the demonstration ended, Truman snapped out two sentences that set off renewed cheering.

"Senator Barkley and I will win this election and make those Republicans like it," he declared confidently. "Don't you forget that."

Much of his speech was predictable, dealing with his legislative program and the opposition to it in Congress. Then he started talking about the platform adopted by the Republicans in this same hall three weeks earlier. That platform, he noted, called for legislation to meet the housing problem, turn back the inflationary trend, and increase social-security benefits.

"There is a long list of these promises in the Republican platform," he went on to say. "If it weren't so late I would tell you about them. I have discussed a number of these failures of the Eightieth Congress. Every one of them is important. . . . My duty as President requires that I use every means at my disposal to get the laws the people need on matters of such importance and urgency."

He paused to set his sights on the Eightieth Congress.

"On the twenty-sixth day of July," he announced, "I am going to call Congress back and ask them to pass laws to halt rising prices, to meet the housing crisis—which they are saying they are for in their platform. If there is any reality behind that Republican platform, we ought to get some action from a short session of the Eightieth Congress. They can do this job in fifteen days, if they want to do it. They will still have time to get out and run for office."

The President, having delivered his political statement at a political convention, went back to Washington that night. The delegates scattered to their homes, half-believing that maybe Harry Truman could pull it off after all.

But the momentary enthusiasm could not hide the fact that the Democratic party was deeply divided. The day after the convention ended, southerners held a convention of their own in Birmingham, with 6,000 rebels thundering their approval of denunciations of the civil-rights plank adopted in Philadelphia. They nominated as candidates, on what came to be called the Dixiecrat ticket, Governor Strom Thurmond of South Carolina for President and Governor Fielding Wright of Mississippi for vice-president.

A week after the Democratic convention Henry Wallace's newly formed Progressive party moved into the hall in Philadelphia for its own affair. Out of several wild sessions, participated in by an incredible assortment of idealists, nay-sayers, pacifists, boys and girls barely old enough to vote, and a hard core of Communists and fellow travelers working behind the scenes, came a platform closely paralleling that of the U.S. Communist party. Wallace inevitably was nominated for President and Glen Taylor, a guitar-playing United States senator from Idaho, for vice-president. Wallace told a news conference that he welcomed Communist support. He explained, "They support me because I say we can have peace with the Russians."

With this group hitting away from the left, the Dixiecrats nibbling from the right, and the Republicans to be met head-on, Democrats everywhere sagged with discouragement during that torrid summer.

Not Harry Truman.

"I am going to fight," he said sturdily, "and I am going to give 'em hell."

* * *

The political special session of Congress lasted twelve days. Half the time was spent in a filibuster by southern Democrats to prevent consideration of a bill outlawing the poll tax. Nothing of consequence was accomplished except authorization of a loan to help finance the building of the permanent headquarters of the United Nations in New York City. Truman's demand for legislation on civil rights, minimum wages, extension of social-security coverage, public housing and inflation curbs went unanswered by the hostile Congress. He had expected nothing else. He was satisfied that he had gained additional fire power "against," as he said, "the special interests, as represented by the Republicans, and the record of the Eightieth Congress."

Through the dog days of August plans were laid for the campaign. Democratic headquarters were set up in New York at the Biltmore Hotel, with McGrath in charge. Matt Connelly helped him to maintain liaison with key political figures over the country. Another Missourian and old crony of Truman's, Bill Boyle, operated the Washington campaign office. The important and, under the circumstances, grueling post of finance chairman was assumed by Louis Johnson, a West Virginian who was getting rich from his Washington law practice. Clifford, chief of staff and principal speech writer, headed a group of idea men and workers who would accompany the President on his tours of the nation. Oscar Chapman, undersecretary of the Interior, took leave of absence from his job to serve as advance man for the President.

Bleak though the outlook appeared, these men were prepared to devote themselves wholeheartedly for two months to the task of trying to elect a President. Because they were professionals, they did not deceive themselves about the magnitude of the task. It would be an uphill fight all the way. But their very professionalism led them to think all the time not of losing but of how to win.

In the Dewey camp the atmosphere was permeated with calm optimism. A slick, well-financed organization was functioning to move the New Yorker into the presidency with a minimum of fuss and flurry. Strategy had been carefully worked out by Herbert Brownell, campaign manager, and Russel Sprague, long a powerful figure in New York Republican circles. Nobody was to get excited. In going after the nomination, Dewey had vigorously attacked the domestic and foreign policies of the Truman administration in order to draw strength from Bob Taft. But now things were different. In the campaign itself, he and his advisers agreed, such attacks would not be necessary. He was going to win anyway; the less he discussed issues, the less committed he would be to definite courses of action as President. Truman was to be ignored. Dewey would not lower himself by getting down in the gutter for hand-to-hand combat.

Both candidates had their special trains, and in September they started off on their campaign travels. Both early made major speeches in Iowa, and Joe Alsop, the newspaper columnist, who covered the two rallies, reported: "There was something sad about the respective campaign debuts here in Iowa. The Truman show was visibly unsuccessful—the Dewey show was opulent.... The contest was really too uneven." Most reporters accompanying the candidates concurred. Yet Truman was uproariously cheered by an audience of 75,000 people who heard his speech at the national plowing contest at Dexter, Iowa. Dewey was pleasantly but sedately received by a much smaller crowd at Drake University Field House in Des Moines.

Truman went on the offensive every waking moment. He had been making the issues for months, making them almost singlehandedly. Except for his veto of Taft-Hartley, there would have been no labor issue. He had created the civil-rights issue by his repeated demands that Congress enact legislation to protect the rights of minorities. Even the inflation issue had become his own when he came out, however reluctantly, for price controls. He took charge of the farm issue a few days after the campaign began by berating Congress for not giving the Commodity Credit Corporation authority to acquire additional storage warehouses and thus forcing farmers to throw their grain on the market when it was harvested instead of being able to hold it for higher prices.

Attack, attack, attack—that was Truman's strategy. He campaigned for thirty-five days, making two major transcontinental tours and a number of less ambitious forays into various sections of the country. He averaged about ten speeches a day, many of them delivered from the rear platform of the train at station stops. On one record-breaking day he gave sixteen speeches.

In every speech he blasted the "good-for-nothing, Taft-Hartley Eightieth Congress"—"the worst Congress since Thaddeus Stevens." He told good-natured, laughing crowds that "If you send another Republican Congress to Washington, you're a bigger bunch of suckers than I think you are." In earthy, blunt language, he shouted that he, Harry Truman, was fighting the people's battles with this no-good Congress. The Republicans, he said, wanted to put all the people of the country "in one big union and run it for the benefit of the National Association of Manufacturers." The Republicans were "the errand boys of big business." The Republicans had "stuck a pitchfork in the farmer's back."

Truman had set out to get his message "to the people in a personal way," and he did. His audiences listened and cheered. They yelled, "Give 'em hell, Harry!" He yelled back. His throat grew raw, and he almost shouted himself out of voice. Sometimes he showed signs of crankiness; at a midnight stop in Ogden, Utah, he interrupted a scorching attack on the Eightieth to scold into silence a group of roistering boys who had climbed into a tree. But mostly he was perky and cheerful, out of bed before six o'clock in the morning for an eighteen-hour day, filled with an energy that put the younger men on the campaign train to shame.

The Dewey train, modestly dubbed the *Victory* Special, meanwhile was moving through the country with leisurely assurance. Dewey also spoke from the back platform to good —but only good—crowds. They were attentive and cordial but showed none of the impulsive enthusiasm of Truman's audiences. Mostly Dewey offered the same speech, appealing for unity and promising honest and competent government. His basic theme was that only the election of a Republican President and a Republican Congress could give the kind of unified strength the country needed to insure peace in the world. He was given to uttering sentences like "Our country is at the crossroads of history" and "We need a rudder to our ship of state and a firm hand on the tiller."

He talked and acted like a man who had already been elected and was merely waiting for the time to take office. His speeches and his manner indicated that the election would be only a formality to confirm a known decision. While Truman was running against the Republican Congress, Dewey did not appear to be running against anything or anybody.

One of the jokes of the campaign was that it represented one more triumph of mind over matter: Truman didn't mind what he said, and whatever Dewey said didn't matter.

In truth, much of what both said was irrelevant nonsense. But Truman shouted his slashing attacks with fury and conviction. Dewey spoke his platitudes with an air of pleasant remoteness. Truman caused people to feel that everything would be absolutely terrible if he was not returned to the White House. Dewey assured people that everything would be lovely after they elected him. Truman communicated a passionate desire to win, Dewey a calm certainty that he *would* win.

Few observers thought that Dewey's confidence was unfounded. The political pollsters had started predicting his victory as soon as the conventions were over. One of them, Elmo Roper, said as early as September 9, "Mr. Dewey is just as good as elected." Sixty-five per cent of the nation's newspapers, with nearly 80 per cent of total newspaper circulation, supported Dewey. Three weeks before the election, *Newsweek* published the results of a poll of fifty leading political reporters; every one of them predicted a Dewey victory.

Only a few signs here and there might have been taken, if they had been known or noticed, as indicating that it might be well to hold the election after all.

Joe Martin pleaded vainly for Dewey to accept the Eightieth Congress as a campaign issue and defend its record. He declared Dewey was making a mistake not to talk about the constructive aspects of the Republican Congress. But the candidate and his advisers felt otherwise.

In October, as the *Victory* Special came into Massachusetts, it was boarded at Worcester by Frederick Ayer, Jr., a young lawyer and member of a prominent Boston family, and Thomas A. Pappas, Massachusetts businessman. The two were engaged in raising money in their state for the Republican campaign and they were worried. "We can't find that there's any interest at all in Dewey," Ayer told campaign aides. "He's not stirring the people with the kind of campaign you're running." Pappas agreed, but his and Ayer's protestations were brushed aside. The main idea, they were told, was not to rock the boat. Dewey would win all right.

Earl Warren, who had no part in shaping campaign strategy, privately expressed concern. As attorney general and governor of California, he had been accustomed to campaigning hard. He did not understand the blandness of Dewey's speeches. "Maybe they know what they're doing," he said to Gerald Cullinan, a family friend in Dallas, Texas, "but I can tell you I never won any of *my* campaigns this way."

Another experienced man, Bob Taft, was made angry by Dewey's refusal to answer Truman's denunciation of the Eightieth Congress. He was running a campaign, Taft declared, based on the proposition, "We Republicans can do everything the Democrats want to do and do it better." He told his friend Bill White that he knew three weeks ahead of the election Dewey would lose. "I knew it for certain," he explained to White, "when Martha told me she could no longer listen to Dewey's speeches or watch him on television."

Carl McCardle, national correspondent for the Philadelphia *Bulletin*, spent much of the fall traveling with Dewey and Truman, switching back and forth from one train to the other. He was one of some half dozen reporters who looked at the crowds, saw their reception of the candidates, and arrived at an independent conclusion. McCardle went to his editor in October and told him Truman was going to win. "Don't write that!" the editor exploded. "Don't talk to me about it. Don't even think about it. You're wrong!"

As the campaign neared an end, the disparity between the crowds began to give rise to wonder among other reporters. Truman's audiences were consistently bigger than Dewey's. In St. Paul, 21,000 people turned out to hear the President "give 'em hell." He drew 50,000 at an outdoor rally on a cold night in Indianapolis. In Chicago, 30,000 jammed the stadium, with 10,000 more standing outside to hear his speech broadcast.

Bob Albright, wily political writer for the Washington *Post*, noted that some reporters had started asking themselves, "Could we be wrong?" But most of them thought not. People just wanted to see and hear a President of the United States, they told one another. Besides, his wife and daughter were with him as an additional attraction. It was true that Truman's crowds were not only larger than Dewey's but also much more responsive, laughing with the candidate, shouting exhortations to him, and in general behaving like Democrats who found joy in a political fight. But that was because the President made himself one of them—just Harry Truman, a common man's common man.

Richard Rovere of the *New Yorker*, after spending some time on the campaign trail, wrote that the people of the United States were ready to give Truman anything in the world except the presidency of the United States. That statement probably summed up the feeling of most of the reporters.

Just before the election the Gallup poll showed Dewey the winner with 49.5 per cent of the vote to 44.5 per cent for Truman. *Time* correspondents in all forty-eight states said Dewey would carry twenty-nine states with 350 electoral votes; 266 were needed to win. Gamblers gave odds of fifteen or twenty to one against Truman. *Life* went to press before election day with a picture caption identifying Dewey as the next President.

Dewey himself devoted most of his efforts during the last part of the campaign to urging the election of Republican senators. In Louisville, he said he wanted Kentucky voters to concentrate on returning John Sherman Cooper to the Senate. "Don't worry about me," he added confidently. In his final campaign speech, in Madison Square Garden, he seemed ready to name his Cabinet. He gave a benign résumé of the campaign and said: "I am very happy that we can look back over the weeks of our campaign and say, 'This has been good for the country.' I am proud that we can look ahead to our victory and say, 'America won.' "

The Chicago *Tribune*, beating the gun with its first edition for the day after election, ran the headline that was to become famous all over the world: DEWEY DEFEATS TRUMAN.

All the savants were wrong, all the prophets discomfited. When the vote counting started on the night of election day, Truman picked up a lead which, though it went up and down, was never lost. He went over the top at 9:30 the next morning with 270 electoral votes when Bob Taft's Ohio moved firmly into his column. In all, he received 304 electoral votes in twenty-eight states to Dewey's 189 in sixteen states. Thurmond carried four southern states with thirty-eight electoral votes. Wallace carried none. It was the closest presidential election in popular votes since 1916: 24,045,052 for Truman, 21,896,926 for Dewey—49.5 per cent to 45.1 per cent.

Truman's was a truly national victory, won with a combination of eastern, central, midwestern, southern, southwestern and Pacific states. It was a personal victory almost without parallel in American politics, the victory of a fighting spirit and a dogged never-say-die determination. The underdog had triumphantly come through. Harry Truman was one of a slim handful of Americans in public life who could crow after election day, "I told you so!"

1949

A MIXED BAG

Hubris supplanted humility in the White House.

The postelection Truman was far removed from the humbly abject man of 1945 who spoke of being inadequate to carry the responsibility that had fallen on his shoulders and implored every casual visitor to pray for him. Now, having defeated the Republican who in 1944 garnered more votes against Franklin D. Roosevelt than anybody had ever got before, Truman's self-confidence soared. He wore the air of a man who had learned his job and shown that he could keep it. There was a new snap to his decisions. This was the Truman administration, not a holdover operation, and he made big plans for it. With *his* Congress ensconced on Capitol Hill, *his* selections manning the Cabinet, *his* appointees in key positions in Washington and elsewhere, the President set out to write the Fair Deal into the nation's history.

Jaunty and self-assured as he was, Truman maintained some appearance of his natural modesty. In an informal talk to a group of contributors to the Democratic treasury, he conceded that there might be a million people in the United

States who would make a better President. "But," he added, "I have the job and I have to do it." The knowledge filled him with elation.

The presidential inaugural, America's substitute for a coronation, was a lavish affair. A generous appropriation of funds had been made by the Eightieth Congress in the expectation that a Republican would become President on Inauguration Day. When matters turned out otherwise, the Democrats gleefully planned a day to be remembered. After all, sixteen years had passed since a new President was inaugurated, so a gala celebration was in order.

It was Harry Truman's day from start to finish.

For him, Inauguration Day began at a breakfast with ninety-seven veterans of his artillery battery in France in 1918. The aging ex-soldiers traveled up from Missouri in special railroad cars in response to a command invitation from the White House. They crowded around a grinning Truman, shaking hands with him and addressing him as "Mr. President." He would have none of that, he declared with mock asperity. They must call him "Captain Harry" in the manner of thirty years before. Same old Harry, they told one another happily.

After the oath-taking ceremony at noon and lunch at the Capitol, Truman and Barkley boarded a limousine for the mile-long ride downtown to the grandstand in front of the White House from which they would review the inaugural parade. More than a million people came out for the parade, which included thirty bands, thousands of marching troops and civilians, state governors and other dignitaries eager to salute the President. Tanks rumbled along Pennsylvania Avenue in the bright winter afternoon. Six hundred and fifty military aircraft formed an umbrella overhead.

The President, in overcoat and silk hat, watched it all for three hours from the enclosed and heated reviewing stand.

Resting his hips against a high stool, which was invisible from outside, he let the people see that he was enjoying the show. He exchanged cordial waves with officials passing along the street below, applauded the state floats and bands, smiled broadly at the antics of a veteran who had liquidly fortified himself for the event. He and Barkley sipped coffee and, as the afternoon wore on, did a bit of fortifying themselves. The ubiquitous Harry Vaughan, hovering behind him, told a joke that caused Truman and Barkley to break into uproarious laughter. All who looked could see an intensely human President having a very good time.

Twice during the long afternoon he also revealed that he remained an intensely political President. As the car bearing Governor Herman Talmadge of Georgia drew near the reviewing stand, Truman abruptly found he had something confidential to say to Barkley. While he whispered to the new vice-president, the two men turned momentarily away from the parade, leaving the southern governor saluting the presidential and vice-presidential backs. And when Governor Strom Thurmond, the Dixiecrat candidate for President in the recent campaign, lifted his hat as he passed the reviewing stand, Truman stared straight ahead, his face grimly expressionless. Backsliding Democrats, he was saying, would get no comfort from him.

At the inaugural ball, Truman stayed up past midnight enjoying the gaiety. He did not dance. As he once explained, "I'm a Baptist but not a lightfoot one, so I didn't learn to dance." But he watched from his box as everybody who was anybody cavorted below. A stream of the important and would-be important came by his box, anxious to be seen having a word with the President. Truman smilingly accepted congratulatory words from many men who, as he knew, a short time ago had been pleading that the Democratic party nominate anybody but him.

His sprightly aggressiveness stayed much in evidence after Inaugural Day. Appearing at the Democrats' Jefferson-Jackson Day dinner, he showed himself fully aware that the proposals made to Congress in his State of the Union message were encountering a less than enthusiastic reception: "The central issue of the campaign last fall was the welfare of all the people against special privilege for the few," he said. "When we made it clear where the Democratic party stood on that issue, the people made it clear where they stood with us." But now, he went on, "We are meeting determined opposition."

Who was at fault? The Republicans, of course. Ignoring the circumstance that the Democrats were back in control of Congress, the President launched into the familiar attack against the "special interests" which were trying to block repeal of the Taft-Hartley Act, fighting or watering down his welfare proposals, refusing to enact his low-rent housing program, working to keep minimum wages at starvation levels, seeking to destroy the farm price-support program. As usual, he added, these "special interests" enjoyed the support of newspaper editorial writers and columnists—his well-worn whipping boys.

It was hardly a new speech, but the assembled Democrats gave the President a reception vastly different from the per-functory applause that had greeted his address before the 1948 Jefferson-Jackson Day dinner. The speech had worked during the campaign, so it must be good—and, besides, the man giving it was going to be President for four more years. So Truman received an ovation.

A short time later he attended a dinner given by the Reserve Officers Association to honor Harry Vaughan. The jovial general had been under severe attack by Columnist Drew Pearson for accepting a medal from President Juan Perón of Argentina. Pearson said acceptance of a medal by a member of the President's staff from a tyrant like Perón was not in keeping with Truman's role as a champion of democratic principles. The Reserve Officers Association reacted to this by presenting Vaughan with a scroll naming him "Minute Man of 1949," and the President reacted by going to the dinner and making an off-the-cuff speech.

He spoke in language that the reserve officers had no trouble understanding: "I am just as fond of and just as loyal to my military aide as I am to the high brass, and I want you to distinctly understand that any S.O.B. who thinks he can cause any of these people to be discharged by me by some smart-aleck statement over the air or in the paper, he has another think coming."

His casual name calling elicited a number of self-righteous newspaper editorials about the use of such language by the President of the United States. But Truman was pleased with himself, and Pearson thereafter made much of the fact that he was the columnist singled out for being called S.O.B. by the President.

These alarums and excursions were symptomatic of what Arthur Krock labeled "Mr. Truman's expanding self-assurance." Writing in the *Times*, the distinguished columnist noted that the President's speeches and his bearing proclaimed that he had arrived at some new beliefs. Krock proceeded to list them: "He is right and all opponents are wrong, spiritually and factually; he can beat any politician or set of politicians at their common trade; he is boss and intends to assert it; the American majority and most men and women of good will support him down to the item; and if his friends are criticized, with or without good basis, it is a virtue to make a blanket defense of them and to keep them in the places to which they are assigned."

To other objective observers, if not to the President himself, this gently barbed summing up seemed a fair statement of Truman's attitude. His innate qualities were perhaps unchanged, but they were enlarged and intensified by his triumph at the polls. He became even more stubborn, even less tolerant of any opposition to his program, even more convinced that any criticism supposedly directed at his friends or appointees was actually aimed at him. Or, to say it another way, he remained firm in his beliefs of what was right for America, vigorous in his efforts to make those beliefs prevail in the government, and unashamedly loyal to his friends. There was little of the paradoxical about Truman; how he looked depended almost entirely on the point of view.

* * *

The Eighty-first Congress was a mixed bag. The Democrats had a strong majority, but it was numerical and not ideological. Sam Rayburn, again occupying the Speaker's chair with accustomed ease, announced bravely at the start of the session that "we are going to have only one kind of Democrat in this Congress." For once Rayburn was wrong—or, more likely, was not wrong but was simply trying to put a bold face to the situation—in his estimate of a body that he knew better than any other man.

Many of the members had got to Congress on their own, owing nothing to the President. More than a hundred of the 263 Democrats in the House of Representatives had polled more votes than Truman in their respective districts. Some new members in both branches had based their campaigns largely on opposition to the President's policies. It was not a New Deal Congress and, after Truman provided his own slogan for his program by stating, "Every segment of the population and every individual has the right to expect from our government a fair deal," not a Fair Deal Congress either.

Old familiar faces appeared at the heads of committee tables, but more often than not they belonged to Democrats who had a minimum of sympathy for the Truman program. Most of the committee chairmen were southerners, thanks to the seniority system and to the still prevailing one-party South's pleasant habit of keeping their congressmen in office term after term. And most of these southern chairmen were conservative, some would say reactionary, in their approach to domestic issues.

At the head of the enormously powerful House Ways and Means Committee was Robert Doughton of North Carolina, whose nickname—"Muley"—was a tribute to his hardheadedness. Demagogic John Rankin was chairman of the Veterans Affairs Committee, and another Mississippian, William Whittington, held the corresponding position on Public Works. The Armed Services Committee was in charge of the "Old Swamp Fox," Carl Vinson of Georgia. Clarence Cannon, seventy years old and starting his thirteenth term in the House, was no southerner, coming from Missouri, but he brought to the chairmanship of the Appropriations Committee a frosty attitude toward big spending by government.

Southerners also predominated in the Senate committee chairmanships: thrifty Walter George of Georgia, Finance; eighty-year-old, penny-pinching Kenneth McKellar of Tennessee, Appropriations; Millard E. Tydings of Maryland, who, like George, had survived a purge effort by Franklin D. Roosevelt, Armed Services; Olin Johnston of South Carolina, Post Office and Civil Service. Pat McCarran of Nevada broke the southern pattern, but as head of the Judiciary Committee, which controlled more than a third of the Senate's business, he looked with little favor on most aspects of the Fair Deal.

Scott Lucas, a senator from Illinois, succeeding to the majority leadership post left vacant by the ascension of Barkley to the vice-presidency, was sympathetic enough to Truman's program. However, although he was well liked in the

Senate and on the golf course at the Burning Tree Club, Lucas was too amiable to be a really forceful leader.

Some of the new senators were no more tractable than the old entrenched members. Lyndon Johnson moved over from the House after a Texas campaign in which he laid heavy emphasis on his support of the Taft-Hartley Act and his opposition to Truman's civil-rights proposals. From Oklahoma came Robert Kerr, a Bible-quoting, desk-thumping teetotaler who had made many millions in oil before being elected governor of his state and who had no intention of allowing himself to be lost in as small a crowd as the United States Senate. Brash, talkative Hubert Humphrey, fresh from a resounding victory in Minnesota over Republican Joe Ball, was ready to use the Senate to change the nation. Paul Douglas, a University of Chicago economics professor, was also a freshman senator, having defeated the Chicago *Tribune*'s personal spokesman, notorious for his reactionary isolationism; Truman would get support from Douglas, but not always. Russell Long, son of Huey and looking remarkably like the Kingfish, at thirty the youngest member in the body, was smoother than his father but no more inclined to wear any other man's collar. Estes Kefauver of Tennessee, another former House member, had shown his unorthodoxy by taking on and defeating Democratic Senator Tom Stewart, mouthpiece for hitherto unbeatable Memphis Boss Ed Crump.

Such men as these, coming in with their own ambitions and not beholden in any way to the man in the White House, some of them indeed hoping to live there themselves one day, could never be easy to handle. They and others no less dissimilar, in both Senate and House, made the Eighty-first the most unmanaged and unmanageable Congress in history.

Harry Truman, working with and through congressional leaders, tried hard. He was full of bounce as he submitted two dozen proposals for legislation, ranging all the way from new controls on the economy to a broadened civil-rights program, from repeal of Taft-Hartley to a compulsory-health-insurance bill. The President scheduled regular Monday morning meetings with Barkley, Rayburn, Lucas and John McCormack, House majority leader, to discuss upcoming legislative measures and how they could be passed. He frequently wrote letters to other members of Congress to solicit their support for a particular bill. He invited committee chairmen to the White House to give progress reports.

In the beginning the outlook seemed promising when Rayburn was able to force through the House a measure curbing the power of the Rules Committee. The conservative majority in this committee frequently bottled up legislation simply by refusing to clear it for consideration by the whole House. Now an agreement was reached that the panel could sit on a bill only twenty-one days without action. After that period the chairman of the legislative committee holding jurisdiction over the bill in question could ask the House for permission to bypass the Rules Committee and bring the measure directly to the floor.

This victory cheered the President. So did congressional approval of a pay raise for him. The presidential salary was increased from $75,000 to $100,000 a year and the sum of $50,000—tax free, no questions asked—was added to the old $40,000 travel-expense allowance. Truman was glad to get the raise, having found it costly to be President without private means to supplement his salary. Little opposition was voiced, although Senator Morse took advantage of the occasion to inveigh against cocktail parties and social activities. "There is entirely too much high living in Washington," argued the man from Oregon.

Steps also were taken to improve the President's living quarters. The Executive Mansion, rebuilt in 1818 after being burned by the British, was in danger of falling to pieces.

Ceilings sagged dangerously, floors shook beneath the tread of a heavy man, stairs quivered when a group of people walked up or down them. Alarmed that the structure might collapse around them, the Trumans had moved into Blair House shortly after the election. Early in 1949 the President asked a committee of building experts to make a thorough examination of the White House. After they reported that it was in deplorable condition, Congress established its own committee to decide what should be done. Although some members wanted to tear it down, a decision finally was reached to save the exterior and have the interior completely rebuilt.

So Truman had more money of his own and would have a better place to live. What he did not have was the cooperation of Congress in getting his Fair Deal proposals acted on instead of just being talked about.

By late spring it was evident that the program was bogged down. Action on major legislation was stymied by an effective coalition of southern Democrats and northern Republicans.

The prevailing southern attitude was expressed by a man no longer part of the Washington scene. Jimmy Byrnes, preparing to run—successfully—for governor of South Carolina, spoke up in accepting an honorary degree from Washington and Lee University: "We are going down the road to statism. Where we will wind up no one can tell. But if some of the new programs proposed should be adopted, there is danger that the individual—whether farmer, worker, manufacturer, lawyer or doctor—will soon be an economic slave pulling an oar in the galley of state." This statement, coming from a man who had done much to steer the New Deal program through Congress, infuriated Truman and did not aid his own program.

The House took a thirty-day recess in the middle of the session to enable the Senate to catch up with it. Majority

Leader Lucas went to the hospital with well-earned gastric ulcers. The President fumed and stewed and threatened to get on a train and "go to the people" again.

Rayburn advised against it. The Speaker, who had a super-lative sense of the "feel" of the House, suggested a two-point strategy: to hold Congress in session, let the members talk themselves out, and blame Republican obstructionists for con-gressional inaction; to let Congress know it had to get to work on what was left of the Truman program and the sooner it went to work the sooner the members could go home.

To a limited extent this strategy worked. Before Congress adjourned in October, after the longest peacetime session in history, the minimum wage was raised, increased appropria-tions were made for public power projects, and the authority of the Commodity Credit Corporation to build storage bins for grain was restored. The National Security Act passed the year before was amended, as Truman wanted, to increase the authority of the Secretary of Defense over the military forces. A public-housing bill was passed, but only because Taft sur-prisingly joined Democrats in fighting for it. Other Republi-cans, Vandenberg and John Foster Dulles, who had been appointed senator from New York to fill the vacancy caused by Wagner's resignation, played important roles in bringing about extension of the Marshall Plan. The North Atlantic pact linking the United States and eleven other nations in a defensive alliance was approved—again with the assistance of Vandenberg.

Against these pluses were balanced numerous glaring minuses. Repeal of the Taft-Hartley Act, high on the list of Truman's priorities, was refused by Congress despite a rare and impassioned appeal by Rayburn himself. No civil-rights legislation was enacted. Standby authority for price controls was refused the President and only a compromise extension of rent control was granted. The compulsory health control bill failed, although the American Medical Association was sufficiently exercised by its threat to assess each of its members twenty-five dollars to finance a $1.1 million campaign to fight the proposal.

Yet Truman was able to bring himself to say at the end, "I'm happy about the record of Congress. It's accomplished more than I expected."

And an especially political-minded Fair Dealer, concerned more with creating issues than with enacting legislation, chortled, "We haven't lost a Negro vote. We haven't lost a labor vote. We haven't lost a farmer vote."

Nevertheless, the Democratic party as represented in Congress was running out of control. A striking demonstration of loss of party support by Truman was given during the session when he nominated Leland Olds for a third five-year term on the Federal Power Commission. Lucas, in tune with Senate sentiment, warned the President against this action; but his warning went unheeded.

Olds was first appointed to the commission by Roosevelt in 1939 and had served as member, vice-chairman and chairman. Under his prodding the FPC had tightened up on government regulation of utilities, brought about substantial reductions in wholesale natural gas and electricity rates, and successfully opposed legislative attempts to exempt the booming natural-gas industry from federal control. Naturally, the oil and gas industry was not kindly disposed toward him.

Colorado's Ed Johnson, chairman of the Senate Interstate and Foreign Commerce Committee, named Lyndon Johnson chairman of a subcommittee to hold hearings on the nomination. Lyndon Johnson was from Texas, where the oil-and-gas industry was very big indeed. Moreover, the young senator, who had won his primary victory in 1948 by the breathtakingly narrow margin of 87 votes out of more than a million cast, needed to build himself up in the esteem of the men who ran the industry. The Olds nomination afforded him an ideal opportunity to do so.

The nominee could hardly be opposed on the ground that he took his job seriously, which was the main count against him. But at a time when there was a vague but widespread uneasiness among Americans about what Communist Russia was up to, Olds was vulnerable in another area. Twenty years before, like many other men who were to become part of the New Deal administration, he had held and expressed some radical views about the capitalist system. Lyndon Johnson's subcommittee dug up an article he had written for a labor news syndicate in which he said, "Capitalism in the United States is rapidly passing into a stage which has marked the decay of many earlier social orders." Olds had gone on to berate the capitalists themselves, who, he wrote, composed "a privileged class of parasites whose idleness and dissipation become an increasing stench in the nostrils of the people."

The commissioner, although surprised to hear the words he had written two decades before quoted back to him at the subcommittee hearing, refused to repudiate his old opinions. He only went so far as to say that for shock value he had phrased them a little too intemperately. He firmly denied that he had ever been a Communist and labeled Communism a "negation of democracy."

It was no use. Big Ed Johnson thundered: "Personally I regard Leland Olds as a warped, tyrannical, mischievous, egotistic chameleon whose predominant color is pink." Lyndon Johnson, making sure that Washington reporters for Texas newspapers were listening, sternly declared the commissioner's record was "an uninterrupted tale of bias, prejudice and hostility directed against the industry over which he seeks control." Olds, a prickly man, inspired invective.

Belatedly alarmed, Truman had Bill Boyle wire every

Democratic national and state committeeman and every Democratic governor and mayor to say that Olds' defeat would be "a victory for the power lobbyists and the Republican party." At a news conference he barked that the Olds case was a question of party policy and party discipline.

But the Democrats in Congress wanted to have a hand in making party policy and they had no thought of submitting to discipline from the White House. Lyndon Johnson's subcommittee voted 7 to 0 to reject the nomination, Ed Johnson's full committee voted 10 to 2 against it, and in the Senate the vote was 55 to 15 to deny confirmation. It was a stunning defeat for the President, administered by his own party on a matter which he himself had made a party issue.

He had other troubles during the year. His chum Harry Vaughan was called before a Senate subcommittee which was investigating the activities of influence peddlers in wangling lucrative contracts with departments of the federal government. The postwar period was a flourishing time for the "five percenter," a person who, for a percentage of the sum involved in a given project, would undertake to obtain favored treatment for his clients through his friendship, real or purported, with top government officials. Some five percenters were sleazy, small-time operators like John Maragon, a one-time Kansas City bootblack. Others, like James V. Hunt, who had been a colonel in the Quartermaster Corps during the war, drew down heavy retainers plus huge contingency fees and worked from offices adorned by the autographed pictures of prominent personages in Washington. What Maragon and Hunt and others of their kind had in common was friendship with Major General Harry Vaughan, military aide to the President of the United States.

The subcommittee looking into these matters was headed by Senator Clyde Hoey of North Carolina. Hoey was a southern gentleman of the old school and looked it with his high-top shoes, wing collar and frock coat, a friendly man who was often seen in the morning riding a streetcar to Capitol Hill and chatting amiably with his seatmate. Behind his soft manner, however, lay experience as a newspaper editor and lawyer, assistant United States district attorney, and governor of his state. Soon the reports of his subcommittee hearings were appearing on the front pages every day.

Testimony centered around the activities of the five per-centers in the Defense Department, the War Assets Administration, the Reconstruction Finance Corporation, and other agencies involved in disposing of surplus war properties and making decisions about allocations of scarce materials. Even before Vaughan was called before the panel, it was made clear that he had dashed off reams of letters on White House stationery to give his friends a helping hand. A client of Maragon's had sent deep-freeze units not only to Vaughan but also to the White House in Washington, the "little White House" in Independence and several officials in the Executive Branch. The client was a Chicago perfume firm for which Maragon had once tried to smuggle into the United States a quantity of valuable perfume oil under the guise of "champagne for Mrs. Truman." Vaughan explained to the subcommittee that he had been told the deep-freezers were experimental models and had no commercial value. He did not deny trying to help his friends, including Maragon and Hunt. "Why pick on Hunt," he inquired plaintively, "when there are three hundred people in Washington in the same business?"

The 240-pound general sweated on the witness stand for two days. Aside from the deep-freeze, he said, he got nothing for the help he gave except cigars. Despite the headlines, this admission more or less typified the whole proceedings. Nothing big was uncovered by this investigation, just cases of petty favors done by and for little men. The whole thing was only

97

sordid, not really scandalous. Hoey concluded that Vaughan, for a man so close to the President, was too quick with his favors, but the quiet North Carolinian's verdict was that no corruption was involved.

Even though egregious wrongdoing was not proved, Truman was damaged by the investigation. It was the most natural reaction in the world for him to stand by Vaughan and to proclaim that the special interests and the kept press were trying to get at him through his military aide. As an organization politician, Truman had been unquestioningly loyal to those above him when he stood at the bottom of the political ladder. Now that he was on the top rung he was just as unhesitating in his loyalty to those below him, so long as they were on the same ladder. Sam Rayburn often admonished, "Every man should stay with his own crowd," and it was advice that Truman instinctively followed. Attacks on his associates simply hardened his defense of them. He stoutly denied that there was a "mess in Washington."

The administration also came under heavy fire during the year for its alleged "softness on Communism." This development was in part a hangover from investigations conducted by the House Un-American Activities Committee when the Republicans controlled Congress. Former Communist agents were paraded before the committee. One of them, a brooding man named Whittaker Chambers, testified that some years before he had received from Alger Hiss, then a trusted employee of the State Department, transcripts of secret documents for transmission to Soviet Russia. Hiss denied the charge. Truman called the investigation "a red herring" dragged up by his opponents for political reasons. Now, in 1949, Hiss was tried for perjury, eventually was convicted and sent to prison. The administration was further embarrassed by a statement by Dean Acheson, the new Secretary of State, that he would never "turn my back" on Alger Hiss.

Apprehension grew among the American people about the extent to which subversive influences were at work within the government. This feeling of alarm was intensified by almost daily stories about spies and communist cells within the most sensitive agencies. Truman, becoming acutely uncomfortable under charges that he was coddling Communists inside the government, issued a set of "loyalty" regulations and established a board to enforce them. But when loyalty investigations and trials were held, he said at a press conference that they were nothing but headline-hunting affairs. The whole uproar, he declared, was typical postwar hysteria, which, he added huffily, was not evident in the Executive Branch of the government.

Hysterical or not, it seemed to many Americans that Communism was winning in the struggle for power in the world. It became evident that mainland China was lost to the Communists. Truman and the State Department were charged by Republicans and many Democrats with responsibility for the loss. They alleged that Chiang Kai-shek and his Nationalist Chinese had been "sold out" by a pro-Communist clique in the United States government. A young congressman named John Fitzgerald Kennedy made a speech in Salem, Massachusetts, detailing events leading up to the downfall and concluding: "This is the tragic story of China whose freedom we once sought to preserve. What our young men had saved, our diplomats and our President have frittered away."

In the fall came the grim news that an atomic explosion had occurred in the Soviet Union. The Communists had the Bomb, ushering the world into a new era of the atomic age. Scientists had known the United States could not forever retain its monopoly, but now the cry arose, not without justification, that Russia would not have been able to break that monopoly so early without the help of spies in America. And who persisted in fighting against attempts to expose and root out these subversives? Truman, cried the administration's opponents. He was soft on Communism. He babied the Reds. Dark mutterings were heard about treason in high places.

Events combined to take most of the fun out of being President.

* * *

On the Republican front, Guy George Gabrielson, who had succeeded Hugh Scott as National Chairman, paid a visit to Chicago in October and passed on to the assemblage of Cook County political bosses a suggestion he had received from Dwight Eisenhower. "I hope," said the president of Columbia University, "the Republicans now will develop party principles so that even a person as dumb as I am can tell the difference between the Republican and Democratic parties."

1950-51

EVERYTHING COMING LOOSE

Republican members of Congress traditionally fan out over the country during the week in which Lincoln's birthday falls to bring the party gospel to whatever audiences can be drummed up for them. In February of 1950 a routine request for such a speaker reached the Republican National Committee from the Republican Women's Club of Wheeling, West Virginia. On the list of congressmen who had indicated they were available for such engagements was the name Joseph Raymond McCarthy, a first-term senator from Wisconsin. He was little known outside his own state, but then Wheeling was not the crossroads of the world.

So the speakers' bureau sent Joe McCarthy to West Virginia.

McCarthy had gone to a country school in his native Wisconsin, dropped out to run a chicken farm, then at the age of nineteen enrolled in high school. According to his self-prepared biography in the *Congressional Directory*, he completed the four-year course in a single year while working during off-school hours in a grocery store and a movie

101

house. After graduation from Marquette University in 1935 he was admitted to the Wisconsin bar. Four years later he was elected a circuit judge. He enlisted as a private in the Marine Corps in 1942 and while still in service ran unsuccessfully for the United States Senate. He was again a candidate in 1946, this time against Senator Robert M. La Follette, Jr., son of the legendary old Progressive from Wisconsin. In that state of perpetually surprising politics, McCarthy defeated La Follette and entered the Senate.

In his three years in the body he had done nothing to distinguish himself. His committee assignments were negligible. He displayed no oratorical ability and had no comprehensive understanding of the problems which came before the Senate. He was generally regarded by his fellow senators as just another man swept into office on the 1946 wave of anti-Truman sentiment. They accepted him amiably enough, but it was clear in those early years that he was not likely to become a member of the inner circle which, effectively and quietly, ran the Senate.

But obscurity did not suit the black-browed Wisconsin senator. He wanted to be known. He restlessly sought for an issue which would bring him the publicity he longed for. He found the issue in his Wheeling speech and at age forty-one was off on a brand new career as a professional anti-Communist.

It was not that he possessed, then or later, any real knowledge of the nature of Communism. McCarthy was no student of dialectic materialism, had no inside track to Communist subversion. Most of his speech in Wheeling was devoted to a rehash of the loyalty investigations and congressional committee hearings on Communists in government.

Then suddenly he was flourishing a sheet of paper in the air before the startled Republican ladies and rasping, "While I cannot take the time to name all of the men in the State

102

Department who have been named as members of the Communist party and members of a spy ring, I have here in my hand a list of two hundred and five—a list of names that were made known to the Secretary of State as being members of the Communist party and who nevertheless are still working and shaping policy in the State Department."

When accounts of the speech appeared in the newspapers, Truman promptly and categorically denied that any such list had been "made known" to Secretary Acheson. But the Wisconsin senator traveled westward to repeat his charges in Reno and Salt Lake City. He fired off a telegram to the President—released to the press, naturally—demanding a "housecleaning" in the State Department. When he returned to Washington to find a gratifyingly large stack of front-page newspaper stories on his desk, he rose in the Senate chamber to talk about "known Communist agents in the State Department." He now placed the number at eighty-one.

The Secretary of State was the focal point of his continuing onslaught. "Red Dean" Acheson, as McCarthy labeled him, formed the perfect target. He not only occupied the post of Secretary of State, in itself grounds enough for suspicion in the minds of the people to whom McCarthy appealed, but in addition he looked and acted like the king of all striped-pants cookie pushers. Standing an erect six feet, always immaculately dressed and possessed of a truly imposing guardsman's mustache, he instantly aroused the combative instincts of a street brawler like McCarthy. Day after day the senator bore down on his charge that Acheson habitually used his office to protect Communists working in the State Department.

Nor were other government agencies and departments immune from the lash of McCarthy's tongue. He shouted that the government was honeycombed with Communists and that they were to be found even in the White House. Truman, he confided to the Senate, was the victim of "a bunch of twisted intellectuals telling him only what they want him to know." Congress could and should rescue the President by exposing and throwing out the Communists in his administration.

Most of the letters and telegrams pouring into the White House and congressional offices about such charges expressed support of McCarthy. They reflected a widespread public belief that Communists who had infiltrated the government did indeed influence its policies to the detriment of national security. This belief was based on many facts which had been brought to attention before McCarthy spoke in Wheeling. Since the end of the war Communist spies in the United States *had* been flushed out from their cover—although not by McCarthy—and one did not have to be a crank to wonder if others not known had wormed their way into the government and stayed there. Persons still on the public payroll *had* admitted their seduction in the past by the Communist party line. Their vows of repentance and their repudiation of former views may have satisfied their superiors in office, but many other Americans were not so sure. They resented the attitude of Truman and Acheson that the whole issue of Communism in government was an absurdity. Besides, McCarthy was so convincing. He named numbers if not names, and he never let up.

That the administration was being damaged could not be doubted. Word was passed among the Democrats that action would have to be taken to put down the McCarthy menace.

Within two weeks after the West Virginia speech the Senate unanimously passed a resolution instructing the Foreign Relations Committee or an authorized subcommittee to conduct "a full and complete study and investigation as to whether persons who are disloyal to the United States are or have been employed by the Department of State." A special subcommittee was established to conduct the investigation. Millard E. Tydings of Maryland was named chairman. Other members were Theodore Francis Green of Rhode Island and Brien McMahon of Connecticut, Democrats, and Republicans Henry Cabot Lodge, Massachusetts, and Bourke B. Hickenlooper, Iowa. Of these only the last had ever expressed sympathy for what McCarthy was doing.

The Tydings subcommittee held hearings for four months, producing testimony covering more than 1500 printed pages. McCarthy was the star witness, but it quickly became evident that he had no new information to offer. He dealt constantly in what Winston Churchill was once pleased to call terminological inexactitudes. He based a long list of unsubstantiated charges on material his staff had dug out of the files of investigations conducted by several House committees during the Eightieth Congress. It was old stuff, but it got an excited rerun in the newspapers.

At a typical session McCarthy would reel off his accusations and suggest that the committee search the files of the FBI and Civil Service Commission for proof of their accuracy. Then he would stride off across the street to the dining room of the Carroll Arms Hotel to down two fast Manhattan cocktails and gobble a hamburger, happy in the knowledge that he had met the deadline for the afternoon papers.

He spoke frequently in the Senate to repeat and enlarge upon the charges he made before the Tydings subcommittee. He was rarely challenged by other senators, especially those who were up for re-election in the fall. He had a few stout supporters, including William E. Jenner of Indiana, a fair demagogue in his own right, and Kenneth Wherry. Even the respected Bob Taft, to whom the tactics and general bad manners of McCarthy were repellent, said the Wisconsin senator should "keep talking and if one case doesn't work out he should proceed with another." Muted approval came from other senators. Ralph Flanders of Vermont, a progressive Republican, conceded that he found some of McCarthy's charges "disturbing." Alexander Smith of New Jersey, a legislator of great repute, defended his colleague from some of the Democratic outbursts and said he was doing his "obvious duty."

Another Republican, Margaret Chase Smith of Maine, felt differently. The only woman in the Senate, she got to her feet one day to say, as a still and white-faced McCarthy listened, "The American people are sick and tired of being afraid to speak their minds lest they be politically smeared as 'Communists' or 'Fascists.' The American people are sick and tired of seeing innocent people smeared and guilty people whitewashed." The spunky lady senator made it plain that she spoke as a Republican, declaring that the Democratic administration had in fact substantially lost the confidence of the American people. "The nation sorely needs a Republican victory," she added. "But I don't want to see the Republican party ride to victory on the Four Horsemen of Calumny—Fear, Ignorance, Bigotry, and Smear."

Half a dozen other senators subscribed to Mrs. Smith's "Declaration of Conscience," but the Republican leadership ignored it.

After four months of hearings, the Tydings subcommittee issued a report which had the effect of clearing the State Department with respect to McCarthy's charges of Communist infiltration and its refusal to take action to stop it. Lodge and Hickenlooper declined to sign the report, declaring the investigation had not been broad enough to justify the issuance of a clean bill of health for the department. McCarthy put out a press release in which he said, "Today, Tydings tried to notify the Communists in the government that they are safe in their positions." But the Wisconsin senator said that promise could not be kept: they would be exposed, "regardless of how frantically Tydings screams for their protection." To McCarthy the whole matter had become a personal issue between him and Tydings.

The Maryland senator was up for re-election in 1950, and McCarthy moved into the campaign with vigor, guile and determination. Tydings had been in the Senate twenty-four years. His opponent was a rather dim Baltimore lawyer, John Marshall Butler. Butler was regarded by political observers as a weak candidate with little chance of defeating the veteran incumbent.

But McCarthy was determined to bring Tydings down, and he approached the welcome task with the full force of his crafty political mind. His campaign against Communism had attracted the support of rich right wingers throughout the country. McCarthy now called on them to help finance Butler's campaign. The response was excellent. McCarthy also put a heavy hand on strategy, which consisted almost entirely of depicting Tydings as either the dupe or the accomplice of Communists. A political publicity man from Chicago, Jon M. Jonkel, was hired to go into Maryland to make sure that McCarthy's ideas were put into effect. Jonkel did such an effective job—including the faking of a photograph which apparently showed Tydings and Joseph Stalin in amicable conversation—that later he was fined $5,000 for violation of the Federal Corrupt Practices Act. Regardless of that, Tydings was defeated by more than 40,000 votes.

Maryland was not the only state where the McCarthy influence was felt. He campaigned hard against Scott Lucas, Senate majority leader, who by virtue of his position was in the front row of congressional defenders of the administration. Other factors entered into the Illinois Senate campaign, with Lucas making the mistake of saying over and over, "A vote for me is a vote for Harry Truman," but McCarthy claimed credit for the result. In California, Helen Gahagan

Douglas, Democratic nominee for the Senate, had been scored by her primary opponent as "the pink lady." McCarthy helped Richard M. Nixon, striving to move over from the House of Representatives, make the most of this label, and the liberal Mrs. Douglas lost.

It was a happy election day for Joe McCarthy and for the Republican party. The Republicans gained five seats in the Senate and twenty-eight in the House. Over the nation as a whole, they had a majority of 54 per cent of the popular vote. The Democrats were able to hold their majority in Congress with a minority vote because of light balloting in the South, where many of their candidates were unopposed. They might have been better off if they had lost Congress. As it was, they faced the prospect of two years in which they would have great responsibility without much power. Although nominally in control, they were in fact at the mercy of a strong Republican minority abetted by Democrats from the South.

McCarthy typically overstated the part he played in the election campaign, but even Republicans who disliked his methods and distrusted him personally admitted he had been a great asset in vote getting. In just nine months McCarthy had elevated himself from the obscurity he hated to a position of prestige and power in his party and in the nation.

Given a new weapon by Communist aggression against South Korea, which he said was a result of the "sellout" of Chiang Kai-shek by the United States, he pressed his attack against Truman and his appointees. Speaking before the American Society of Newspaper Editors in April 1951, he matter-of-factly described the Secretary of State as "incompetent." He also remarked that it was "pathetic" that General George C. Marshall should have been called again from retirement to serve as Secretary of Defense. McCarthy received only perfunctory applause as he concluded his address, but at the end of a question-and-answer period which followed, the editors exhibited much greater enthusiasm. Arthur Krock wrote in the *Times* that one newsman commented, "His hearers apparently concluded that though he is a barroom fighter who pays no attention to the rules designed to make fighting fair, he has something."

In another session with reporters, McCarthy offered to name twenty-six State Department officials and underlings who were being investigated for loyalty. He was asked if he would list the names in a statement off the Senate floor, where he enjoyed immunity against being called legally to account for anything he said. Certainly he would, McCarthy rejoined, if the reporters would publish the entire list in their papers.

"I assume that twenty would sue you for libel," McCarthy said, with his wolfish smile. "You could win, of course, but the cost might be a couple of hundred thousand dollars. I'd be sued too, but I'm willing to take the chance."

The reporters were not willing, so McCarthy proceeded to read the list of names in the Senate.

A spokesman for the State Department promptly said that one of those named had never worked in the department, some had quit, fourteen had been cleared by the loyalty board, and the remainder were "in process through the loyalty program." Even the senator's detractors could not hail this as a very stirring rebuttal—and the newsmen had their story, the senator his publicity.

In his talk before the newspaper editors McCarthy had called Marshall "a great general," but by June he had changed his mind about the old soldier and public servant. Now he came up with the astounding charge that Marshall for years —all through the war and during his 1946 mission to China— had been a conscious agent of Soviet Russia. Marshall, said

McCarthy, was involved in a "conspiracy and an infamy so black as to dwarf any previous such venture in the history of man."

This was strong stuff. McCarthy had never gone so far before, and the Democrats hopefully told one another that in his accusations against Marshall he had at last overreached himself. His blatant irresponsibility would now be generally recognized and the McCarthy figure would topple of its own weight. But Senator William Benton of Connecticut thought it needed a hard push.

After weeks of studying the record of the Tydings subcommittee investigation and other material which had accumulated about the activities of the Wisconsin senator in his quick rise to fame, Benton offered a resolution to expel McCarthy from the Senate for perjury, deceit, fraud, and lack of fitness for office. The resolution was referred to the Rules Committee by a straight party vote.

The ensuing investigation went on desultorily for sixteen months. Benton was the only witness to testify publicly. McCarthy, not in the least bothered by the expulsion resolution, insolently refused to appear before the committee. Instead he attacked its members for conducting an investigation which was merely part of the continuing Communist-inspired effort to silence him. It would never work, he declared.

After the sixteen months, the committee issued a report slapping McCarthy on the wrist for the derogatory statements he had made about the panel. No recommendations were offered. The report said of itself that it "should speak for itself," adding, "The issue raised is one for the entire Senate."

It was an issue the Senate was not yet prepared to meet.

Joe McCarthy was like a surfboard rider who watches keenly for the biggest wave to carry him ashore. The purpose is not to get to the shore but to thrill to the ride, and

McCarthy had no particular destination in mind. Most politicians are imbued with a certain lust for power or they would be in some other business, but McCarthy never seemed especially greedy for power. What he wanted, and what for a time he got, was just the glory of it all: the newspaper stories, the television appearances, the crowd cries of "Give 'em hell, Joe," the grasping of his elbow in rough manly approval by individuals lurking outside committee hearing rooms, the opportunity to be bought a drink by a rich man with a pathological fear that any show of liberalism was a manifestation of Communism.

McCarthy lusted to be in the limelight, that was all. To this end he destroyed a few individuals, impaired the usefulness of others, brought vast uneasiness to the minds of many more, did substantial harm to the U.S. Foreign Service, and increased public distrust of the American government.

In the process he severely damaged the Democratic party, which may also have been part of his purpose. Eventually he was to do even greater damage to the Republicans.

* * *

Truman was forced to reckon with a MacArthur as well as a McCarthy.

Rayburn, who in his time judged the characters of many men, once said of General Douglas MacArthur, "The only trouble with him is he's always thought he was a man of destiny." Then, the Speaker's uncontrollable honesty breaking out, he added, "And he just about was too."

The handsome general with the introspective eyes and noble profile had long been absent from the United States, but his exploits during the war and his remarkable achievement of turning Japan around, governmentally and economically, after the war—plus skillfully managed publicity—had made his name a household word among Americans. The American

111

image was given added sheen by the grandiloquent pronouncements on honor and duty and loyalty which the general occasionally issued from his Pacific command headquarters. Anything he said made news. His picture was often on the front pages. Except to some men who had served under him, he was the embodiment of all the American people wanted their military leaders to be. They even admired his imperiousness, his unself-conscious arrogance.

In 1948, enmeshed in the problems of Occupied Japan, MacArthur had said: "My major advisers now have boiled down to two men—George Washington and Abraham Lincoln. If you go back into their lives, you can find almost all the answers." The general never gave any sign of doubt that he had found the answers. His faith in his own judgment was supreme.

He was the man on horseback when the North Korean army swept across the 38th parallel into South Korea in June of 1950.

The invaders were well trained and were equipped by the Soviet Union with tanks and other modern weapons of war. U.S. forces stationed in South Korea and the South Korean soldiers themselves were quickly routed. The North Koreans pushed steadily down the peninsula until finally checked by a narrow defensive perimeter around the port city of Pusan far into the south. Then, in a stunning reversal, MacArthur carried out a boldly conceived landing in Inchon behind the enemy and hurled the invaders back across the demarcation line. The military genius had worked his magic once again.

In the United States, the people rallied behind Truman. His quick reaction to North Korea's aggression won widespread approval from both Democrats and Republicans. The United Nations was formally committed to the war, although its armed contingents never made up more than a small fraction of the total forces participating in it. The UN was also committed to the reunification of all Korea. A push began toward the Yalu River, the border between Korea and Manchuria. Total victory was the watchword.

Truman decided that he should have a personal conference with MacArthur. "I thought," he wrote later, "that he ought to know his Commander in Chief and I ought to know the senior field officer in the Far East."

The President had never met MacArthur, although he had tried to meet him. On two occasions shortly after the end of the war with Japan he instructed George Marshall to suggest that MacArthur come to the United States for a visit. The first invitation included a suggestion that the general might appear before congressional committees concerned with the postwar national defense. MacArthur declined the invitation and added that when he did come to the United States he would not care to make any committee appearances, "involving me in controversial issues which I do not feel I should undertake at that time and under such circumstances."

A month later, Truman had Marshall send a second message to MacArthur. This one was somewhat stronger: "The President has asked me to inform you that he wishes you to understand that he would like you to make a trip home at such time as you feel you can safely leave your duties." It was suggested that Congress would want to invite him to address a joint session. In his reply, MacArthur expressed himself as grateful for the President's sympathetic attitude and said he would like very much to come home for a visit, but "The desperation of the coming winter here cannot be overestimated. I would feel that I were failing in my duty and obligations were I to delegate this responsibility."

Five years later, on an island in the Pacific, the President and the general finally got together.

The Wake Island meeting was hardly the historic event that contemporary news accounts made it appear. The two posed for photographs, MacArthur wearing his famous peaked cap and a shirt unbuttoned at the throat, Truman managing to look simultaneously determined and good humored. The general imparted an air of stately condescension toward the civilian, who tried without rancor to put over the idea that he was the man in charge. They talked alone for an hour or more, but no momentous decisions were made, no grand strategy designed.

In his *Memoirs*, Truman's account of the meeting was uncharacteristically succinct. "We discussed the Japanese and Korean situations," he reported. "The general assured me that the victory was won in Korea. He also informed me that the Chinese Communists would not attack and that Japan was ready for a peace treaty. He said he wanted me to understand that he was not in politics in any way—that he had allowed the politicians to make a 'chump' (his word) of him in 1948 and that it would not happen again."

The President appeared, at least in afterthought, to have been less than charmed.

Five weeks later, on November 24, MacArthur started the Eighth Army on a major attack, announcing it as a general offensive "to win the war." He told one of his commanders to inform his troops that they would be home by Christmas.

They were not home by Christmas and many never reached home at all. As the attack moved northward it met with increasing resistance not only from the regrouping North Koreans but also, and more alarmingly, from massive numbers of "volunteers" from Communist China. United States losses of men and equipment were extremely heavy. Only timely preparations for retreat by the field generals averted total disaster.

MacArthur wanted to bomb the bases in Manchuria beyond the Yalu River, which might well have moved Communist China into full-scale war. Permission was not granted from Washington, but MacArthur talked about the possibility to such an extent that many people in the United States and elsewhere believed the government would change its policy.

Truman tried to shut him up. He issued an order to all government agencies that no speech, press release or other public statement regarding foreign policy should be issued for public consumption without being cleared by the State Department. He followed this up with a more specific notice calling on U.S. officials overseas, "including military commanders," to be extraordinarily cautious in their public statements "and to refrain from direct communications on military or foreign policy with newspapers, magazines, or other publicity media in the United States." Neither of these orders mentioned MacArthur, but the point was clear.

As the American people came incredulously to realize that the war in Korea was not being won, the bipartisan support Truman had enjoyed at its beginning faded away. He had made the mistake in a news conference of calling the war a "police action." The term was hurled against him as a sneer. Now it was "Truman's war." Casualties mounted. The President came under heavy attack from some members of Congress and much of the press. So did certain members of his Cabinet.

Louis Johnson, the 1948 campaign fund raiser for Truman who had succeeded Forrestal as Secretary of Defense, was roundly denounced for the country's state of military unpreparedness. It was true that when he made up his defense budget for the 1951 fiscal year—early in calendar 1950—he had responded too heartily to widespread demands for economy. Now he was attacked by men who at the time had thought the defense budget was too high. Truman finally asked for his resignation in an effort to appease public opinion. George Catlett Marshall was called back into service as his successor.

The President would not fire Dean Acheson. "They wanted Acheson's scalp because he stood for *my* policy," Truman declared. "The men who struck out against Acheson were in reality striking out at me." In the House of Representatives, Joe Martin introduced a bill to stop payment of Acheson's salary.

The soreness of the people over the way things were going in Korea was exacerbated by controls and inflation at home. Price and wage controls were brought back. Sugar, meat, tires, gasoline and other common consumer items were again rationed. The excess-profits tax so hated by business was reimposed. Money in circulation multiplied at the same time that possible and legal uses of money were dwindling. Prices shot up. The dollar bought less.

It was a winter of discontent. The coming of spring brought no improvement.

On March 24, 1951, General MacArthur issued a statement, in effect threatening Communist China with an ultimatum and saying he was prepared to cross the Yalu and carry the war to the Chinese. This was an expression of open disagreement with U.S. government policy, and Truman noted it with set jaw.

On April 4, Chairman Connally of the Senate Foreign Relations Committee and Speaker Rayburn, obviously without prior consultation together, spoke about the state of the world. Connally said, "The course of world events is uncertain, but it is my view that there will be no world war this year. The Russians will not defy the free nations of the world." Rayburn said, "I think that we stand in the face of terrible danger and maybe the beginning of World War III." He expressed grave fear that Soviet Russia would move aggressively in Europe if the United States became embroiled in open warfare with Red China.

The next day Joe Martin read in the House a letter he had received from MacArthur and which he had been worriedly carrying around in his pocket for several days. The letter was in reply to one he had written the general to advocate the use of Chinese Nationalist troops in Korea. He asked if Mac-Arthur agreed with that view.

Yes, said MacArthur, he agreed. "It seems strangely difficult," he wrote Martin, "for some to realize that here in Asia is where the Communist conspirators have elected to make their play for global conquest, and that we have joined the issue thus raised on the battlefield; that here we fight Europe's war with arms while the diplomats there still fight it with words; that if we lose the war to Communism in Asia the fall of Europe is inevitable, win it and Europe most probably would avoid war and yet preserve freedom. As you point out, we must win. There is no substitute for victory."

Truman had his mind made up. MacArthur must go. On April 11, at a press conference hastily called in the middle of the night because he had been advised that the story of Mac-Arthur's dismissal would appear in a Chicago paper the next morning, the President gave out this announcement:

"With deep regret, I have concluded that General of the Army Douglas MacArthur is unable to give his wholehearted support to the policies of the United States Government and of the United Nations in matters pertaining to his official duties. In view of the specific responsibilities imposed upon me by the Constitution of the United States and the added responsibility which has been entrusted to me by the United Nations, I have decided that I must make a change of command in the Far East. I have, therefore, relieved General MacArthur of his commands and have designated Lieutenant General Matthew B. Ridgway as his successor."

The fight predicted by Acheson started immediately and

furiously. Involving emotion, personality conflict, partisan maneuvering and political buncombe, it quickly aroused the entire nation.

The news caused shock waves around the world. Harold Nicholson, the British journalist and indefatigable diarist, noted in his journal, "In the morning I do my overseas talk, devoted entirely to the dismissal of MacArthur. Of course the Republicans are going to exploit all this against Truman, and will say that MacArthur was dismissed owing to our representation. This will make us the more suspicious of American leadership, while the fortunes of the world may be at the mercy of some senatorial lobby or some press stunt." Foreign governments, fearing that if MacArthur had his way the war would spread, were generally pleased by his dismissal.

That was a foreign viewpoint. But in the United States Senate, Jenner of Indiana cried in semi-hysteria, "Our only choice is to impeach President Truman and find out who is the secret invisible government which has so cleverly led our country down the road to destruction." McCarthy sneered that MacArthur was fired as a result of the machinations of a White House clique operating under the influence of "bourbon and benedictine." When Dewey Short of Missouri merely mentioned MacArthur's name in the House chamber, Republican members jumped to their feet and applauded for three solid minutes.

Ladies marched in front of the United Nations headquarters in New York carrying signs with such admonitions as "Truman should quit and take Acheson and Alger Hiss with him" and "Bring MacArthur back to tell the truth." Indignant newspaper editorials exploded everywhere, and flags were lowered to half mast in towns from one end of the country to the other. State legislatures passed angry resolutions. Truman was burned in effigy in many places. The White House and Congress were snowed under by fiery letters and telegrams calling for impeachment of "the little ward politician stupidity from Kansas City," "the imbecile," "the pig in the White House." One letter writer thoroughly vindicated Harold Nicholson: "This is just another sellout of our country to those dirty Britons who run the Far East while our sons give up their lives for British domination and dirty dollars."

John Foster Dulles, who had been brought into the State Department as a Republican adviser, said MacArthur's recall was "irreparably damaging" to the U.S. cause in Asia. He talked of resigning in protest, but did not.

Republicans started a vociferous demand that MacArthur be invited to address a joint session of Congress. The congressional Democrats wanted nothing less, but they lacked the strength to prevent it. After consulting with Ernest McFarland, the Arizona senator who succeeded Lucas as majority leader, and Rayburn, Truman announced that he was pleased Congress had extended the invitation to the deposed general.

"I shall return," MacArthur had dramatically stated when he was forced out of the Philippines soon after the beginning of the war with Japan. He had returned, and now he was making another return—this time to the United States, where he had not set foot in fourteen years.

His address before the joint session of Congress was delivered on April 19. Attendance was so complete that twenty House members had to stand, and Senators Douglas and Butler sat on the floor in an aisle. The great showman had a sellout house.

Nobody had expected MacArthur to offer a defense of his conduct, and he did not. Although, he said, he had not been consulted prior to the President's decision to intervene in support of the Republic of Korea, that decision, he grandly conceded, "proved a sound one." But when soldiers from Communist China re-enforced the battered North Korean army, a new war was created, calling for "new decisions in the diplomatic sphere to permit the realistic adjustment of military strategy."

"Such decisions have not been forthcoming," he declared.

MacArthur outlined the steps he considered mandatory, including the imposition of a naval blockade against the China coast, removal of restrictions on bombing bases in Manchuria, and getting Nationalist China forces into the war. He denounced "appeasement" of Communist China, praised the courage and fortitude of the Korean people, spoke movingly of the American fighting men as "splendid in every way."

Then, in the hushed chamber, he concluded with words that brought tears to the eyes of more than one hard-bitten politician:

"I am closing my fifty-two years of military service. When I joined the army even before the turn of the century, it was the fulfillment of all my boyish hopes and dreams. The world has turned over many times since I took the oath on the plain at West Point, and the hopes and dreams have long since vanished. But I still remember the refrain of one of the most popular barrack ballads of that day which proclaimed most proudly that 'Old soldiers never die, they just fade away.'

"And like the old soldier of that ballad, I now close my military career and just fade away—an old soldier who tried to do his duty as God gave him the light to see that duty.

"Good-bye."

MacArthur did not exactly fade away. He made triumphal tours of a number of cities and for some time continued to stir deep emotions among the American people. Some of his admirers, among them several rich Texas oil men, hoped he would be the Republican candidate for President in 1952. But a joint congressional committee, headed by the greatly respected Russell of Georgia, made an investigation of the facts concerning MacArthur's dismissal and put them dispassionately on record. MacArthurism, unlike McCarthyism, never developed as a strong political issue.

All the same, during this emotional period, when Harry Truman took his wife to a baseball game at Griffith Stadium in Washington, he was lustily booed by the spectators. He had never been more of an antihero.

* * *

Truman's hair turned white during these two years, and the lines in his face deepened. The cocky grin that creased his cheeks still flashed on, but at times it seemed forced and meaningless. In public he grew increasingly imperious and resentful of criticism. At press conferences he lectured newsmen, advising them to turn to their history books to see an analogy between him and Lincoln. The Civil War President, he pointed out, refused to fire Seward from his Cabinet just as he refused to fire Acheson.

His touchiness was shown in a stinging letter he wrote in his own hand to Paul Hume, music critic for the Washington *Post*, taking him to task for an unfavorable report on Margaret's singing. Nobody could pick on Harry Truman's womenfolk with impunity.

When a foreign ambassador canceled his acceptance of a White House dinner invitation because the envoy of his country's traditional enemy was also to be present, Truman telephoned Acheson to demand that the ambassador be recalled because he had been rude to Mrs. Truman. The Secretary of State went to the White House and tried to calm the President by assuring him that it was the fault of Stanley Woodward, chief of protocol, for putting two known enemies on the same guest list. Truman refused to be soothed.

While he and the Secretary were talking, the telephone

rang; Mrs. Truman was on the line. The President, after exchanging a few words, handed the phone to Acheson. "You must not let Harry do what he's going to do," Mrs. Truman said. Acheson replied that he was in sympathy with her view. Then the quick-thinking Secretary began saying aloud, for the President's hearing, comments that the American press might make about the diplomat's recall. He pretended that he was repeating words uttered by Mrs. Truman, who actually remained silent. "Too big for his britches—oh, no, no!" exclaimed the nefarious Acheson at one point. Truman finally gave up. He took back the phone and said to his wife, "All right, all right. When you two gang up on me, I haven't got a chance."

Afterward he showed Acheson a photograph of a young Bess Truman inscribed on the back to a young Harry Truman, then on his way to France to fight in World War I. "Anybody who's rude to this girl is in trouble with me," he said with a combination of tenderness and truculence.

In his public appearances the truculence was uppermost, as the President reacted to the flood of criticism pouring in on him from much of the press, from Republicans, and from many Democrats. He missed Clark Clifford, whose financial necessities forced him to leave government service in 1950. Clifford came close to being the indispensable man, and although he was still in Washington and available, Truman sorely needed his daily counsel.

Younger Democrats in Congress, sensing a leadership vacuum, sought for ways to advance themselves by attacking unpopular administration policies. This undertaking was not without danger, for they almost certainly would need at some time in the future to point to a record of party loyalty. Yet, driven by impatient ambition, they felt they had to make names for themselves, and in the existing atmosphere some thought they could best attain this end by belaboring, if not the President himself, his policies and appointees.

Truman was vulnerable, all the more because he stubbornly resisted and resented charges that any of "his people" would be anything but completely honest and aboveboard in their official conduct. Congressional investigations on several fronts showed that not all the people the President so stanchly defended were worthy of his trust.

A Senate Banking and Currency subcommittee headed by Fulbright of Arkansas dug deeply into activities of the Reconstruction Finance Corporation. Since the end of the war this agency had gone into the business of making speculative loans on a large scale. In 1950 total loans amounted to more than half a billion dollars. Whispers about the purposes of some of these loans—to build a racetrack, to construct an elaborate resort hotel, to "bail out" enterprises of questionable value—and how they were obtained had been going around Washington for some time. The Fulbright panel sought for whatever substance lay behind the whispers.

After a year of looking, the subcommittee issued its report. A conclusion was reached that RFC's operation was infected by favoritism and dominated by outsiders bringing political pressure on the agency's officials. The report charged that this pressure stemmed from the White House itself, that Donald Dawson, a Truman assistant, "tried to dominate" the RFC. It noted that E. Merl Young, who had been chief RFC examiner before setting himself up as a business consultant and whose wife had worked for Truman since his Senate days, was "the individual named most frequently in the reports of alleged influence." Young was an intimate of Dawson's.

Truman called the report "asinine." At a vacation news conference in Key West, he rapped out that there was no truth in tales of fraud in his administration. His house was always in order; it was a clean house. "My people are all honorable—all of them are," he declared defiantly. "I wouldn't have them if they were not."

However, he ordered a reorganization of the RFC, abolishing the five-man directorate which had been running it and placing one man in charge. He appointed Stuart Symington, a successful Missouri businessman who had been the first Secretary of the Air Force and now was chairman of the National Security Resources Board, as RFC Administrator. Symington's instructions were to clean up the agency.

A few months later another Senate panel, the one headed by Hoey, conducted an investigation of the RFC and revealed that, before Symington took over, Bill Boyle had been paid a fee to help a St. Louis printing firm get a loan. At the time of his intervention with the RFC, Boyle was vice-chairman of the Democratic National Committee. He had since become chairman. The Hoey investigation showed that the St. Louis company's application had been rejected by the lending agency until a telephone call from Boyle to its chairman reversed the decision. The Democratic official beyond doubt had profited from his party position. Demands for his resignation as chairman rose from all sides, but Truman came to his friend's defense and Boyle announced that he would stay. He resigned a few months later, giving poor health as the reason.

Charges of corruption in the administration now flared up everywhere. A special subcommittee of the House Ways and Means Committee started turning up evidence of irregularities and worse in the Bureau of Internal Revenue. The subcommittee, with Cecil King of California as chairman, found a definite pattern of dishonesty, bribery and political favoritism in the government's tax-collecting arm. The threads of the pattern extended over into the Department of Justice. Before this sordid chapter came to an end sixty-six persons, many of them high-ranking officials, were discharged from their jobs. A number of them eventually went to prison.

Truman complained bitterly to Rayburn that he had been betrayed, "stabbed in the back," by people he trusted. Rayburn was sympathetic, but he was also deeply concerned about the effect on the future fortunes of the Democratic party. The Speaker told Truman that he had no choice but to "get rid of the bad eggs."

The President tried to do as his old friend advised. But he was on the defensive. When pressed by news reporters about the removal of Internal Revenue Bureau collectors and employees, he lost his temper and rebuked the press for magnifying disclosures of corruption in his administration. There was nothing unusual, he insisted belligerently, about the spate of firings and resignations. This kind of personnel turnover was normal and to be expected. And, he added, his administration, not Congress, was responsible for cleaning up whatever wrongdoing had been found to exist.

"I'm not going to be pushed into doing anything by anybody," the President, his jaw set, told the reporters.

Another investigation, while it was not focused on the administration itself, did reveal proof of unsavory links between organized crime and political figures. Estes Kefauver introduced in the Senate a resolution instructing Congress to investigate crime on the national level. After some delay the resolution was approved, and a special committee was created with its membership drawn from the Judiciary Committee and the Interstate and Foreign Commerce Committee. Kefauver was named chairman. For eleven months he was the central figure in a political road show extravaganza such as the country had never seen before.

During those eleven months the committee roamed 52,000 miles, holding open hearings in a large number of major cities. The hearings brought to light stories of bribed policemen, payoffs to political leaders, sheriffs indifferent or even involved, and honest officials made helpless by others who worked in partnership with criminals. A police captain in Chicago had received $30,000 for unexplained services from a high-up figure in a racing wire service. The sheriff of Dade

County, Florida, whose salary was $7,000, boasted a total annual income of $35,000. A Louisiana sheriff kept $150,000 in cash in a strongbox in the attic of his home. In these cities and others, the offending lawmen and politicians were mostly Democrats. In New York City, William O'Dwyer, the former mayor who had been named ambassador to Mexico, squirmed under cross-examination about alleged connections with the underworld. A bribe charge was not proved, but O'Dwyer was forced into some embarrassing admissions. Newspapers clamored for his recall as ambassador, but Truman paid no attention.

Denizens of the underworld also were called before the committee. The hearings were televised, and millions of Americans—in their homes, in offices and bars—peered with horrified delight at dark-jowled, shifty-eyed gentlemen rejoicing in such nicknames as "Greasy Thumb," "Trigger Mike," "The Camel," "Dandy Phil." Most of them, including Frank Costello of New York City, who was regarded as king of gangland, were largely inarticulate and revealed themselves as having remarkably poor memories. None of them had ever so much as heard of an organization called the Mafia, the Sicilian secret society reputed to be engaged in crime on an international scale.

It was an entertaining show and, with all that television coverage, produced great publicity for Chairman Kefauver. Some dispassionate columnists wondered in print just how a committee of the United States Senate had come to be involved in this particular kind of investigation of local law enforcement. Some senators questioned the value of the committee's work; old Tom Connally, for example, rumbling that its members were "off chasing crapshooters" instead of attending to their duties in the Senate. But nobody wanted to be in favor of crime, so in general the committee's press was good, and the Senate obligingly confirmed the contempt citations issued by the committee to recalcitrant witnesses.

If, as some said, the principal purpose of the Crime Committee was to make Kefauver a nationally known political figure, it was successful. The Tennesseean's earnest face and plodding, painstaking manner with witnesses was impinged upon the consciousness of television viewers throughout the nation. He wrote a best-selling book, *Crime in America*. The National Junior Chamber of Commerce gave him a good-government award. *Time* Magazine put him on its list of the Senate's "ten most valuable members." The Washington press corps voted him the second-best member of the Senate, standing below only Paul Douglas.

Kefauver told newsman, "There is a definite possibility I may run for President."

Other congressional committees—all, of course, headed by Democrats—caused trouble for the Democratic administration. In the Senate, McCarran's Internal Security Subcommittee was loudly on the hunt for Communists, fellow travelers and subversive influences on U.S. policy. Lyndon Johnson's newly created Senate Preparedness Subcommittee was making headlines with its investigation of favoritism in military procurement and racketeering in hiring employees for overseas bases. In the House, Porter Hardy, Jr., of Virginia played the same side of the street by turning a spotlight on the high cost of military construction. The House Un-American Activities Committee and a dozen lesser groups were alert for opportunities to attack unpopular administration policies.

Harry Truman, known for his advice that anyone unable to stand the heat should stay out of the kitchen, had proved that he could endure heat. But he felt it. As De Lawd said to Noah in Marc Connelly's *The Green Pastures*, "Everything dat's fastened down is comin' loose." Hardly anything was fastened down any more in the Truman administration.

1952

THE GENERAL'S YEAR

The madness that sweeps college campuses in the spring of the year took the form in 1952 of panty raids by male students on girls' dormitories. On one campus after another, in all sections of the country, large groups of excited young men rampaged through rooms occupied by happily squealing coeds and demanded that they hand over their undergarments. Two thousand University of Missouri students, not content with raiding the dormitories on their home grounds, journeyed to nearby Stephens College and Christian College; a call went out for the militia. At the University of Georgia, manly members of the football squad planted themselves at the doors of the coeds' quarters to block raiders, but the young women tossed their intimate apparel from the windows of their rooms. At Toledo University, the coeds went on the offensive and stormed into a men's dorm to take away their shorts.

Dr. Alfred O. Kinsey, the noted sexologist, was asked for an explanation of such goings on. "It is somewhat," the doctor said cautiously, "out of my field."

128

A similar seizure, although less openly frenzied, held politicians in its grip from the beginning of the year through the first Tuesday after the first Monday in November.

Bob Taft and Earl Warren had been for months in open pursuit of the Republican presidential nomination. At the beginning of the year, Harold Stassen, for whom running for President was already becoming a hobby, announced "with all humility" that he would try again. Earlier he had proposed that neither he nor Taft should seek the nomination if General Dwight D. Eisenhower would become a candidate. Some took his announcement in January to mean that Eisenhower, now in Paris as commander of the supreme headquarters of the Allied powers in Europe, still stood by his refusal to consider political office.

But even before Eisenhower left Columbia, Dewey, who as governor still retained control of New York's political machinery, had proposed him as the 1952 nominee. The general once more declined, saying plaintively, "I don't know why people are always nagging me to run for President. I think I've gotten too old." A month before he went to Paris he told Hugh Roy Cullen, a Houston oil multimillionaire, that he had no political ambitions. "I've had all the honors I want or need," he said, "and I would wish—if I had the chance—to bow out of the picture." This time, however, he made a significant addition to his usual statement. "If the Republican party doesn't trot out someone to beat Truman," he said, "then, if they want me to run, I'll run."

Cullen did not immediately report this conversation, although he advised Eisenhower, "You can be nominated and elected if you refuse to talk politics with anyone. Remain just what you are, a soldier." Cullen, who fancied himself as a kingmaker and who bore a deadly hatred toward New and Fair Deal policies, showered the general with letters of advice and admonition, cautioning him in particular not to allow himself to be taken over by Tom Dewey and "the professional politicians."

A steady stream of visitors came to see Eisenhower at his command headquarters to try to push him onto the political stage. It was reliably reported that an influential Democrat from Washington brought word that the general could have Truman's support for the Democratic nomination. Eisenhower retorted, "You can't join a party just to run for office." But it was still true that no one knew what his party affiliation was or whether he had one.

Henry Cabot Lodge, the senator from Massachusetts, was a frequent visitor. He told Eisenhower he represented the known views of many large groups of American citizens and that they were anxious to start organizing a nationwide movement. Unless the Republicans could come up with a winning candidate, Lodge declared, continued existence of the two-party system was endangered. The Democrats had been in power too long. Their dominance had increased paternalism in the federal government's relations with the citizens. Constant deficit spending threatened the government with bankruptcy.

Eisenhower had often spoken in this vein while he was president of Columbia, so he was a receptive listener as Lodge skillfully played the record back to him.

(Basil Brewer, ultraconservative publisher of the New Bedford, Massachusetts, *Standard-Times*, wrote Lodge that he had heard the senator might be the convention floor manager for Eisenhower, and he hoped the report was untrue. Taft was the man, Brewer said. Lodge wrote back that he had no intention of injecting himself into convention party fights and, anyway, that if Eisenhower should indeed be nominated it would be by acclamation at the convention. When the full extent of Lodge's activities on behalf of Eisenhower became evident, Brewer was so enraged that he threw the support of his paper to John F. Kennedy in his race against Lodge for the Senate. This unexpected dividend to Kennedy may well have made the difference that carried him to victory and placed him in the Senate at the age of thirty-five.)

On January 6, Lodge called a press conference in Washington to announce that Eisenhower's name would be entered in the Republican presidential primary in New Hampshire in March. "He will not withdraw," the Massachusetts senator emphasized. "He is in the race to the finish."

In Paris, the general stated that Lodge was correct in saying that he was a Republican by conviction; he had voted that way since his relief from active military duty in 1948. He was not seeking, and would not seek, nomination to public office. But, he added, American citizens had a right "to organize in pursuit of their common conviction," and "I realize that Senator Lodge and his associates are exercising the right in an attempt to place before me next July a duty that would transcend my present responsibility." This seemed to mean that he would take the nomination if "Senator Lodge and his associates" could get it for him. He said that under no circumstances would he ask for relief from his assignment in Europe to engage in political activity.

The tempo of the pro-Eisenhower effort picked up sharply. Citizens-for-Eisenhower clubs were formed in a number of cities. In February, a mass meeting was held at midnight in Madison Square Garden, arranged and financed by a group of men who wanted to show the general that he would receive tremendous popular support. A special train filled with whooping fans came up from Texas, paid for by oil men with a special interest in getting Truman out of office. The public-relations team of Tex McCrary, an ambitious native of Texas who long before had moved on to the opportunities of New York, and his wife, Jinx Falkenberg, noted for her prowess on the tennis court, put together a carefully staged show which was a combination of vaudeville and an old-fashioned revival meeting. The 15,000 men and women assembled in the Garden were coached in chanting "I like Ike" at the top of their voices. The whole show was filmed and the film was then flown to Paris by the famous flier Jacqueline Cochran. Eisenhower and his wife Mamie looked at it and were impressed.

Eisenhower went to London for a conference with General Lucius Clay, a trusted friend, about the fast-moving developments that were transforming a military man into a candidate for President. Sid Richardson—another of those Texas oil millionaires, this one from Fort Worth—and George Allen, rapidly shifting his affections, were present. They said the time had come for Eisenhower to return to the United States. He agreed that he would do so in the near future.

The New Hampshire preferential primary came in March. It was a clear-cut contest between Eisenhower and Taft. The general's campaign was managed by Governor Sherman Adams. This primary was the first of the year and received extensive press coverage. Eisenhower rolled up 46,661 votes, almost 11,000 more than Taft. The ship was launched.

A primary was held in Minnesota that same month. Eisenhower was not on the ballot, but nearly 107,000 voters wrote in his name. In New Jersey, Taft withdrew from that state's primary after Governor Driscoll announced that he was for Eisenhower. And in Paris, the general said, "The mounting numbers of my fellow citizens who are voting to make me the Republican nominee are forcing me to examine my personal position and past decisions." He asked to be relieved of his command effective June 1 so he could return to the United States.

Taft sent his lieutenants out over the country to line up hard-and-fast support among delegates to the July convention, regardless of how many popularity contests might be won by the man who now loomed as his chief rival for the nomination. Stassen was on the edge of the stage, again hoping for a deadlock. Warren, standing on the sidelines with the large California delegation behind him, allowed himself the same hope.

* * *

Among the Democrats, Estes Kefauver was out in front. He paid a visit to the White House in January and told Truman he was thinking of trying for the nomination if the President did not plan to seek re-election. Truman was non-committal about his own intentions, but Kefauver got the impression, possibly because it was the one he wanted to get, that the President would not oppose his candidacy. A week later, he formally announced that he was a candidate and would enter primaries in all states were they were to be held. New Hampshire was first.

When the President sneered at the preferential primaries as "eyewash," Kefauver began to suspect that his hope of no opposition from Truman was only wishful thinking. The suspicion became certainty when Truman permitted the state Democratic organization to enter his name in the New Hampshire primary.

After this happened, strong pressure was exerted to get Kefauver to withdraw, one administration official stating publicly that it was an insult to the President for him to stay in the race. The Tennessean did not see matters that way, but he offered to get out if the Democratic organization in New Hampshire would withdraw Truman's name and let the delegates to the national convention decide for themselves whom they would support. The state organization rejected this proposal and the primary campaign proceeded.

Truman made no personal foray into the state. Kefauver,

on the other hand, came as close as he could to greeting individually every voter in New Hampshire. He traveled through the towns and villages and over the hilly countryside in a long and arduous quest for votes.

Bob Taft once said of presidential primaries, "No man who holds a responsible federal or state office can spare the time from it to campaign in a majority of the states and still do justice to his job." But Kefauver felt that his job in 1952 was running for President. He devoted virtually full time to it, showing no sign of being concerned about his record of absenteeism in the Senate. And he ran for President in just the same way that he had run for office back in Tennessee.

When he first became a candidate for the Senate, Kefauver was hardly known in the state outside his own congressional district. One of his few supporters among the state's newspaper publishers, Silliman Evans of the Nashville *Tennesseean*, advised him that the way to overcome this handicap was to shake hands with at least 500 people every day of the campaign. Following this counsel, Kefauver won. He carried with him to Washington the habit of shaking hands with everybody in sight, becoming known among irreverent Senate pages as The Hand.

That spring he roamed through New Hampshire with right hand outstretched and the words "My name is Estes Kefauver and I'm running for President" falling readily from his lips. The reaction of a roadside diner counterman showed that the people he met at least listened. "President of what?" the counterman demanded. "President of the United States." "Hey, Ma!" cried the counterman to his helpmeet in the kitchen. "Here's a guy who says he's runnin' for President— and he ain't kiddin'."

Kefauver's direct and folksy appeal to the voters amused the political writers who followed him around the state. They had no thought that he could win, but he was entertaining to write about and they sent back a great mass of copy to their papers. Most of them stressed human-interest angles. They wrote gleefully about the candidate making a talk in neighboring Vermont by mistake and, back in New Hampshire, shaking hands with two convicted gamblers in a county courthouse and asking for their votes; about his attractive wife Nancy, who was in the campaign party and made speeches of her own; about a housewife who, after Kefauver had shaken her hand and gone his way, sighed, "You just know he's honest."

The reporters predicted that Truman, backed by the state organization and labor, would win three to one. But on election day it was Estes Kefauver by a vote of nearly five to four.

Shortly afterward, at the Jefferson-Jackson Day dinner in Washington, Truman appeared before some 6,000 Democrats to announce near the end of a characteristically hard-hitting speech that he would not be a candidate for re-election, he would not accept nomination.

Some political pundits drew the conclusion that his decision was caused by the result in New Hampshire combined with a deep drop in his standing in nationwide popularity polls. He had in fact decided not to run again long before the surprise announcement at the dinner—as early, he said, as the day of his inauguration in 1949. In a memorandum to himself fifteen months later, he wrote, "Eight years as President is long enough."

He did not tell anybody about his decision until November 19, 1951, when, vacationing at Key West, he informed some of his staff members and enjoined them to secrecy. Immediately after that he started looking for a candidate to take his place. His first choice was his old friend, Chief Justice Vinson. But Vinson, after some consideration, told Truman his doctors had warned him that his heart was not good. "So I'll stay on the Supreme Court," he decided.

The President, although disappointed, was not at a loss. Early in January, he asked Governor Adlai Stevenson of Illinois to come to see him.

The two men were not well acquainted personally, but Truman had been deeply impressed by the vote-getting ability Stevenson displayed in 1948. In his first try for an elective office, running as an internationalist-minded Democrat in Chicago *Tribune* territory, he piled up the largest majority ever received by any candidate for the Illinois governorship. He even pulled Truman through in Illinois that year. He was making an excellent record as governor. He cleaned out the corruption which had marked the regime of his Republican predecessor, eliminated useless positions, put state buying on a businesslike basis, improved the school system, and started an ambitious road-construction program. He seemed the ideal man to give the Democratic party a clean new look.

Stevenson was planning to run for a second term as governor and told Truman so when he visited the President in Blair House. Truman did not take this very seriously, feeling that no politician worthy of the name would rather be a state governor than President of the United States. The presidency was the most powerful office in the world. It naturally followed that anybody who was in politics would want to be President. He did not understand Stevenson's hesitancy, but the best he could get out of the governor was a promise that he would think it over.

Stevenson left Blair House a perplexed and troubled man. The next day he went to see Barkley, to whom he was distantly related, and told him the gist of his conversation with the President. "I think," he said, "I probably ought to announce right now that I will not be a candidate under any conditions." The vice-president advised him not to make such a categoric statement, at least not until Truman publicly stated his own intention not to run. Barkley added that if Truman really did not run he might become a candidate himself.

In March, Stevenson again visited the President and told him that he was committed to running for re-election and did not feel he could honorably go back on his commitment. And at Illinois' own Jefferson-Jackson Day dinner in Springfield, he said, "I want to run for governor of Illinois—and that's all."

In private as well as in public, he reiterated that he would not be a candidate. Soon after Truman announced his non-availability, Thomas Dawes Blake, a man-about-Washington who had attended Chicago Latin School with Stevenson, ran into the governor at a cocktail party in Chicago and said, not at all jokingly, "Well, Ad, it looks as if the way is left wide open for you." Stevenson firmly replied that he was going to run for a second term as governor. Later in the spring, Blake, an old Washington hand who had served as a press officer in the State Department and briefly as an assistant to Steve Early, Roosevelt's press secretary, reported this conversation to Senator Richard Russell of Georgia. Russell, an announced candidate for the Democratic presidential nomination, was naturally interested and perhaps skeptical; at any rate, he telephoned Stevenson, who confirmed Blake's report.

As late as two weeks before the national convention, Jake Arvey, a leading promoter of the movement to make Stevenson the nominee, called Barkley to say that the governor had told him he definitely must be considered out of the running. Arvey said he thought Stevenson should nominate Barkley at the convention and volunteered that he would ask him about doing so. Barkley liked the idea, but heard no more about it.

If Stevenson was reluctant, some other Democrats were not.

Barkley himself was among the most willing, and his chances looked good. Soon after the telephone call from Arvey, he met by invitation of the President with Truman, National Chairman Frank McKinney, and several members of the White House staff to discuss the coming convention. McKinney announced that Truman had decided to back Barkley. He would make no public statement, but would urge the Missouri delegation, of which he was a member, to support him. "What about Governor Stevenson?" Barkley asked. "In my judgment, he has not eliminated himself." No, McKinney assured him, Stevenson had made it clear that he would not accept the nomination. The little gathering reached a comfortable agreement that Barkley would be nominated on the third ballot.

Estes Kefauver did not see how the convention could fail to give him the nomination. He had entered sixteen primaries and won all but two, having been bested by Russell in Florida and by Harriman in the District of Columbia. He would go to the convention with more committed delegates than any other candidate. The party bosses might not like him, but the people did. He listened gladly when his publisher supporter, Silliman Evans, predicted, "The delegates will be forced by public opinion to accept you, regardless of what they want personally." Evans, too, foresaw a third ballot victory—but for Kefauver, not Barkley.

Dick Russell would enter the convention with a substantial block of votes pledged to him. Unfortunately, the eminent Georgian, considered by many political observers to be the ablest man in the Senate, suffered from the handicap of being a sectional candidate. He was not helped by the attitude of some of his supporters. At a fund-raising affair for Russell in Atlanta, a speaker from Mississippi bawled out, "If the South can't sit at the head table, we won't come to dinner!" This remark, with its implied threat of refusal to support in November any Democratic candidate other than Russell, was headlined in eastern newspapers. Tom Blake, joining the Russell headquarters staff as public-relations director, tried desperately to bring an element of professionalism to the campaign, but the overriding atmosphere of magnolia blossoms and honey-chile talk was never dissipated. Speaking of Russell, Sam Rayburn remarked to a friend, "Too bad he doesn't have a chance. Good man, but from the wrong part of the country." And the Speaker added, "Like me."

Some thought that Rayburn did in fact consider himself a possibility. "He has his lightning rod out a mile," Russell confided to a member of his staff. But there was never any possibility that the seasoned old Speaker was so unrealistic as to expect the nomination to come to him. Averell Harriman, who had filled many important appointive positions but never an elective one, held a faint hope. The New York delegation was prepared to place his name before the convention, and he asked Truman if he would object. Not at all, said the President later, "but when the time came for the convention to nominate its candidate for President I wanted him to be in line to help nominate that man." Bob Kerr, the rich senator from Oklahoma, wanted the nomination and saw no reason why he should not have it. He felt he had at least as much ability as any of the others and knew he had more money, with the possible exception of Harriman.

The Democrats thus went down to convention time with at least four serious contenders for the nomination. The Republicans approached their quadrennial blood-letting ceremony with only two.

*　　*　　*

A national political convention is comparable to no other event known to the American people. Four to five thousand men and women, delegates and alternates from all the states, are loose in a city with nothing to do except during the comparatively few hours when the convention is formally in session—and even then their roles permit few ad libs. Restlessness overtakes them. Inhibitions fall away. The delegates hold innumerable and largely meaningless caucuses. They exchange rumors, overdrink, fight for seats in restaurants, trade confidences with persons they never knew the day before yesterday, try ineptly to shove themselves close to the individuals they believe are running things, push through jampacked hotel lobbies and onto impossibly crowded elevators; sweating, quarreling, running out of money, running out of patience, forever waiting to be told what to do. Frenzied noise bedevils them. Sleep escapes them. A fortunate few achieve short-lived fame through being interviewed by press and radio-TV representatives, who likewise have descended upon the city by the thousands and are trying with little success to make sense out of what is going on. But most of the delegates come, stay and go in unrelieved anonymity.

Bands march and blare through the day and much of the night. Placard-carrying pickets advocate causes that were lost before they started. Important personages are swept in from the airport in hired limousines preceded by shrieking police cars. Garishly clad and semiclad girls hand out taffy candy, miniature flags, striped walking canes, bubble gum, Georgia peaches, California oranges, Texas pecans. Candidates feverishly give interviews, pose for photographs, haunt the television screens, yelp into telephones, speak before state caucuses—and ceaselessly, endlessly strive to impress upon delegation bosses visiting their hotel suites that now NOW! is the time to get on the bandwagon.

All the while, the managers—the very few who have some reason to believe they know what they are doing, or at least trying to do—are at work in seclusion from the accredited delegates and alternates, away from the press, out of range of the television cameras.

The managers are of vital importance. They must submerge themselves in the intricacies of the convention and at the end come up with a candidate for the presidency of the United States. Without the managers a national political convention would be impossible. Thanks to their skill and knowledge, it is only highly improbable.

* * *

The Republicans were first in Chicago.

Of the 604 votes need for the nomination, Bob Taft could count about 530 committed or pledged to him. Although he knew—none better—the pitfalls that could open before any candidate at a convention, Taft expected to win this time. The Republicans had muffed their big chance of victory by refusing him the nomination in 1948. He figured that they would hardly make the same mistake again, especially since that year's loser, Tom Dewey, was prominent in the leadership of the Eisenhower forces. Other Eisenhower managers were also members of the Eastern Establishment: Lodge and Governor James H. Duff of Pennsylvania. They were suspect by all true-blue midwestern and southern Republicans. A convention victory over them would be doubly sweet.

The Ohio senator was aware, rather bitterly but not uneasily, of the "—but Taft can't win" propaganda going around the convention. He knew he could win.

Taft's own management team consisted of two Ohioans, his cousin David Ingalls and Representative Clarence Brown; Carroll Reece, the bumbling former representative from Tennessee and chairman of the Republican National Committee during the time of the Eightieth Congress; and Tom Coleman of Wisconsin. All were solidly Old Guard in their con-

141

victions. The convention issue, as they and their candidate saw it, was between a man whose adult life had been devoted to the principles of the Republican party and a newcomer who until very recently had not known whether he was a Republican or a Democrat. It was, they liked to say, as simple as that.

Simplistic doctrines often give rise to abrasive conflict. It was so in Chicago. The bitterness engendered during those scorching July days and nights was deep and intense. For the first time a national political convention was fully covered by television, and millions of Americans shared in the agonized suspense as the Old Guard and the "new Republicans" clashed in bloody battle.

Yet that fight—so all-absorbing to the participants, so thrilling to the television viewers—was already lost by the Taftites. The seeds of defeat had been planted weeks before at a state Republican convention in the little city of Mineral Wells, Texas.

In Texas, Taft's preconvention campaign was directed by Henry Zweifel, state Republican chairman. Zweifel was a shrewd and experienced political organizer. His flaw was that in one-party Texas he had developed a minority-party mentality. The Republican party was deliberately kept small in Texas so that it could be easily controlled. Zweifel regarded it as a matter of course that in any year the sparsely attended precinct conventions would send "regular" Republicans to the county conventions, which in turn would send to the state convention delegates pledged to the candidate favored by the party organization. That was the way it always worked.

This year was different. The precinct conventions were jammed with people who had never before been seen at any kind of Republican gathering. For the first time since Reconstruction days, attendance was larger at Republican than at

Democratic precinct conventions. Moreover, as the uneasy Zweifel noted, the Taft-committed delegates were being outvoted at one meeting after another. For months a well-financed campaign, headed by H. J. "Jack" Porter, a Houston oil operator, had been carried on all over the state on behalf of Eisenhower. Zweifel was aware of Porter's effort, but it had not worried him unduly. He was confident that the regular organization would follow the customary course, its purpose being not to deliver Republican votes in November but to deliver committed delegates at the national convention.

Now, when the old-line party leader saw what was going on, he instructed his followers to hold rump sessions at the precinct meetings to name Taft delegates. The same procedure was followed at the county conventions. It became clear that two sets of delegates would appear at the state Republican convention in Mineral Wells. That happened. Zweifel's executive committee, a holdover from the previous convention which had been solidly pro-Taft, promptly and enthusiastically threw out the Eisenhower delegates on the ground that they were not really Republicans at all but Democrats who had invaded Republican meetings. Thirty-five Taft delegates to the national convention were named to replace the invaders. Zweifel made the gesture of giving three remaining openings to Eisenhower supporters.

The Eisenhower forces then held a rump convention of their own, naming a full slate of delegates pledged to the candidate of their choice.

Both delegations went to Chicago. By that time the cool professionals in charge of the Eisenhower campaign had fully exploited the story of "the Texas steal." Much of the national press cried scandal. Taft took no action to condemn the tactics of his political sponsors in the Lone Star State, a failure which gave his opponents full opportunity to press their moral issue at the convention.

In the showdown floor fight, after Lodge rejected a last-minute compromise offer by Taft's managers, the Eisenhower backers won the Texas dispute and a similar one in Georgia. Taft lost 56 indispensable votes and his chance for the nomination.

At the end of the first ballot Eisenhower had 595 votes, 9 less than he needed to win. Taft had 500, Earl Warren 81. As the roll call ended, Senator Edward Thye, chairman of the Minnesota delegation, was recognized by the convention chairman. He announced a change of Minnesota's nineteen votes from Harold Stassen, the state's favorite son, to Eisenhower. That started a flood of vote switching, and the Republican party had a nominee for President.

Eisenhower, following the instincts of a public-relations sense which had served him well in the Army, went immediately to Taft headquarters in the Conrad Hilton Hotel on what he said was "a call of friendship on a great American." The two men shook hands, the old soldier looking concerned and almost apologetic, the old politician wearing a strained smile. "I want to congratulate General Eisenhower," Taft said. "I shall do everything possible in the campaign to secure his election and to help in his administration." Only he could know what effort the words cost him.

Nothing remained to be done except to select a vice-presidential nominee. Richard M. Nixon, who had helped persuade the Warren-committed California delegation to vote in favor of unseating Taft's Texas and Georgia delegations and who had voiced the opinion that Eisenhower was likely to be nominated on the first ballot, was chosen.

The delegates, many of them still furiously angry, then vacated their hotel rooms to make way for the Democrats.

The Democrats came in confusion and anxiety. For the first time in twenty years at a national convention the signals were unclear. Not since 1932 had they been called upon to nominate as their candidate for President any man not already holding the office. Adlai Stevenson, the known favorite of their party leader, was resoundingly applauded when he gave an eloquent welcoming address; but he continued to maintain that he was not a candidate. Estes Kefauver had shown that he knew how to go out among the people for votes, but his standing with party professionals was low. Dick Russell had the South solidly behind him, but little strength elsewhere. Bob Kerr opened a noisy headquarters in Chicago, but nobody except himself took his availability seriously. Harriman? Barkley?

The delegates writhed with uncertainty. There was nobody to tell them what to do.

Barkley was the first to go down. He arrived in Chicago at the head of his Kentucky delegation feeling that he had an excellent chance to win despite his seventy-four years. He carried with him assurances of backing from numerous old-timers in the Democratic party. He expected Truman to rally to his side. He had always been strong with organized labor and counted heavily on its support.

His happy dream soon evaporated, blown out of existence the day before the convention officially opened by a statement from labor spokesmen that, although Barkley was a great man, he was too old to be their candidate for President. A few hours later Barkley was called on by a group of men who had actively urged his candidacy. They were Les Biffle and three Kentucky officials, Senator Earle Clements, Governor Lawrence Wetherby and Lieutenant Governor Emerson Beauchamp. Hesitantly they told him the labor statement was causing an unfavorable reaction on delegates from the big industrial states. "Do I understand," Barkley asked painfully, "that you have come here to ask me to withdraw?" Yes, that was the purpose of their visit. That evening Barkley issued a statement taking himself out of the race.

A bumper crop of rumors sprang up among the delegates. Russell was making a determined bid for the support that had been denied Barkley. Kefauver was trying desperately to win over some of the big state delegates to add to the delegates he had picked up in the primaries. Harriman would get the nod from Truman in case of a deadlock. Stevenson would be placed in nomination after all. Stevenson had repeated firmly that he wanted only to run for governor of Illinois. Stevenson had been in touch with Truman.

All these rumors may have had some factual basis. The last *was* a fact.

In midweek, hours before nominations would begin, Stevenson telephoned Truman at the White House. His mind made up at last, he asked if the President would be embarrassed if he allowed his name to be placed before the convention. Truman was understandably irritated. He replied, as he recalled later, with "some rather vigorous words." Finally he told Stevenson, "I've been trying since last January to get you to say that. Why would it embarrass me?"

But it looked as if the indecisive governor had waited too long. At the end of the first roll call Stevenson had only 273 of the 616 votes needed to win. Russell received 238, Harriman 123½. Kefauver was on top with 340 votes.

"I think I'm going to win," the Tennesseean said, watching proceedings on television in a hotel near the convention hall.

In Washington, Harry Truman also was in front of a television set. To him the result of the ballot shouted, "Deadlock!" He was determined to prevent that.

He and Mrs. Truman flew to Chicago the next day. The second ballot was taken while they were on the presidential plane. It was no more conclusive than the first. Kefauver picked up 22 votes and Russell added 56. Stevenson received 51 fewer votes than before.

Sam Rayburn, serving again as convention chairman, recessed proceedings after the roll call was completed—officially for dinner, actually to give the party leaders a chance to regain control. Truman, heading the meeting of these leaders, insisted that Stevenson must be the nominee. And, he added, on the next ballot before the convention flew completely apart. He instructed Harriman to swing his votes to Stevenson.

When the third roll call began at nine o'clock that night, it became immediately apparent that significant vote switching had taken place. Stevenson started at once to forge sharply ahead. As the balloting proceeded, Kefauver and Senator Paul Douglas, a strong supporter, entered the hall and moved toward the platform. Their appearance before the vote was finished threw the convention into turmoil, intensified as it became evident that Kefauver wished to address the delegations.

Rayburn's political instinct told him that the Tennesseean, realizing he no longer had a chance, proposed to withdraw and make a last desperate effort to be named as Stevenson's running mate. The Speaker had no intention of permitting this to happen. He would not interrupt the balloting. With a grimace he motioned the two senators to seats on the platform. There they remained, silent and angry, as the voting went on and Stevenson was chosen.

Kefauver's tactics at the convention completed the alienation between himself and the established party leadership. He had appeared on television after the first ballot and declared, in white-faced rage, that he did not like the way the convention was being run, he was being discriminated against, Rayburn was handing down unfair decisions from the chair. Then he compounded his errors by appearing in the convention hall while he was still a candidate, which was contrary to all of Rayburn's ideas of protocol. Coming to Chicago with high hopes that his nomination could be rammed through on the basis of popular support, the unhappy Tennessee senator was not even given a chance for the vice-presidential nomination.

Stevenson, Truman, Rayburn, Jake Arvey, Scott Lucas and Frank McKinney met privately after midnight to select the party's candidate for vice-president. Rayburn, presiding over the meeting, threw out the name of his protégé and fellow Texan, Lyndon Johnson, but his suggestion was met by silence. Stevenson then said he would list four possibilities and leave the final choice up to the group. He wrote down the names of four senators: Kefauver, Fulbright, John Sparkman of Alabama, and Mike Monroney of Oklahoma. Truman and Lucas expressed unyielding opposition to Kefauver, and Rayburn backed them up; he complained that the Tennessee senator had been rude to him. As the discussion went on, Truman left the meeting but not before he had remarked, "This fellow Sparkman would be a good man." And Sparkman it was by selection of the informal committee and by acclamation of the convention on a voice vote.

Truman had effectually asserted control over the Democratic party by carrying the convention for the two men he wanted. But at the very moment of doing so he lost future control. From now on other Democrats would be running things, and not always to his satisfaction.

* * *

After the ceremony uniting Vice-President Alben Barkley and Jane Hadley in marriage, the vivacious young bride was aghast at the prospect of leaving the church to face the television cameras and the crowd of excited women gathered outside. "I don't see how I can stand going out into that mess," she said nervously to the bridegroom. "Why, my dear," boomed Barkley, "that's no mess. That is the great American people."

148

To Adlai Stevenson, try as he might to rise above his instinctive reaction, noisy crowds and political activity in general were always that mess, and he approached it cautiously and at arm's length.

The reason was not immediately apparent. He came from a political family. His father had been active in Illinois politics. One grandfather, the first Adlai Stevenson, had been vice-president of the United States; another, James Fell, had been an adviser to Lincoln. Stevenson himself had served with various New Deal agencies. He had been assistant to the Secretary of the Navy and special assistant to the Secretary of State. In the latter position, to which he was named in 1945, he helped to work up a program to arouse popular sentiment for creation of the United Nations Organization. Going from appointive to elective politics, he had been chosen governor of Illinois by an unprecedented majority.

Yet he remained a curiously nonpolitical figure. He was at home neither with cigar-chomping politicos who growled out cryptic orders about voter registration and precinct organization nor with loud gatherings of the common man who traditionally gave the Democratic party its strength. The charm, wit and urbanity which shone brightly in personal conversation tended to make him appear before large crowds as a man who did not take himself or the cause he represented with appropriate seriousness. Yet he could be extraordinarily moving and forceful, as in his Chicago acceptance speech. He consistently gave more attention to the substance of his speeches than to their delivery, often laboring over an address almost up to the moment he was to give it.

Stevenson considered his speeches far more important than mingling with the voters. Once during the campaign he was in a Minnesota town to address a local gathering when the district congressman rushed into his hotel suite to demand that he come downstairs to meet a group of miners. Stevenson ex-

149

plained that he was working on a speech and unable to spare the time. The congressman exploded. "It doesn't make a damn bit of difference what you say in your speech," he roared, "but it will make a lot of difference for you to come down and shake hands with these people." Stevenson was astounded by this concept. The astonishment projected a perfect reflection of his basically nonpolitical nature.

Dwight Eisenhower was no politician either at this time, but at that point any resemblance between the two presidential candidates stopped. Eisenhower, at sixty-two (ten years older than Stevenson), radiated vigor and sunny self-confidence. His ruddy face, expressive blue eyes and wide smile made people feel good just to look at him. He was fully aware of the market value of his smile, and he wanted people around him to appear equally pleased with life. At his first staff meeting after his nomination, he insisted that everybody should wear "a ready grin." "In Europe," he added, "I sent some otherwise able leaders home because they went around all the time with long faces." But even if his own grin was at times more ready than heartfelt, its appeal was irresistible.

While Stevenson was so little known by sight at the beginning of the campaign that his manager, Wilson Wyatt, was frequently mistaken for the candidate, people recognized Eisenhower anywhere. He had been a world figure for a decade. Now he traveled the country as a national hero as well as the Republican candidate for President. Cries of "We like Ike!" greeted him everywhere. He responded by extending his arms above his head as if to embrace everybody in sight. His grin grew broader as the cheers continued. In a year when the chemical industry was profitably engaged in making all America kissing sweet by the injection of chlorophyll into everything from toothpaste to cigarettes, from diapers to dog food, Eisenhower's personality held a deep appeal for a people desperately wanting respite from troubles encountered after the war was won. They believed in Eisenhower. They had faith that this man, who had led in the liberation of Europe, could lead the United States out of the shadows and into the sunlight. No matter that he was far from a polished speaker or that he sometimes became mired down in subjects about which he knew little. The people "liked Ike" and that was that.

Eisenhower the candidate was not in any way a phony creation. He was genuine in his patriotism, his honesty, his longing for peace in the world, his concern for integrity and efficiency in government. So was Adlai Stevenson. Their vast differences in education, background and personality were reflected in the campaign, but both had qualities that fitted them—if any man can be truly fitted for the terrifying responsibility—to be President of the United States.

Eisenhower's campaign was the better organized from the start and it so remained. This nonpolitician was surrounded by men thoroughly versed in the art of politics. They had put together the basic campaign organization long before the Chicago convention. They kept control, but at the same time made use of the ecstatic support of hundreds of thousands of amateurs drinking the heady juice of political activity for the first time. Nor was the campaign hindered by any scarcity of funds. Contributions poured in from the usual Republican sources in the East but also from other areas, Texas and California in particular.

Money was not a problem, but Bob Taft's silence was. After the convention the defeated candidate went for a vacation to the family summer home in Quebec. No word came until Edwin Lahey, veteran political writer for the Chicago *Daily News*, went to Canada to visit his old friend. Taft talked to him, and Lahey wrote a story beginning with a sword-thrust: "General Eisenhower's chances of winning the support of Senator Robert Taft are about zero." He reported

151

that Taft felt Eisenhower should start talking like a Republican and acting like a man running for President.

The Eisenhower managers already were alarmed by the sharply expressed editorial judgment of the Scripps-Howard newspaper chain that their candidate was "running like a dry creek." After Lahey's story appeared, they agreed Eisenhower must meet with Taft to iron out their differences. An invitation issued to the sulking senator to visit Eisenhower at his home in Morningside Heights, Manhattan, was duly accepted, and the meeting was held.

After it was over, Taft outlined at a news conference the points on which he and Eisenhower had reached an accord. They included a pledge that there would be no reprisals against Taft supporters and no discrimination in appointments when the new administration took over. The federal budget would be reduced from $80 billion to $60 billion within two years. This reduction would be followed by a cut in taxes. The basic principles of Taft's beloved labor law would not be compromised. And, finally, there would be no tolerance of "creeping socialism."

As Taft read to the reporters the concluding section of the written agreement, even his flat, matter-of-fact manner could not conceal a note of triumph. The words were those he had used in many a speech: "The price of liberty, including the free enterprise system, is the reduction of federal spending and taxes, the repudiation of arbitrary powers in the executive, claimed to be derived from Heaven, and the stand against the statutory extension of power by the creation and extension of federal bureaus; the protection of the people against any arbitrary excess of power which may be developed by big business or by big labor or other pressure groups is also essential."

A widely published photograph of the two men showed them sitting together on a sofa with the document on which they had agreed. Eisenhower, his arms folded, was frowning deeply as he looked with obvious distaste at the paper Taft held. Taft wore a cat-that-ate-the-canary smile which gave his face an expression of smugness no one had ever seen there before.

The Democrats joyously hailed the agreement as "the Surrender of Morningside Heights." Stevenson commented, "Now we have the spectacle of the candidate who won the nomination seeking out his defeated rival and begging for a kind word. It looks as if Taft lost the nomination but won the election." But underneath the surface chortling of the Democrats was the uneasy certainty that the Republican campaign had been given a strong forward push by the rapport established between the candidate and the king of the Old Guard wing of the party.

The Democrats' own campaign had got off to a fumbling start. Their national committee suffered the effects of having been without a candidate for months after Truman had taken himself out of the picture. Stevenson himself, a noncandidate until the national convention was half over, boasted neither organization nor campaign plans. He discussed these lacks with members of his staff and a few close friends at a meeting in Springfield shortly after the convention. They agreed that he could not afford simply to pick up the Truman organization. Stevenson was determined to make it clear that he was not "Truman's man."

He began by firing McKinney as chairman of the national committee and appointed Stephen Mitchell, a Chicago lawyer. He set up his campaign headquarters in Springfield instead of Washington. He tried to avoid placing on his staff men known for their connection with Truman. Wyatt Wilson of Louisville, chairman of his personal staff, was one of the few campaign leaders who could be considered a professional in politics.

Truman, keeping a close eye on developments, was considerably irritated. "Stevenson's attitude toward the President he hoped to succeed was a mystery to me," he later declared. He said he did not know whether this attitude was caused by Stevenson's listening to poor advice or receiving bad information, or by "the contagion other good citizens were suffering as a result of reading the anti-Democratic press." The miffed President concluded, "By alienating many influential Democratic political leaders at the outset Adlai may have thought he was attaining full freedom of action. But in reality he needlessly sacrificed basic political backing and perhaps millions of votes."

Stevenson was indeed running the risk of a fragmented campaign. Little or no coordination existed between his Springfield headquarters and the national committee in Washington. Many important state organizations were in sad disarray. Early in the game Stevenson made a statement to a reporter which seemed to agree with the Republican contention that there was in truth a "mess in Washington," and this further affronted Truman.

Still the campaign wagon creaked along. Stevenson announced that, after "prayerful deliberation," he had decided upon the issues which he would stress. These included patriotism and loyalty, civil rights, social welfare, relations between business and government, relations between the states and the federal government, political morality, and above all the war in Korea and foreign policy in general. The Democratic National Committee offered no overt objection to this admirable compendium, but significantly one of its most elaborate and costly pieces of campaign literature was headlined "You Never Had It So Good!" and made a frank appeal to the belly instincts of the voters.

None of this mattered much. It was a year for the opposition to set the campaign issues. The Republicans quickly settled on stopping the Korean war and cleaning up "that mess in Washington" as holding maximum appeal to the majority of the voters.

Eisenhower and many Republicans had at first approved of Truman's policy in Korea. But as the fighting continued much longer than anyone had expected, public-opinion polls showed that the Democratic administration was being blamed. Eisenhower, prodded by his managers, began to stress administration mistakes in conducting the war. In the heat of the campaign he finally came to the point of suggesting that it could have been avoided.

"The biggest fact," he said, "about the Korean war is this: It was never inevitable, it was never inescapable. No fantastic fiat of history decreed that little South Korea—in the summer of 1950—would fatally tempt Communist aggressors as their easiest victim. No demonic destiny decreed that America had to bleed this way in order to keep South Korea free and to keep freedom itself self-respecting."

(*Fantastic fiat of history? Demonic destiny?* Stevenson was said to compose his own speeches. No such claim was made for Eisenhower.)

The Republicans were successful in turning the Korean conflict into "Truman's war" in the thinking of a large part of the American public. The tragic blunder, Eisenhower insisted, could be remedied only by a new administration headed by himself. "I shall go to Korea," he promised, and millions of people thrilled to the drama of his pledge.

The general was learning about politics. In Indianapolis, attacking the administration harder than he had ever done, for the sake of party harmony he stood on the platform with a man he despised—Senator Jenner of Indiana, who had called George Marshall a "front man for traitors." Jenner, up for re-election, planted himself at Eisenhower's elbow, slapped his shoulder in a gesture of intimacy, and got himself photographed with the presidential candidate. In Milwaukee, Eisenhower yielded to urgent pleas by advisers to delete from his speech a friendly reference to Marshall because its inclusion might offend Joe McCarthy.

The political Eisenhower was routinely criticized by Democratic orators, but for the most part the thrust of their campaign was against the Republican party of Bob Taft. Similarly, the Republicans campaigned harder against Truman than against Stevenson. They were more pleased than not when the President finally took to the stump and attacked Eisenhower as a candidate who "doesn't know anything about most of the issues." "He has betrayed his principles," Truman said of the popular hero, "and he has deserted his friends."

The Republicans promptly created a "Truth Squad" to follow the President around and issue statements discrediting his speeches. The congressmen serving in this group possibly were not acquainted with Dean Swift's pamphlet, *A Treatise on the Art of Political Lying*, in which the satirist advised, "The people have a right to private truth from their neighbors and economical truth from their own family, but they have no right at all to political truth." In fact, Swift concluded, "The proper contradiction to a lie is another lie."

Stevenson might well have quoted Swift just as, to the dismay of old-fashioned Democratic politicians, he was already citing pronouncements by Shaw, Disraeli, Oliver Wendell Holmes, Robert Browning, and the London *Times Literary Supplement*. He spoke seriously about the issues he had raised in the beginning, but his tone grew flippant when he talked about the Republicans as a political party. Their slogan, he remarked, was "throw the rascals in." He said their desire for a change was understandable, for "I suppose if I'd been sewn up in the same underwear for twenty years I'd want a change too." As to their platform, he quipped, "Well, nobody can stand on a bushel of eels."

These lighter notes could not obscure the fact that a tough, bitter political campaign was being waged. One of the most sanguinary battlefields was in Texas, which had a direct and substantial dollars-and-cents interest in the outcome.

For some years a dispute had raged over whether the federal government or the states owned the tidelands oil reserves in the submerged shelf outside the three-mile territorial limit. Many millions of dollars were at stake. Texas naturally wanted the state revenue that would come from development of the tidelands. Oil producers preferred to be under state rather than federal regulation. The U.S. Supreme Court had ruled that the federal government held "dominant rights" in the area. When Congress enacted legislation to give the tidelands to the states, Truman vetoed it.

Stevenson said he would follow the same course if he was President and the legislation was again enacted, but Eisenhower told Texas political leaders that he believed the tidelands oil belonged to the states. As a result, the State Democratic Committee, under control of Governor Allan Shivers, officially recommended that Texas Democrats work for the election of Eisenhower. During the campaign the state group operated in tandem with the strong Eisenhower organization set up by Jack Porter. A new campaign committee had to be established for Stevenson and Sparkman; Rayburn was its chairman.

Despite its solidly materialistic base, the Texas effort was portrayed as a crusade with a high moral purpose. In addition, a strong appeal was made to state pride, never an inconsiderable factor in Texas. Eisenhower was claimed as a Texan by virtue of his having spent the first few months of his life in the state. "Vote Texan—Vote Ike!" exhorted windshield stickers on Fords and Cadillacs alike. When Eisenhower visited the state, he found himself coerced into having his picture taken with a ten-gallon hat perched on his head. He grinned and bore it.

Virtually all of the important daily newspapers in Texas—

as throughout the country—and most of the less-important dailies and the weeklies came out with editorial endorsements of Eisenhower. Amon Carter, publisher of the powerful Fort Worth *Star-Telegram*, sent word to Lyndon Johnson, whom his paper had strongly supported for years, that unless he announced for Eisenhower, future support would be lacking. Johnson's answer was to travel with Stevenson on his campaign train through Texas and to make a radio network speech calling for a Democratic victory. Carter never forgave the senator. His paper blasted Johnson at frequent intervals until the dictatorial old publisher died in 1955.

Other lifelong friendships were disrupted, husbands and wives fell out, Democrats reluctant to switch to Eisenhower were threatened with the loss of their jobs, and fist fights broke out among small fry on school playgrounds as the campaign in Texas and over the nation swept on to its end and the inevitable outcome.

The popular vote of more than 61 million was the largest in the nation's history. Eisenhower ran far ahead of his party, Stevenson far behind the Democratic ticket. The victor took thirty-nine states with 442 electoral votes, including Texas and the southern states of Florida, Virginia and Tennessee. The hapless Stevenson was left with nine states and only 89 votes in the electoral college.

Sam Rayburn spoke accurately for the Democrats when he told a friend the morning after election day, "We just got the *hell* beat out of us."

1953

NEW BOYS IN TOWN

"Our Republic," wrote the perceptive and sometimes impertinent Margaret Halsey in her book *The Folks at Home*, published shortly before the Eisenhower administration came in, "is not a pastoral, not a military, not an agricultural, not a nomadic, but a business civilization. Nor is there anything random, casual or accidental about the U.S. as a business society. It is thoroughly well integrated—organized from top to bottom for the maximum efficiency of making money. We are so accustomed to the infiltration of business into every single area of human living that we take it for granted. It seems to us the natural, the inevitable—indeed, the only conceivable—way for a nation to be organized." *

Certainly it seemed so to the men who came to Washington in January 1953 sharing a deep-rooted conviction that the application of business thinking and business methods to the operation of the federal government would surely cure all its problems. They were businessmen and they knew how to

* Margaret Halsey, *The Folks at Home* (New York, Simon & Schuster, Inc., 1952). Quoted by permission.

eliminate waste and duplication of effort. They would trim down the federal bureaucracy, get rid of incompetent employees, cut spending and reduce taxes. They would throw out the subversives who had succeeded in infiltrating the government. They would deal resolutely with the threat of Communism. They would clean up the mess.

It was all so simple. Just use plain horse sense. Stay with the principles of the American system. Put more business in government and less government in business. Plan your work and work your plan.

Immediately after the election, Harold Talbott, a New York financier and an important fund raiser for the Republican party, hired a management consultant firm to find out how many jobs the new administration would need to fill in order to control all policy making. The firm also was instructed to prepare a report explaining in detail the nature of each job and the qualifications needed to fill it. The management consultant came up with an estimate that 250 to 300 men in the right positions would be able to control the government. The President-elect was given a fourteen-volume analysis of every top policy-making job he would have to fill, an outline of qualifications needed by applicants, and a statement of the chief problems they would face.

Since this was to be a business administration, its leadership naturally was recruited largely from the business community. Within days after his election Eisenhower, at work in his headquarters in New York's Commodore Hotel, began building his Cabinet. He broke precedent by announcing his selections as they were made.

Key appointments were John Foster Dulles as Secretary of State and George M. Humphrey as head of the Treasury Department.

Dulles was to be given a free hand with respect to the new administration's foreign policy, with special reference to the conduct of the Cold War. In Eisenhower's words, the New York lawyer had "been in training for this job all his life." As a youth of nineteen he was a secretary at the second Hague Peace Conference in 1907, was sent by President Wilson to Central America to negotiate for the protection of the Panama Canal at the beginning of World War I, served as counsel for the United States at the Versailles Peace Conference, was an adviser to the U.S. delegation at the organization meeting of the United Nations, and helped to negotiate the peace treaty with Japan. Eisenhower came to consider him, as Truman had thought of Acheson, as the greatest Secretary of State ever to serve the nation. Dulles was not in deep disagreement with this judgment. He told Eisenhower before his appointment was announced, "With my understanding of the intricate relationships between the peoples of the world and your sensitiveness to political considerations involved, we will make the most successful team in history."

Just as Dulles was responsible for foreign affairs, Humphrey was the man in charge of matters affecting the domestic economy. He knew the business world inside out. He was the prototype of the successful businessman, with a hard-driving, no-nonsense approach that solved problems and a smiling, frank personality that made friends. Humphrey held as a basic tenet of faith that prosperity depended not on government initiative but on creating an atmosphere in which flourishing business enterprise would provide wealth-creating jobs. Eisenhower had complete confidence in him and never lost it. On Capitol Hill, Humphrey became one of the most popular members of the Cabinet. He and congressmen knew how to talk to one another.

Charles E. Wilson left the presidency of General Motors to become Secretary of Defense. When he came up for confirmation, Democrats on the Senate Armed Services Committee happily focused on the fact that the nominee, although he had severed his connection with the automobile firm, still held $2.5 million in stock and rights to more than $600,000 in bonuses and other benefits. Wilson demurred at selling his stock because of the heavy tax liability that would result. Democrats on the committee wondered aloud if the Secretary-designate could avoid a conflict of interest, considering that General Motors was the beneficiary of nearly 8 per cent of the dollar volume of Defense Department contracts. Wilson retorted that in any decision coming before him he would place the government interest first. Besides, he added, "For years I thought that what was good for our country was good for General Motors, and vice versa." Thanks to Democratic briefing of newsmen, this statement was turned around to say, "What's good for General Motors is good for our country," a misquotation that plagued Wilson as long as he stayed in government. He sold his stock.

A Cabinet appointment creating some dissension was that of Martin P. Durkin, president of the Plumbers and Steamfitters Union, as Secretary of Labor. Taft, already irritated because he had not been consulted about the appointment of Humphrey, a fellow Ohioan, blew up on this one. Durkin was a Democrat and had been a strong supporter of Stevenson in the 1952 campaign. He had been among the leaders of organized labor's long fight against the Taft-Hartley Act. Moreover, he had been recommended for Secretary of Labor by Harold Stassen, for whom Taft had little use. Durkin's appointment was "incredible," Taft raged, and many Republicans agreed. Eisenhower's hope was that, with a union leader occupying the Labor Department post, organized labor would take its problems there instead of bringing them to the White House. The appointment did not work out. Durkin resigned within nine months, charging the President with bad faith in connection with plans to revise the Taft-Hartley Act.

Herbert Brownell, Jr., named Attorney General, was the

only Cabinet member with long political experience, although Arthur Summerfield, the Michigan automobile dealer appointed Postmaster General, had been prominently identified with Eisenhower's presidential campaign. Summerfield wanted to be both Postmaster General and Republican National Chairman, but Eisenhower instructed him to choose between the two positions.

The first Eisenhower Cabinet was rounded out with Douglas McKay, a former governor of Oregon, as Secretary of the Interior; Ezra Taft Benson, a Mormon Church elder from Utah, Secretary of Agriculture; and Sinclair Weeks, a rather nondescript businessman from Massachusetts, Secretary of Commerce. In April, Oveta Culp Hobby, publisher of the Houston *Post*, was added to the Cabinet as Secretary of the Department of Health, Education and Welfare after that department was created to replace the old Federal Security Agency.

"Our kind of people are now in power," rejoiced Randolph Burgess, formerly of the National City Bank in New York City, who served in the Eisenhower administration as deputy Secretary of the Treasury. But some of the Old Guard were less pleased. Taft, their perennial spokesman, expressed their uncertainty: "I'm not at all sure that all these businessmen are going to work out. I don't know of any reason why success in business should mean success in public service."

Nevertheless, these were men liked and trusted by Eisenhower, and they were men he understood far better than he did the politicians. They were practical. They knew what they were talking about. And they were patriotically willing to place themselves at the service of their country.

The President carried his liking for the company of businessmen into his social as well as his official life. When he was relaxing, he did not care to have either politicians or intellectuals around. His recreations were bridge and golf, and he enjoyed them with men like General Alfred Gruenther, his old friend from the Army; George Allen, who suspended his predilection for politics when he was in Eisenhower's company; Alton Jones, chairman of the board of Cities Service; and James C. Black, Washington representative of the U.S. Steel Corporation. George Humphrey had a plantation in Georgia, and the President liked to visit there. When he went on a golfing vacation away from Washington, he played with such kindred spirits as Humphrey, William Robinson, Coca-Cola board chairman, and Clifford Roberts, who headed the Augusta National Golf Club.

The great advantage to the new President of companionship with these men was that they did not constantly badger him. They wanted nothing of him, he felt, except that his administration be businesslike and efficient—that is, successful. Politicians, on the contrary, were constantly at him about patronage or legislation or other matters equally distasteful. Eisenhower had no choice but to contend with them during the course of the working day, but the experience of ten thousand evenings in Army officers' clubs drew him in off-hours to the pleasant, undemanding company of men who knew how to play a bridge hand or swing a golf club.

Sherman Adams, chief of staff at the White House, might have served as a link between the President and the politicians, but in the view of the latter he was more often a barrier than a connection. The former New Hampshire governor, at age fifty-four, was imbued equally with physical energy and moral rectitude. He spent twelve intense, work-filled hours or more at his desk every day. He received up to two hundred telephone calls daily, and according to some Republican congressmen, his answer to 199 of the calls was a flat "No." To personal visitors he was no less uncommunicative, continuing as the caller presented his case to go through the stack of papers that never completely disappeared from his desk. He decided who was to see the President and who was not, and a negative decision was delivered curtly and without any mollifying phrase. He was a man who, quite simply, seemed not to care in the slightest whether he was liked or disliked by other men.

Still there was another side to Adams, revealed at small dinner parties he regularly gave at the Occidental Restaurant for sub-Cabinet members of the administration. At these gatherings he was the perfect host, talking with knowledge and understanding of the problems his guests encountered in their daily activities—problems which, he said, after all were his as well as theirs and, finally, the President's.

No one questioned Adams' integrity or his undeviating loyalty to Eisenhower. But many disgruntled politicians doubted that he should be so seemingly proud of an utter lack of the milk of human kindness.

Characteristically, at the first meeting of the White House staff called by Adams, he lectured on how staff members should comport themselves. There must be no gossip sessions among secretaries, he warned, no smoking in the corridors and no propping of feet on desks. "He sounded like the headmaster of a very tough school for boys who had not behaved themselves or were on the verge of not behaving themselves," one staff member reported.

Major General Wilton B. "Jerry" Persons had the responsibility of soothing congressmen ruffled by Adams. He brought to the post of congressional liaison between the White House and Capitol Hill years of similar duty for the Army. His experience had taught him respect for congressional sensibilities, and his warm, gregarious nature fitted him admirably for working out the delicate compromises and negotiations so necessary in establishing a viable relationship between the presidential office and temperamental congressmen. Persons was ably assisted by Gerald Morgan, an attorney who had been deeply involved in drafting the Taft-Hartley Act, and Bryce Harlow, a former staff director of the House Armed Services Committee.

Even with these buffers between him and Congress, the President could not escape the necessity of dealing with politicians. The administration had taken office with the announced intention of making a substantial reduction in the size of the federal establishment. This would not be hard to accomplish, the country was assured, because under the new administration the federal government would do only what the states or the people could not do for themselves. It was proposed to cut out several hundred thousand jobs. Yet deserving Republicans themselves were hungry for government positions. To satisfy them, the Republican National Committee and some of the younger members of the presidential staff planned to take over thousands of top federal career jobs. At one time an order went out that all promotions in and appointments to jobs above a certain civil-service level must be cleared with the Republican National Committee. Adverse newspaper publicity caused this plan to be abandoned, but congressmen still wanted jobs for their constituents.

The entire concept of political patronage was painful to Eisenhower. He had selected and appointed his Cabinet members without consulting Republican members of Congress, and he was more than slightly irritated when an imposing delegation of senators, including Taft, Styles Bridges of New Hampshire, and Leverett Saltonstall of Massachusetts, visited him to protest. He talked soothingly to them, but there was no doubt that he thought this was his business and his alone.

Taft in particular felt that too many of the new men being brought into the government were from the eastern seaboard. He considered that administration people were not living up to the Morningside Heights agreement between him and Eisenhower that there would be no discrimination against Taft men. He spoke up harshly at one of the weekly meetings between the President and Republican congressional leaders when Eisenhower remarked that he was having trouble in finding the right person to head the Veterans' Administration and somebody suggested the name of a military man. "He doesn't have to be a general," Taft barked. "We've got too many generals around here already."

There was constant grumbling among the congressional Republicans that they were rarely shown the courtesy of being consulted about job openings in their own districts. Soon after the administration came in, Joe Martin, again Speaker of the House, picked up a newspaper from his district and read that a lawyer there had been appointed an assistant attorney general. It was the first he knew of it. "What a way to go about strengthening the local Republican organization!" moaned the old party regular.

"I was troubled by the fact that too many sons of rich families were getting the jobs," Martin said later. "For the good of the party I wanted to see some of them go to the boys who were mining the coal and sawing the wood for the Republican organization. How was the party being strengthened by passing them by?"

So Martin had a ready answer when Saltonstall asked him if he had been able to get any new jobs for his constituents. "New jobs?" Martin snorted. "I lost two that I got when Truman was in office."

At the White House meetings, Eisenhower and his aides rarely brought up the subject of patronage. They talked about jobs only when forced to do so by pressure from the congressmen attending. To Eisenhower, the nonpolitician, the attitude of the congressmen reflected "the same old narrow, inflexible view of partisan politics," which he neither shared nor liked.

167

The President noted also that some Republicans not in Congress resented the citizens' groups which had played so large a part in his election. A few weeks after he took office a visiting group of prominent Republicans declared that steps must be taken at once to get rid of "these volunteer politicians," scornfully called "hangers on" by one speaker. Eisenhower was taken aback. He recalled how helpful the amateurs had been in his campaign and said he hoped they could be induced to continue their activities in the future.

A lady among the visiting group retorted, "All they want is to get their fingers in the patronage pie. It's time we let them know that the Republican party is in charge."

In no uncertain terms the President told his visitors that, while people seeking jobs for themselves or others had laid heavy siege to him, not a single member of the citizens' groups had asked for any kind of official or unofficial favor. Most of the campaign "hangers on," he declared, were Independents and Republicans. They would have to be courted, not rebuffed, if the Republican party was to be built up. The visitors went away dissatisfied.

In his first weeks in office Eisenhower was greatly annoyed to find some of his decisions reported in the press before he announced them. The news leaks must stop, he said. He laid down the law that anyone under his authority or enjoying his confidence who gave out information about matters reserved for White House release should consider that his resignation had been tendered and accepted or that the confidential relationship was terminated. The report of this strict policy was promptly leaked to the newspapers and published. Washington reporters as a matter of course stepped up their efforts to get information about presidential decisions before it was officially released.

Jim Hagerty, who had been borrowed from Dewey for the

campaign, stayed on as the President's press secretary. The forty-three-year-old former newspaperman brought to his work not only a high degree of technical competence but also a completely pragmatic attitude. He saw his job as being one of making the President look good in the eyes of the public, and to that purpose he dedicated all his waking hours. He brought the cultivation of relations between the President and the communications media to a fine art. If some complaints were voiced that he was a bit *too* artful at times, they were submerged in the general approval by working reporters of his skill and his readiness to be helpful.

Hagerty worked out with the President a plan to release the transcripts of his press conference for full quotation. This had never been done before. It took some doing now because Eisenhower preferred not to have press conferences at all. He did not hold his first until almost a month after his inaugural, and then only under steady persuasion by Hagerty.

The presidential press conference was not established as an institution until Franklin D. Roosevelt's time. Woodrow Wilson for a while held intermittent meetings with the press, not with great success, but ended them when the war started in 1917. Harding began by permitting limited quotation of his statements at news conferences, but soon adopted a policy of answering only questions submitted in writing in advance. Coolidge and Hoover generally had poor relations with newsmen and saw as little of them as possible. Roosevelt, who enjoyed fencing with reporters, gave his news conferences an air of freedom and informality, but actually kept them under tight control. He often spoke off the record and also showered reporters with background information which they could use without attributing it to the President. No direct quotations were allowed except when specifically authorized. Roosevelt was more adept than any other President in using his press conferences to promote his own ideas and objectives. Truman tried to operate the same way, but he was never as successful.

The wide-open nature of Eisenhower's meetings with the communications people was better in theory than in practice. The transcripts contained all the errors in syntax and awkwardness of expression that might fall from the lips of any man bombarded with impromptu, often covertly hostile questions, and trying to answer them fully and honestly. The gentlemen of the press, never noted for their kindliness, fell with ferocious glee on sentences that wandered, participles that dangled, and verbs that were in disagreement with their subjects. This ridicule was damaging to the President's standing as a national and world leader, and eventually so exasperated him that he sharply reduced the frequency of his meetings with reporters. They thus succeeded in cutting off their news-seeking noses to spite their laughing faces.

But that was later. Eisenhower, as he had promised, went to Korea after his election and before he assumed office, took the first step toward an uneasy armistice—and the people were glad the fighting had stopped. The elimination of wage and price controls, to which the new administration was committed, began early in February. White House groundkeepers kidnapped the gray squirrels disturbing the President's backyard putting green and transported them to new woodland freedom in the Virginia countryside.

Meanwhile, in Congress . . .

* * *

The Republicans were in control of both bodies of Congress, although not by impressive majorities. The division in the Senate was nearly equal: forty-eight Republicans and forty-seven Democrats. Wayne Morse, beginning to phase himself out of his party, announced that he was a member—

the only member—of the Independent party. However, he voted with the Republicans in organizing the Senate for the session, giving them all the committee chairmanships.

In the House, the slight Republican majority meant that those old political antagonists and personal cronies, Sam Rayburn and Joe Martin, exchanged places again. If there had to be a Republican Speaker, Rayburn preferred Martin to any other. The devoted friendship of these two men, one from New England, the other from rural Texas, was one of the wonders of Capitol Hill. Once an enthusiastic Democrat suggested in a campaign year that Rayburn go into Massachusetts to make a speech urging the election of Martin's Democratic opponent. The Texan stared at the man in disbelief. "Speak against Joe Martin!" he exclaimed. "Hell, if I lived up there, I'd vote for him." Rayburn never felt a doubt that in Texas he would get Martin's vote.

Bob Taft decided that in this Congress he would take the post of Senate floor leader. Under the Republican organizational system, doing so meant he had to relinquish the chairmanship of the Policy Committee. But, as he said, with a Republican in the White House, most of the policy would come from there anyway. He was determined that this Republican administration should be a success. Naturally, the best assurance of realizing this objective lay in the full use of his own power to steer the administration on a conservative course. His kind of Republicans held the majority of the committee chairmanships. Taft was satisfied that he had the Senate Republicans well in hand.

This year marked the beginning of Lyndon Johnson's rise to power. In Arizona, McFarland had been defeated by Barry Goldwater, leaving a vacancy in the post of Democratic floor leader. Johnson, after two years as party whip—assistant leader—in the Senate, badly wanted the leadership. But he knew that pushing directly for it would be considered presumptuous on the part of a first-term senator. So he followed a characteristically indirect course.

Immediately after the election, he phoned Dick Russell from Austin and suggested that the Georgian announce his availability for the position. "Of course you won't want to do all the legwork and water carrying," Johnson said. "But that's all right. You be the leader and I'll do the work." As he had expected, Russell rejected the suggestion; as he had hoped, Russell suggested that Johnson himself stand for the leadership.

The Georgia senator went further; he volunteered to get in touch with other senators and ask them to back Johnson. Russell headed the conservative coalition in the Senate which had so often stalemated Truman. He was the acknowledged leader of the southern bloc. After the 1952 election this group held twenty-two of the forty-seven Democratic seats. In addition, Russell had close relationships with a number of western senators. There was no question of his ability to deliver the Democratic leadership to the man of his choice.

Johnson, with his already well-developed instinct for knowing where power lay, had courted Russell assiduously from the time he entered the Senate. Now he was to be rewarded.

Word quickly went out from Russell's home in the little town of Winder, Georgia, that Johnson was the man. Within forty-eight hours he had pledges of support from more than a majority of the Senate Democrats. In their caucus at the beginning of the session, Johnson was overwhelmingly elected floor leader. The feeble opposition was led by Hubert Humphrey, who tried to line up other liberal votes for the elderly James Murray of Montana. The liberals were beaten so badly that at the end of the caucus the vote for Johnson was officially made unanimous and so announced in order to avoid public humiliation of those who had opposed him.

The Texan wasted no time gloating over his victory. He

immediately started wooing the opposition. He asked Humphrey to come to his office that evening to discuss liberal representation on the Steering Committee, which named Democratic members of other Senate panels, and the Democratic Policy Committee. The new leader was ex-officio chairman of both groups.

Johnson, forty-four, was the youngest man to be elected Senate floor leader of either party. A driving, forceful man, whose unbounded energy was matched only by his ambition, he had survived and risen in the political world by his own wits.

He first came to Washington in the early 1930s as secretary to Representative Richard M. Kleberg, one of the owners of the fabulous King Ranch of Texas. After a few years, during which the bright young man learned all there was to know about running a congressman's office, Kleberg became fearful that his employee might be eying his own job and the two parted company. In the summer of 1935, a few days before his twenty-seventh birthday, Johnson was appointed state administrator for Texas of the National Youth Administration.

His performance was outstanding. The organization he built in Texas was used as a model in many other states. The NYA was one of the brighter stars in the New Deal crown. Its purpose was to get young Americans off the street corners and the highways and put them to work, either in school or at jobs. The Texas organization touched the lives of some 30,000 youngsters, many of whom regarded the young administrator as personally responsible for their economic salvation. This sentiment was no small asset for a man who was on the lookout for the political main chance.

The chance came in 1937 when the representative of the Central Texas congressional district that Johnson called home died and a special election was called to name his successor. It was a "sudden death" election in which, no matter how many candidates entered, the man getting the largest number of votes would win; a majority of all votes cast was not necessary for victory. Johnson resigned his NYA job. There were nine other candidates, several of them much better known than Johnson. They had the backing of political conservatives, who were aghast at many New Deal policies.

But then he boldly announced his support of Roosevelt's controversial plan to "pack" the Supreme Court. The other candidates united in turning their fire on him. Johnson got more publicity than any other candidate. With all of his opponents declaring their conservatism, he lined up virtually all of the hard-and-fast New Deal vote. He worked harder than any other candidate. He received almost twice as many votes as the runner-up—but not a majority of all votes. He had skillfully tailored his campaign to the kind of election it was.

In Washington, although he was a Roosevelt favorite because he had expressed support for the President's doomed Supreme Court plan, he found service in the House rather less satisfactory than he had anticipated. He wanted to move up and he was in a hurry. In 1941 he tried unsuccessfully for the Senate in a special election to fill the vacancy caused by the death of Morris Sheppard. Swallowing his defeat, he remained in the House until his election to the Senate by an almost invisible margin in 1948. During the years since then, he had become known as hard-working, eager to please his seniors, and willing to listen deferentially to their opinions and advice. He lived Senate politics and Texas politics during all his waking hours.

Some unfriendly observers thought that the exigencies of Texas politics unduly influenced his approach to his new responsibilities as Democratic floor leader. It was true that in speaking before the Democratic conference after he had been chosen, he rejected out of hand a policy of opposition for opposition's sake. "We are now in the minority," he said. "I have never agreed with the statement that 'it is the business of the opposition to oppose.' I do not believe the American people sent us here merely to obstruct." The more ardently partisan Democrats muttered that this expression showed Johnson was still listening to the presidential election returns from Texas. But there was more to it than that.

Johnson and, in the House, Sam Rayburn knew that the Democratic leadership in Congress faced a wholly new set of problems. Their party was disorganized, deeply in debt, and without effective leadership except for the two of them. The schism between the southern and northern wings of the party had deepened. Recriminations over the manner in which the losing national campaign had been waged were still being hurled back and forth. The two Texans did not deceive themselves about the difficulties they faced. Nevertheless, they had no intention of acting as referees in bankruptcy for the Democratic party. In their separate ways, and conferring together every day, they sought to bring some degree of unity to the party without automatically opposing every proposal that came from the White House.

Rayburn had the easier task. He had been around so long and had fought so hard for New Deal and Fair Deal programs that his credentials as a party loyalist could not be doubted. Johnson, on the other hand, was ruefully aware that the liberal bloc in the Senate viewed him with considerable apprehension. His first task, as he saw it, was to lull so far as possible the suspicions of the liberals while retaining the confidence of the larger group of conservatives.

He began by demonstrating forcibly that, with all due respect to tradition, he was not afraid to depart from the beaten path in Senate procedure. Important committee assignments customarily were made on the basis of seniority. But Johnson, when he made the assignments at the beginning of the session, was able to persuade some of the Democratic

175

elders to surrender their claims to choice committee spots. That left the way open to give desirable assignments to the freshman senators who had won in 1952 in spite of the party's national defeat.

Every Democratic senator wound up with appointment to at least one major committee. With perhaps one or two exceptions, everyone was pleased. The new members were especially happy. Their reaction was important to the success of Johnson's plan to persuade Democrats to get along.

Even the old hands who had complained about Johnson's departure from tradition came to approve his policy on committee assignments. They found to their surprise that they could work with the more-or-less militant young liberals. Harry Byrd, the deep-dyed conservative from Virginia, grumbled good-naturedly to Johnson, "Lyndon, I'll never understand how you got me to liking Hubert Humphrey so much."

He was on excellent terms with most of the Republicans in the Senate. He and Taft regarded each other with genuine liking and friendship. Outwardly two men could hardly have been more different. Johnson was gregarious, sentimental, persuasive, all fire and energy. Taft was usually withdrawn and often tactless, constantly giving the impression of a man who was not in the least concerned about whether other men liked what he was doing or the way he did it. Yet Johnson and he not only got along well in performing their official duties but also enjoyed a warm personal relationship.

This feeling came to life only after they had assumed the Senate leadership of their respective parties. Before that they had not really known each other at all. Each approached the other warily during the early days of the 1953 session. All his life Taft had been associated with dour Republicans who would have blanched at the thought of finding fun in politics. Yet before long he was able to grin wryly as Johnson, leaning across the aisle space that separated their schoolboylike desks at the front of the Senate chamber, teased him about not being able to line up enough Republican votes to put over an administration measure which the Ohio senator probably did not really favor in the first place. Johnson in turn came to feel a deep respect for the other man's stubborn integrity and forthright manner.

Old Guard Republicans and conservative Democrats believed hopefully that the pre-election meeting at Morningside Heights between Eisenhower and Taft had resulted in an agreement that New and Fair Deal laws would be scrapped wholesale. They were soon disillusioned. The Eisenhower messages to Congress in the first weeks of his administration failed almost completely to draw a stiff line between the positions of the Republican and Democratic parties. Most messages merely recommended continuing old programs, although on a reduced basis. Such controversies as they created were largely within the parties, not between them.

It was wholly unrealistic to suppose that basic reforms enacted into law during the preceding twenty years would be repealed. If Eisenhower had proposed any such action, he would have seriously endangered his relations with Rayburn and with Johnson. Their cooperation was essential if any part of his own program was to have a chance of success. Congressional Republicans had little experience in cooperating with a President. Not one Republican senator serving in the Eighty-third Congress and only nine Republican House members had previously served with a President of their party. In both houses, the Republicans had long been accustomed to saying "Yes" when the President said "No" and to saying "No" when the President said "Please." It was hard for them to change. Taft in the Senate and Martin in the House found themselves constantly having to resist pressure from old friends to oppose Eisenhower on a wide range of issues.

177

One veteran House member in a strong position to cause trouble if he wanted to made it clear early in the session that he had no intention of changing. This was Daniel A. Reed of New York, who had served in Congress since 1919 and now was chairman of the House Ways and Means Committee.

Reed said the Republicans had promised to cut taxes, and he wanted them cut immediately. The preceding Congress had passed a law to reduce the income-tax rate on January 1, 1954. Reed introduced a bill to make the reduction effective July 1, 1953. In his State of the Union message, Eisenhower took a stand against the earlier tax cut on the ground that if taxes went down before expenditures were reduced further inflation would result. Reed was not deterred. His committee reported the bill favorably.

"I don't know what those monkeys up there think they're doing," Eisenhower grumbled to a White House aide. He called a press conference to say that tax reductions should not come until a balanced budget could be at least glimpsed on the horizon. Reed kept up the fight until the House Rules Committee blocked his bill from being considered on the floor. The old New Yorker made vitriolic speeches about unkept promises, and the Democrats thoroughly enjoyed themselves.

Money matters also brought a blast from Taft, although not publicly uttered, during preparation of the administration budget for the coming fiscal year. Truman had recommended a budget which would have resulted in an estimated deficit of $9.9 billion. Eisenhower's revised budget reduced the anticipated deficit to $5.5 billion. At a meeting of several Cabinet members and Republican congressional leaders with the President, George Humphrey and Joseph M. Dodge, Director of the Budget, explained with some complacency that the administration already was beginning to make a turnaround in federal spending. This was evidenced, they pointed out, by the substantial reduction in Truman's proposed budget. But an unbalanced budget for fiscal 1954 was unavoidable because of the necessity for continued heavy spending for military purposes.

Taft's face grew increasingly gloomy as he listened to all this. At the end of the recital he banged his fist on the table and declared he would not accept the theory that no further reductions were possible. His voice rising in anger, he threw his words directly at the President. "With a program like this, we'll never elect a Republican Congress in 1954," he shouted. "You're taking us down the same road Truman traveled. It's a repudiation of everything we promised in the campaign."

Neither as general nor as President was Eisenhower accustomed to being talked to in this fashion. He was instantly angry and his anger showed in his flushed face. However, someone quickly turned the talk to minor subjects until he could compose himself. Then the President defended the budget, dwelling on the point that it would at least halt the upward trend in expenditures. But the proposed military spending was absolutely essential, he told the group, carefully refraining from a direct challenge to Taft, to maintain the national security. Grounds existed for hope that substantial reductions could be made in the 1955 budget, although he added that he would make no firm commitment that such reductions would be possible.

Taft was far from satisfied. Having expressed himself, he went away from the meeting still determined that the Eisenhower administration must be a success—and in his eyes it would be successful only if a Republican Congress was elected in 1954. Eventually this session appropriated $3.9 billion less than Eisenhower requested.

Shortly before the heated encounter with the President,

Taft, ably assisted by Johnson and nearly all other Senate Democrats, saved Eisenhower in a case in which the presidential prestige was squarely on the line.

The President nominated Charles E. "Chip" Bohlen to be ambassador to Soviet Russia. Bohlen was a career foreign-service officer. One of his assignments had been to serve as Roosevelt's interpreter and adviser on Russian affairs at the Yalta Conference in 1945, at which the President and Winston Churchill made concessions to Stalin to induce him to promise to enter the war against Japan. The "Yalta betrayal" for years had been the target of vicious Republican attack. The agreements reached there were denounced in the party's 1952 platform and their repudiation had been promised. Yet here was the Republican President proposing to send to Moscow the very man who went with Roosevelt to Yalta! Blood boiled and tempers exploded.

After the nomination was approved by the Foreign Relations Committee, the fight went to the Senate floor. Joe McCarthy, bawling that Bohlen had been associated with the "old Acheson gang," said labeling him a security risk was "putting it too weak." Styles Bridges, Republican dean of the Senate, called Bohlen a symbol of Yalta; his confirmation would be proof to the country that the Republicans were going back on their promise to change things in Washington. Democrat Pat McCarran, joining right-wing Republicans as he often did, declared in a Senate speech that the State Department security officer had refused to clear Bohlen and had been overriden by Dulles. The Secretary of State denied this. He already had told the Foreign Relations Committee the FBI investigation regularly made of presidential appointees produced no evidence that Bohlen was a security risk.

The uproar crowded other congressional news off the front pages of Washington newspapers. Every time Taft came off the Senate floor he was surrounded by reporters asking endless variants of "What about Chip Bohlen?" The Republican leader had often expressed sharp criticism of the Yalta agreements, but he did not now criticize the appointment of Bohlen. He was busily lining up votes for his confirmation.

"I'm against the appointment," he confided to Johnson. "But the President has asked me to get it through. I believe a President has the right to name his appointees, including ambassadors."

The question of what information was in Bohlen's files at the State Department was answered when Taft and John Sparkman inspected them. The Republican reported to the Senate: "There was no suggestion anywhere reflecting on the loyalty of Mr. Bohlen or any association by him with Communism or support of Communism or even tolerance of Communism."

This unequivocal assurance by a man whose word was never questioned satisfied all but a few die-hards. Bohlen's appointment was confirmed by a vote of 74 to 13. Eleven of the 13 holdouts were Republicans, only McCarran and Ed Johnson joining them from the other side.

After his victory, Taft sent word to the White House that he hoped there would be "no more Bohlens."

McCarthy's gadfly role in the Bohlen case represented only a small part of the trouble he was causing the administration. In the new Congress, he became chairman of the Committee on Government Operations, a dull assignment concerned primarily with matters of administrative procedure and efficiency. It was a spot, Taft said, where McCarthy "can't do any harm." He was wrong. The committee also had jurisdiction over legislative proposals to improve the efficiency of executive agencies. McCarthy appointed himself chairman of its Permanent Investigating Subcommittee, the function of which he saw as investigating anything in the Executive Branch that struck his fancy. Far from being neutralized, as the Republican leadership had hopefully planned, with the ample funds granted the subcommittee he was in a position greatly to extend the scope of his operations.

He hired as chief counsel of the committee a brilliant young lawyer named Roy Cohn, who was admitted to the bar when he was twenty-one and had been a member of the staff of the United States attorney's office in New York City. The pouty-faced, publicity-seeking Cohn engaged a friend, G. David Schine, son of a wealthy hotel man, as the subcommittee's chief consultant. The two brash youngsters were soon off on a tour of Europe to get material on which their boss could base denunciations of the Voice of America and the "subversive" books to be found in U.S. embassy libraries. They distinguished themselves on one occasion by playfully running through a London hotel lobby, shouting and laughing as one whacked the other with a rolled-up magazine. Cohn and Schine received tremendous foreign press coverage, all of it unfavorable to the United States.

While the two young men were thus engaged, McCarthy named J. B. Matthews, a former research assistant for the House Committee on Un-American Activities, as director of investigations for his subcommittee. Announcement of the appointment came only a little ahead of the publication of an article by Matthews, a scholarly type, entitled "Reds and Our Churches" in the *American Mercury*, which was not the magazine it had been under H. L. Mencken's editorship. The first sentence read, "The largest single group supporting the Communist cause in the United States today is composed of Protestant clergymen."

The article caused a great public outcry, especially from Protestant clergymen. McCarthy grinned and stood by his employee—for a time. But Deputy Attorney General William Rogers, encouraged by anti-McCarthy White House aides, arranged for a blistering telegram of protest to be sent the

President by the cochairmen of the National Conference of Christians and Jews. Meanwhile, McCarthy himself had begun to feel the heat. Rumors abounded in Washington that he would fire Matthews. For a time it was touch and go as to whether the White House group could beat him to the punch. However, when the wire came from New York, with Sherman Adams' cooperation an answer went back from the President calling the *Mercury* article "irresponsible" and "alien to America." McCarthy announced Matthews' resignation and went on with his self-assigned task of exposing "Communists and homosexuals" in the State Department, and hammering out new charges against various government officials.

It was a setback for the Wisconsin senator, but only a slight one. Eisenhower despised him, but when he was implored to oppose McCarthy openly, his reply was, "I refuse to get into the gutter with that guy."

Few members of the Senate were ready to take on the bad boy of the Republican party. McCarthy was for a time the most feared man in Washington. He had shown that he was perfectly willing to make any statement, however outlandish, about anybody, regardless of position, regardless of party, so long as he hit the front pages. Taft looked pained when McCarthy's most recent antics were mentioned, but he remained silent. Lyndon Johnson told a friend, "I'm not about to take him on in a debate on the subject, Resolved, Communism is good for the United States, with the Democratic party taking the affirmative side."

Adlai Stevenson, still the titular head of the party, did speak out: "When one party says that the other is the party of traitors who have deliberately conspired to betray America, to fill our government services with Communists and spies, to send our young men to unnecessary death in Korea, they violate not only the limits of partisanship, they offend not only the credulity of the people, but they stain the vision of America and of democracy for us and for the world we seek to lead."

And Sam Rayburn, who was not afraid of anybody, took the floor of the House one day to voice an angry warning. After listening impatiently to talk about how the American people became so disillusioned with the Democrats that they elected a Republican President and Congress, he advised the Republicans to soften their partisan attitude, "because there comes a time when partisanship can be practiced on both sides of the House." The 1952 election, he said, was an Eisenhower victory, not a Republican victory, and there might be a great change in Congress after 1954. "I know how to cause trouble if I want to," Rayburn reminded colleagues who knew it all too well, "for I know something about the rules of the House and the rights of the minority, and I want to see this administration one of these days spread its wings and get off the ground, let us know where they are going, what they stand for, and when they are going to do something about what they stand for."

Nobody could beat the man from Bonham, Texas, in speaking his mind when he felt the right time had come. He recognized the need for cooperating with the administration, but he felt that his party—*his* party—was being unjustly charged with having betrayed the interests of the country, and this he did not like at all.

* * *

Late in June, already suffering from the illness that would prove fatal the next month, Taft surveyed the record of the first session of the Eighty-third Congress. He was not satisfied, but neither was he wholly unhappy. "It's not much of a record," he conceded. "But there was the problem of a new government, of getting turned around." His own skill and loyalty, plus the President's enormous prestige and the fragmented nature of the Congress, had prevented the anti-Eisenhower faction of the Republican party from mounting an organized and effective opposition.

The session was adjourned August 3. William F. Knowland of California, Taft's own choice to succeed him as majority leader, and Joe Martin could report a not unimpressive list of accomplishments. Congress had accepted Eisenhower's defense bill with its controversial reduced goal for the Air Force, accepted the administration's Mutual Security program after reducing appropriations from the amount requested, accepted the President's tax program in spite of Dan Reed's best efforts, extended the Democratic reciprocal-trade program, made good on an Eisenhower campaign promise by giving the states title to offshore oil lands, established the Small Business Administration, and earmarked $200 million to begin the rehabilitation of Korea. The administration suffered only one major defeat during the session when Congress rejected Eisenhower's last-minute request to raise the national debt limit. For the sake of harmony, action was put off until some later date on establishment of the St. Lawrence Seaway, increased postal rates, statehood for Hawaii, extension of social-security coverage, and revision of the Taft-Hartley Act.

On balance, it was a good beginning for the first Republican administration in twenty years. The new boys had more than held their own.

As for the President's personal popularity, the American people still "liked Ike." At the end of the year, Pollster George Gallup sent out interviewers to ask a cross section of the populace, "What man that you have heard or read about living today do you admire the most?" Eisenhower won as many votes as the combined total of the next two men on the list, Winston Churchill and General Douglas MacArthur.

He could well say, as he did say on Christmas Day, "I'm not mad at anybody."

1954

SPRING FORWARD, FALL BACK

"Poor Ike," Harry Truman sighed one day in 1952, when General Eisenhower's victory began to look certain. "It won't be a bit like the Army. He'll sit there and he'll say, 'Do this! Do that!' And nothing will happen. He'll find it very frustrating."

Despite this not altogether disinterested forecast, Eisenhower started the new year with the air of a man on top of his job and enjoying the sensation. In his State of the Union message, he listed and described specific legislative measures on which he hoped for action during the session. The message bore the stamp of a military "by the numbers" precision, setting dates on which subsequent messages on particular subjects would be submitted. "The commitment to deliver specific messages on specific dates kept my staff, at times, working around the clock," Eisenhower noted proudly, "but every message arrived at Capitol Hill on time."

The President's political philosophy, which necessarily had been formed after he took office, became clearer in the series of requests for legislation. In large areas he took a stand some-

186

where between Herbert Hoover and Franklin D. Roosevelt. The keystone of the nation's foreign policy, he said, was unity and strength in the free world's struggle against Communism. Aid would be continued to Nationalist China and also, but on a reduced scale, to Europe. National defense would depend more on atomic power and less on manpower, with consequent monetary savings—a concept which gave rise to the slogan "More bang for a buck." He asked for a broadening of the unemployment compensation and old-age or survivors insurance programs. He proposed a mild "medical reinsurance" plan, although he added, and was enthusiastically applauded by Congress, "I am flatly opposed to the socialization of medicine." His suggested revisions of the Taft-Hartley Act represented a compromise between what labor wanted and what management wanted. With the nation's warehouses bulging with surplus grain crops, he asked for a shift to flexible farm price supports. He proposed a modest housing program.

Congress passed no important law during the session that was not recommended by the President. Many of his proposals were sharply modified, however, and some were defeated. Ironically, he was at first quite skeptical about a measure for which he later received great acclaim. This legislation authorized construction of the St. Lawrence Seaway from Canada to the Great Lakes. The proposal had been before Congress for years in one form or another, and its approval this year added to Eisenhower's reputation as a giant killer.

Some Democrats complained that because of the Johnson-Rayburn policy of cooperation with the Republican President, no worthwhile political issues were being created for the fall elections. But there was no madness in the Texans' method. They could read the popularity polls as well as anyone. They were content to use their strength in revising legislation proposed by the President and to point out from time to time that his program generally received more support from Democrats than Republicans.

It was true that Eisenhower's most vexing problems were caused by members of his congressional majority. One of them, held over from the preceding year, was a proposed constitutional amendment introduced by John W. Bricker, the former Ohio governor and 1944 vice-presidential nominee.

Bricker's amendment would change the constitution to impose drastic limits on the power of the President and the Senate to enter into treaties with other countries. It was born out of the nightmares of the not inconsiderable number of Americans who held a steadfast conviction that the United States had been consistently "sold out" to world-wide Communism. The Bricker amendment, introduced with the co-sponsorship of forty-five senators, quickly became a highly emotional issue. Gathered behind it were all the self-styled patriots, right wingers and isolationists imbued with a dark suspicion that the State Department, working through the United Nations, saw the treaty-making power as a means of circumventing provisions of the very Constitution into which it was written.

The Senate Judiciary Committee held hearings for three months on the resolution, with attention concentrated on two vital provisions. One gave Congress the power to regulate all Executive and other agreements, thus implementing the bitter sentiment of "No more Yaltas." The other provision read: "A treaty shall become effective as internal law within the United States only through legislation which would be valid in the absence of a treaty." The last ten words—the "which clause," as it was known—would in fact virtually strip the President of authority to make even routine executive agreements.

The White House and members of the Senate were subjected to a heavy barrage of letters and telegrams from individuals and organizations incited to support the Bricker amendment. The Daughters of the American Revolution endorsed it. So did an ex-president of the American Bar Association. The *Bulletin* of the Association of Physicians and Surgeons urged doctors to inform their congressmen that they were for it. Hugh Roy Cullen, the Houston oil man who had appointed himself an adviser to the President, wired Eisenhower: "The people of the United States are becoming greatly alarmed over what is happening in Washington. Word has come to me from the North, South, East and West that the internationalists in New York are using all their influence, including 'brain washing,' to pressure your administration; and lined up with these internationalists are the most radical members of Congress. If the Bricker amendment is not passed, the Republican party is wrecked." Cullen, whose every word was news in dollar-conscious Houston, thoughtfully released the text of his telegram to the press, thereby encouraging others to send similar messages to Washington.

For a long time Eisenhower made no public comment on the proposed amendment, but emissaries from the administration were working on Bricker. Nixon, Dulles, Humphrey, Brownell and Weeks met with him repeatedly in an effort to get him to modify his proposal. Bricker was adamant. He had the necessary votes in the Senate, he said, and he would not budge an inch; it was a matter of principle. Once the President, listening to the report of yet another futile visit to the Ohio senator, exclaimed violently, "I'm so sick of this I could scream." Later he tried personally to work out compromise wording with Bricker, but this effort also failed.

Under Johnson's leadership, the Senate Democrats stood aside from the fray. They cheerfully noted that what had started as a move to curb constitutional powers exerted by a Democratic President had mushroomed into an abrasive issue within the Republican party. Johnson himself, although he considered the amendment unwise, told Nixon he would vote for it "because my people are for it." George Reedy, the former United Press reporter who had joined the staff of Johnson's Defense Preparedness Subcommittee in 1950 and now was staff director of the Senate Democratic Policy Committee, gave him a count on the Texas mail about the Bricker amendment. Reedy reported that 1,325 letters, telegrams, postcards and petitions had been received in favor of it. Only ninety Texans expressed opposition.

After the Judiciary Committee favorably reported the amendment, Eisenhower at last wrote Knowland that he was "unalterably opposed" to it. Its adoption, he declared sternly, "would be notice to our friends as well as to our enemies abroad that our country intends to withdraw from its leadership in world affairs." With the President's opposition made so unmistakably if belatedly clear, some senators who had cosponsored Bricker's resolution withdrew their names. The amendment finally fell narrowly short of the two-thirds vote necessary for passage.

A substitute was offered by Walter George, ranking Democrat on the Foreign Relations Committee. It was little less objectionable to the administration than the original proposal, as evidenced by Bricker's support of it. The aging Georgia senator made an emotional appeal in the Senate on behalf of his substitute, at times breaking into tears as he pleaded for its approval. Knowland, moving back from his majority leader's seat to stress that he was acting only as an individual senator, voted for it. Johnson, who had worked closely with George in the drawing up of the new resolution, also supported it by his vote if not by his conviction. But the George substitute was defeated—by one vote.

* * *

At 12:32 P.M. on May 17, 1954, Chief Justice Earl Warren read a unanimous decision of the Supreme Court holding that racial segregation in public schools was a violation of the Federal Constitution.

No other decision in the Court's 164-year history had affected directly the lives of so many American families. In seventeen states and the District of Columbia segregation of schools was written into the law; four other states permitted segregation.

The decision was denounced violently by members of Congress from the South and by state officials in that section. Every senator from the old Confederate South except Lyndon Johnson signed a "Southern Manifesto" protesting the Court's ruling. When the President was asked if he endorsed the decision delivered by his first appointee to the Supreme Court, he replied: "I think it makes no difference whether or not I endorse it. What I say is the Constitution is as the Supreme Court interprets it, and I must conform to that and do my very best to see that it is carried out in this country." This answer displeased many, but it was the honest reaction of a man accustomed to live by accredited authority.

The decision set the country off on a road long sought after with dedication and fervor by Negro leaders and white liberals. It was not to lead straight and true to the Promised Land.

* * *

The position of "leadership in world affairs" which Eisenhower mentioned in expressing opposition to the Bricker amendment was repeatedly put to the test during the year.

In February, on the President's direct orders, some 250 Air Force technicians landed in Indochina from U.S. air bases in Japan. They were the vanguard of a major effort to save French Indochina from Communist forces led by Ho Chi Minh. The United States had been financing the French army in the area since 1950 and sending over great amounts of matériel and large numbers of warplanes, naval vessels, and combat vehicles. But the Air Force technicians were the first American troops dispatched to Indochina.

It was the government's view that Indochina must be kept out of Communist hands. "If Indochina fell," Eisenhower said, "not only Thailand but Burma and Malaya might be threatened, with added risks to East Pakistan and South Asia as well as to all Indonesia." A Democratic senator, Mike Mansfield of Montana, who in 1953 had gone on a study mission to Indochina, agreed that much more than the fate of one country was at stake. "The issue in this war so many people would like to forget," he reported, "is the continued freedom of the non-Communist world, the containment of Communist aggression, and the welfare and security of our country."

The possibility loomed that the United States would be forced out of all Asia and back to Hawaii, which had happened in World War II. The big French fortress of Diênbiênphu was under heavy attack; its fall seemed imminent. In March, the French chief of staff came to Washington to warn that Indochina would be lost unless the United States intervened with armed forces.

Dulles favored American intervention. On the Saturday morning of April 3, the Secretary met in secret with a group of congressional leaders. The President, he told them, wanted Congress to pass a joint resolution permitting him to use air and sea power in Indochina.

Dick Russell, ranking Democrat on the Senate Armed Services Committee, was among those present. As he listened to Dulles outline the plan for American intervention, he grew increasingly concerned, even angry. Only a single air strike, Dulles pleaded, was contemplated against the forces attacking Diênbiênphu. Admiral Arthur W. Radford, chairman of the Joint Chiefs of Staff, proposed to use for the purpose planes from two American carriers then in the South China Sea and land-based aircraft from the Philippines. But it was clear to Russell that "if we went into any of it we would have to take it all," including American aid on the ground. After Dulles had presented the plan, the Georgia senator got to his feet to deliver an impassioned protest. "It's wrong," he said, his voice rising. "I'm tired of seeing American soldiers being used as gladiators to be thrown into every area of the world."

Lyndon Johnson also protested. He gravely pointed out that Knowland and other Republicans kept going around saying that in the Korean War the United States had furnished 90 per cent of the manpower and money. The American people condemned the Truman administration for this, so if Congress was to be asked to approve the kind of resolution Dulles was suggesting, Congress should be told in advance where the manpower for intervening in Indochina would come from. He bluntly asked the Secretary of State if any other nations had been consulted to see if they would join in standing up against the Communist attacks. No, Dulles admitted, they had not. In that case, Johnson argued and the other congressmen present concurred, the Secretary had better find out if the United States would have any allies in such a venture.

Dulles agreed to do so, but Johnson was in a glum mood when he returned to his Senate office. "It looks like war," he told a member of his staff.

Within the next few days, Dulles talked with the diplomatic representatives in Washington of a number of potential allies. He soon learned that Britain for one—and a very big one—was unalterably opposed to the plan for intervention. This fact, combined with the attitude of the congressional leaders, killed it for the time being. The busy Secretary, his hopes blasted for congressional approval of a resolution allowing the President to order bombardment of the attacking forces in Indochina, set about the organization of a Southeast Asia Treaty Organization similar to NATO.

A few days after Dulles' meeting with the congressmen, Vice-President Nixon addressed the annual session of the American Society of Newspaper Editors in Washington. At the end of his talk he offered to answer questions about the situation in Indochina with the understanding that whatever he said would not be attributed to him in print. One editor asked what he called a hypothetical question: In the event of the withdrawal of the French Army, would the United States send over troops to try to save Indochina?

The vice-president's reply was straightforward and to the point. After expressing the belief that the French would not abandon Vietnam, he said, "The United States as leader of the free world cannot afford further retreat in Asia. It is hoped that the United States can avoid direct involvement in Indochina. But if to avoid further Communist expansion in Asia and Indochina, we must take the risk of putting our boys in, I think the Executive has to take the politically unpopular decision and do it."

Nixon's remarks were widely published, at first credited only to "a high administration source." Inevitably, his identity was soon revealed. When the State Department then stated that the vice-president had announced no new U.S. policy, alarm swept the nation and there was a great uproar on Capitol Hill. Instead of the President getting the resolution he wanted from Congress, a rider was introduced to a bill requiring prior congressional approval before American troops could be sent to Indochina or anywhere else. The rider failed to pass, but it spoke the sentiment of much of Congress.

With no allies and no congressional approval, Eisenhower refused to yield to pressure from Dulles and Radford for intervention with air power. Diênbiênphu fell. France was sick of the war. Pierre Mendès-France, the new French premier, promised to negotiate peace at a previously scheduled conference in Geneva of the world's big powers. The Geneva Conference brought a cease-fire agreement between France and the Communists and the "provisional" division of Vietnam into North and South.

The shooting stopped in Indochina on July 21. The first phase of the war was over. But the way had been paved for a second phase, far bloodier and infinitely more tragic.

* * *

John Foster Dulles became the most widely traveled Secretary of State in American history, going nearly everywhere in the world in pursuing his policy of the "containment" of Communism. He did spend some time in the Nation's Capital, however, and on one such occasion—at the Republican Senate congressional campaign committee party for the press—Joe McCarthy came up to him with a warm smile and favored him with a great bear hug. "Foster," said the Communist-baiting senator, who also consistently baited the Department of State, "you've been a pretty good boy over the last six months." Dulles gave his cramped smile. "Joe, that isn't the question," he replied. "The big question is whether you are going to be a good boy for the next six months."

McCarthy would not be.

The Wisconsin senator was out after Harvard professors he suspected of left-wing leanings, after alleged homosexuals and fellow travelers in the State Department, after subversives in the Voice of America, especially out after the Democrats. In a speech in his home state, he declaimed: "The Democratic label is now the property of men who have been unwilling to recognize evil or who bent to widespread pleas from the lips of traitors—men and women who wear the political label stitched by the idiocy of a Truman, rotted by the deceit of an Acheson." This utterance caused Sam Rayburn to serve public notice that he was tired of "it being open season on Democrats" and to send word to Eisenhower, "Some of our backs are getting pretty sore." The President promptly said at a press conference that the times were too serious to permit indulgence in political partisanship to an extreme degree, adding an expression of hope that the sensationalists in his own party would soften their attacks. But he avoided direct reference to the senator from Wisconsin.

McCarthy could hardly have cared less. He dominated the front-page headlines, getting more column inches of space than the President himself. He was determined to make himself the key to the 1954 congressional elections. A public-opinion poll early in the year reported that 50 per cent of the American people approved of his activities. He was riding high.

Yet, all unknowing, McCarthy was approaching the brink of the precipice, led there by Roy Cohn, the young aide on whom he doted, and Cohn's bosom friend, David Schine.

A bad thing happened to Schine in November 1953. Reclassified by Selective Service from 4F to 1A, unable despite the best efforts of McCarthy and Cohn to get a direct commission, he found himself drafted into the Army. He was sent to Fort Dix, New Jersey, for basic training. Private Schine quickly discovered that he did not care for life in the Army, with its close-order drill, obstacle courses, kitchen-police duty, and restriction of personal freedom. He appealed to Cohn to rescue him.

Cohn tried. He bombarded the Army with demands that his friend be given special privileges. He suggested to Army Secretary Robert T. Stevens that Schine be made his special assistant in charge of uncovering subversive soldiers. Stevens recoiled from the idea. Well, then, Cohn persisted, perhaps Schine could be assigned to West Point to keep an eye out

for Communist propaganda in military textbooks. Ste
thought not. Cohn enlisted his employer's assistance in fin
ing Schine a civilian-clothes assignment in New York. But
their undertaking did not succeed.

Nothing was left but to take on the United States Army
in a frontal attack.

McCarthy received a tip that he should look into the
Army's handling of a loyalty case involving Dr. Irving Peress,
a dentist stationed at Camp Kilmer. Peress had been inducted
into service under the doctors' draft law and given a commission in the Medical Corps. When he was issued a loyalty
questionnaire in accordance with regulations, he refused to
fill it out. A loyalty investigation was ordered. While it was
going on, Peress received a promotion from captain to major.
This action was routine, army policy being to try to adjust
the rank of doctors and dentists to conform to their professional qualifications. The findings of the loyalty investigation
caused army officials to decide to discharge Peress at a time
of his own choosing so long as it was within ninety days after
January 18. The discharge would be honorable.

So matters stood when McCarthy roared into the picture.
He called Peress before his subcommittee at a session in New
York. The dentist took refuge in the Fifth Amendment, refusing to answer questions bearing on his alleged past membership in the Communist party. McCarthy sent Stevens a
demand that Peress be court-martialed. But Peress did not
wait around. He immediately applied for an honorable discharge and received it three days after being questioned by
McCarthy. He was safely beyond the reach of military law.

The infuriated senator, throwing off statements left and
right about the Army's "disgraceful coddling of Communists,"
called another committee meeting in New York. In addition
to Peress, witnesses at this closed session included Brigadier
General Ralph W. Zwicker, commanding general of Camp

Kilmer, and three other officers. Peress again refused to answer questions about his Communist affiliations. Now McCarthy bore down on Zwicker, demanding to know the names of all officers involved in Peress' promotion and subsequent discharge. The senator would not for a moment accept the well-founded theory that these blunders were due simply to military red tape and inefficiency, a case of the right and left hands moving independently of each other. He was determined to prove the existence of a deep-dyed conspiracy. "Who promoted Peress?" was his battle cry.

Zwicker refused to produce the names McCarthy demanded, and was immediately accused of shielding Communist conspirators. "You're not fit to wear the uniform," McCarthy grated. When John Adams, army counsel, tried to intercede on Zwicker's behalf, McCarthy ordered him out of the hearing room. He announced that the general would be called before an open hearing.

Stevens obtained an affidavit from Zwicker telling what had gone on at the session. After digesting it, he publicly ordered the general not to appear again before the committee. He himself would go, the Secretary announced. Army officers, he declared, were not to be subjected to such treatment.

Other members of the Investigating Subcommittee decided that matters had gone far enough. The public fight between their Republican chairman and the Republican Secretary of the Army was doing their party no good. They persuaded McCarthy to postpone the announced hearing for a couple of days while they tried to smooth over the situation. A private luncheon was arranged in Dirksen's office, attended only by Republican members of the subcommittee and Stevens. It was to be a secret meeting, Stevens was informed, and he should let no one know about it. He incredibly agreed and went to the luncheon with the businessman's hope that the trouble could be worked out on a reasonable basis.

Stevens, a man of good will who had spent his life in the shelter of a family-owned textile company, could hardly have suspected what he was up against. Present at the meeting were Dirksen, Karl Mundt, and Charles Potter of Michigan—and McCarthy.

The principal point pleaded to the senators by Stevens was that army officers appearing before the subcommittee must receive better treatment than had been accorded Zwicker. He was assured that nobody would quarrel with him about that; witnesses would not be abused, would be treated with respect. Pleased with this assurance, Stevens approved a "Memorandum of Understanding," which Mundt pecked out on an office typewriter. Four points were covered: (1) "Communists must be rooted out"; (2) Stevens was to order that the Army's investigation of the Peress case be completed and would make "everyone involved" available as witnesses; (3) Zwicker's reappearance before the subcommittee would be temporarily postponed; (4) Stevens' proposed appearance would be canceled.

The Secretary was in a complacent mood as he returned to his office. He was quickly disillusioned.

The memorandum was released to the press, unaccompanied by any mention of the agreement Stevens thought had been reached that McCarthy would treat witnesses better. Newspaper stories and editorials indignantly cried out against the Army's capitulation to McCarthy. The senator himself told reporters that Stevens could not have given in "more abjectly if he had got down on his knees." Stevens wept when the statement was read to him over the telephone.

Up to now Eisenhower had been largely shielded by Nixon and White House aides from the developing controversy. The protection could no longer be extended. A general impression was abroad that the President had instructed Stevens to make peace with McCarthy on whatever terms could be obtained. Rumors flew about Washington that Stevens would be asked to resign. The President, boiling mad, summoned the Secretary to the White House the day after the disastrous luncheon, and with Nixon, Sherman Adams and Persons, they worked out a statement for him to issue.

At six o'clock that evening, in Jim Hagerty's office, Stevens read the statement before a hastily assembled press conference. He said he would never assent to the abuse of army personnel or to their being browbeaten and humiliated. He said he did not intend to allow them to be deprived of counsel in appearances before any congressional committee. And he maintained that at the meeting with the Republican senators he had indeed been assured that they would not permit the conditions to which he objected.

McCarthy retorted, through the press, that no witnesses had been abused and that Zwicker had not asked for counsel. He would, he added, continue to oppose Communism "even if it embarrasses my own party."

Statements and counterstatements fell like autumn leaves. The Army charged that Cohn had threatened to "wreck the Army" if it persisted in treating Schine as a lowly private. When army emissaries had warned McCarthy earlier that Cohn was going too far, the senator chose to interpret the warning as an attempt at blackmail. He told members of his subcommittee, "The Army is holding Schine hostage to get me to lay off." He also said Stevens had urged the committee to leave the Army alone and go after the Navy, Air Force and Department of Defense. Stevens called this charge an "unequivocal lie." Defense Secretary Wilson growled that the idea of the Army coddling Communists was "just damn tommyrot." The Army compiled an extensive report detailing repeated instances in which McCarthy and Cohn had pressed for special treatment of Schine. Copies of the report were distributed to the Investigating Subcommittee members, some other senators, and the press. McCarthy and Cohn held a press conference to deny everything except that they were against Communism.

"Even if it embarrasses my own party," the Wisconsin senator had said self-righteously. He was embarrassing his own party all right. Administration Republicans and senatorial Republicans were battling on the front pages every day. The rhetorical gore was frightful.

An end had to be brought to this affair. The other members of McCarthy's subcommittee decided that an investigation should be made of the Army's own investigation of Cohn's activities vis-à-vis Private Schine and of McCarthy's countercharges against the Army. The White House wanted the inquiry to be made by the Senate Armed Services Committee rather than the Permanent Investigating Subcommittee. But Chairman Saltonstall would have nothing to do with it, his patrician aversion for the whole messy controversy intensified by the fact that he would be up for re-election in the fall. So the subcommittee retained jurisdiction, with Mundt temporarily taking McCarthy's place as chairman. McCarthy would, however, sit in on the hearings as a member of the panel. He would also be a witness. With his innate inability to refrain from offering insult, he suggested that all witnesses, himself included, be required to take lie-detector tests. This was not done.

Thirty-six hearing sessions were held, extending over a period of nearly two months. When the hearings were finished, so were McCarthy and Cohn, though this was not immediately evident.

The hearings were televised from the great Senate Caucus Room. Twenty million Americans watched as Cohn sneered arrogantly from the witness chair at Joseph H. Welch, the courtly and accomplished Boston lawyer who had been engaged as counsel for the Army; as Ray Jenkins, the Tennessee lawyer acting in a similar capacity for the subcommittee, brought his tough backwoods competence to the interrogation of witnesses; as McCarthy, alternately scowling and grinning, interrupted proceedings with innumerable and irrelevant "points of order," a parliamentary device which he used to heckle witnesses and to make speeches which were themselves out of order. The television viewers were regaled with accounts of unprecedented weekend passes given Schine so he could frolic with friends at New York's Stork Club. They heard about a stolen letter in McCarthy's files, marked "Personal and Confidential" and addressed not to the demon Communist-hunter but to the Chief of Army Intelligence and signed by the Director of the Federal Bureau of Investigation. They saw a photograph which showed Stevens and Schine posing together amicably, just the two of them; they heard evidence, not controverted, that the picture had been cropped to cut out other persons with them.

All this and much more. The televised hearings offered the best entertainment available that spring. The original charges and countercharges became in the end secondary issues, buried under a mass of personalities and emotion.

The emotional climax was reached one June afternoon as Welch was shooting satiric questions at Cohn about whether the Investigating Subcommittee exposed Communists as fast as they were discovered. McCarthy listened in growing anger. At last he jumped to his feet.

"In view of Mr. Welch's request that the information be given once we know of anyone who might be performing any work for the Communist party," he rasped, "I think we should tell him that he has in his law firm a young man named Fisher, whom he recommended, incidentally, to do work on this committee, who has been for a number of years a member of an organization which was named, oh, years and years ago, as the legal mouthpiece of the Communist party."

He went on to say that he did not know whether Welch was aware of this past connection when he recommended his associate for work with the committee, that he assumed Welch did not know, but that he also was convinced the Bostonian had no conception of the danger of Communism.

As McCarthy talked, Welch remained in his seat at the long table. At the end he stood up and spoke with deep feeling. "Until this moment, Senator," he said slowly, "I think I never really gauged your cruelty or your recklessness."

He proceeded to explain that he had indeed intended to name Fred Fisher to aid him during the subcommittee investigation. However, after Fisher told him that, when he was in law school and for a few months thereafter, he was a member of the National Lawyers Guild, Welch decided against using him. He said he had told Fisher, "If I do, one of these days that will come out and go over national television and it will hurt just like the dickens."

Welch continued to address McCarthy directly. "Little did I dream," he said histrionically, his voice almost breaking, "you could be so reckless and cruel as to do an injury to that lad. It is true that he is still with Hale and Dorr. It is true that he will continue to be with Hale and Dorr. It is, I regret, equally true that I fear he shall always bear a scar needlessly inflicted by you."

Tears shone in the elderly lawyer's eyes as he concluded: "Let us not assassinate this lad further, Senator. You have done enough. Have you no sense of decency, sir, at long last? Have you left no sense of decency?"

Millions of people, sitting transfixed before their tiny screens, saw Welch sink heavily into his chair, saw the combination grin-snarl that McCarthy turned toward the camera. And they heard, after a moment of tense silence, an outburst of spontaneous applause from spectators in the Caucus Room.

Thanks to television, these hearings showed McCarthy as

a ruthless attacker, not a hero fighting against odds to save the country from the Communist menace. Having smeared so many individuals, he was revealed as accusing others of smears. He responded with deception to charges that he had deceived. While crying aloud against diversionary tactics, he repeatedly sidetracked the hearings. Having made a career of blasting "Fifth Amendment Communists," he came perilously close to invoking the Fifth himself in refusing to answer questions put to him by the counsel for the Army. Before the eyes of millions, he fell a victim of his own methods and the outraged eloquence of Joseph Welch.

Not long after the hearings ended, Senator Potter joined Democratic members of the Permanent Investigating Subcommittee in insisting that Cohn must go. The young lawyer, a man McCarthy had called indispensable, turned in his resignation—"a great victory for the Communists," said his erstwhile employer.

McCarthy himself was fast sliding downhill. Within days after Cohn's departure, Ralph Flanders of Vermont introduced in the Senate a resolution condemning the Wisconsin senator for conduct "contrary to senatorial traditions." The Senate voted to establish a six-man Select Committee for the specific and sole purpose of considering this resolution and reporting on it before adjournment of the session. The Republicans were represented on the committee by Arthur Watkins of Utah, a former judge who served as chairman, Carlson of Kansas, and Case of South Dakota. Democratic members were Johnson of Colorado, Stennis of Mississippi, and Ervin of North Carolina. All were conservatives. None could be remotely suspected of the slightest sympathy with Communism.

The committee took evidence for two weeks—without benefit of television cameras. Late in September it recommended condemnation of McCarthy on two counts: contempt of the Senate and his treatment of Zwicker.

After the congressional elections, the lame-duck Senate returned to Washington to dispose of this unsavory matter. The day before debate started on the committee report, McCarthy issued a typical statement. "I would have the American people recognize the fact that the Communist party has now extended its tentacles to the United States Senate," he said. "It has made a committee of the Senate its unwitting handmaiden." There was a long debate in the Senate, accompanied by threats of a filibuster by McCarthy supporters and slowed down when the subject of the committee resolution was hospitalized with a sore elbow.

Finally, on December 2 the resolution—amended so that neither the word "censure" nor Zwicker's name appeared in it —was brought to a vote. The committee report was accepted, 67 to 22. Lyndon Johnson was successful in his determined effort to get the Democrats lined up solidly for the resolution. All of them voted for it except John F. Kennedy, who was recovering in a Boston hospital from a serious operation. Smathers of Florida and Gore of Tennessee were paired with two Republican senators not present for the voting. But of the Republican leadership, Saltonstall was the only member who voted to condemn McCarthy. Knowland, Dirksen and Bridges all voted in his favor. Even as he went down, McCarthy was still heavily dividing the party to which he claimed allegiance.

He hurled defiance at the administration. It was soft on Communism, he said, the same as the Democrats, and he apologized for having supported Eisenhower in 1952. But now McCarthy spoke empty words. The power he once clutched in his fists was gone, the victim of a combination of the Senate vote and the loss of his committee chairmanship

205

in the new Congress. He remained in the Senate, increasingly alone and drinking heavily, until his death in May 1957, but for all practical purposes he died politically in December 1954.

* * *

Richard M. Nixon took the lead for the Republicans in the congressional campaign.

During the past two years the vice-president had become one of the busiest and most influential men in the administration. Eisenhower encouraged him to make a real job out of his office. In dealing with Congress, government departments, even the press, Nixon was in many respects a projection of the President. At Cabinet meetings, if the President was called away before business was finished, he would say, "Dick, you take over." Nixon was the first vice-president in history to preside over Cabinet sessions. He also served on the National Security Council. The first time he was scheduled to act as chairman of a full NSC meeting, at a time when Eisenhower was in Denver on one of his frequent vacations, staff members whispered to one another their wonder about "how Junior will do." They stopped wondering when Nixon conducted the meeting with crisp efficiency. His advice on the government's strategic position in foreign affairs, internal security, labor policy, and general political tactics carried as much weight as that of any man in Washington. In the fall of 1953 he made a good-will trip around the world for the President, and the success of this mission added to his prestige.

He put the prestige on the line in a vigorous, untiring effort to help elect Republicans to Congress. He was the driving force of the entire campaign, not only making a total of more than two hundred speeches in thirty-one states but also cheering on party workers with predictions of victory if they worked hard enough—if they worked as hard, he might have said, as he was working. On a typical fall day, Nixon traveled more than five hundred miles, delivered six speeches, held three press conferences and three meetings with local Republican workers, shook 532 hands by count of a *Newsweek* reporter, "smiled two dozen times for as many photographers, and dictated answers to forty or fifty letters, three press releases and key paragraphs for the next day's six speeches." He kept up this kind of schedule for forty-eight days, getting by on no more than four hours of sleep out of every twenty-four.

The Republicans began by asking for a vote of confidence in Eisenhower and holding up with pride the record of accomplishment by the Republican Congress. But Nixon was a man who instinctively went on the offensive in any combat. He could not be content for long with repeating variations of the theme that the Eisenhower administration was good for the country. Soon he was campaigning hard against "Trumanism."

He shouted to an audience in Michigan that the Truman administration had shown a "hopeless inability" to deal with Communism, corruption, and wage and price controls. In Minnesota, he told a crowd that the basic campaign issue was whether the "integrity, firmness and moderation" of the Eisenhower administration was to be discarded for a return to "discredited Trumanism." In Oregon, he scored Richard Neuberger, candidate for the Senate, as a "left-wing Democrat." He declared that the Eisenhower administration had been "kicking Communists and fellow travelers and security risks out of the government" by the thousands, and warned that they would all be hired back if a Democratic Congress was elected.

The Democrats were not eager to make "Trumanism" an issue, but they were perfectly willing to talk about the record of the Eighty-third Congress. Rayburn said "inept" was the right word.

Adlai Stevenson, who had been appearing regularly at fund-raising functions to help pay off the National Committee's deficit, sounded much as he had in 1952, and it was clear that he was thinking ahead to 1956 and another presidential nomination. He described the administration's "twenty blundering months," and said his 1952 prediction of hard times and disintegration of U.S. foreign policy was already being justified. Nixon, Stevenson said, was pleading that the time had come "for all good men to ratify disorder, contradiction and impotence in order to save the Republican party."

The President had not planned to participate in the drive to keep Republicans in charge of Congress. Taking with complete literalness the constitutional doctrine of separation of powers, he believed it was up to the voters to choose the Congress they wanted. He hoped and expected that it would be a Republican Congress. But he was not anxious to get out on the hustings. He continued to have strong mental reservations about politicians as a class—regardless of their party affiliation. "By golly," he told Jim Hagerty, "sometimes you sure get tired of all this clackety-clack."

Nevertheless, with public-opinion polls showing that a Democratic victory was a distinct possibility, Sherman Adams was pressed by Republican politicians to get Eisenhower actively into the campaign. The President in turn was pressured by Adams and Leonard Hall, Republican National Chairman, and eventually he was out working as no President had ever before worked in a congressional campaign.

The Republican leadership especially wanted Eisenhower to place before the country a picture of a more harmonious relationship between himself and his party members than the one being painted by Rayburn and other Democrats. These worthies persisted in saying that on some key measures the Democrats were better supporters of the President than the Republicans. So, in a Denver speech, the President warned that "a cold war" between a Democratic Congress and the Executive Branch would result in failure for his programs.

Rayburn promptly remarked that the Republicans had become so desperate that "they forced the President to step out of character and make a very partisan speech." He and Lyndon Johnson, as spokesmen for the Democrats in Congress, fired off a telegram to Eisenhower—which, of course, was released for publication—calling his prediction of a cold war "an unwarranted and unjust attack on the many Democrats who have done so much to cooperate with your administration and to defend your programs from attacks by members and leaders of your own party." The two Democrats continued self-righteously: "It may be that you have been placed in your new position of rigid, unswerving partisanship by the frantic pleas of your political advisers to come to the rescue of a party fearful of repudiation by the voters. Nevertheless, we assure you, as leaders of the Democratic party in Congress, that so far as we are concerned there will be no cold war conducted against you by the Democrats when we gain control of both houses of Congress." However, in a radio-television address a few days before the election, the President stubbornly stated: "For the next two years the Executive Branch will be Republican. Confusion can be avoided and steady progress assured only by electing a Republican majority to the Congress."

In some speeches Eisenhower hit the note sounded so raucously by Nixon. "Not one appointee of this administration has been involved in scandal or corruption," he declared. "No longer do we have prosperity pegged to the battlefield sacrifices of our husbands, our sons, and our brothers." He won wild applause from a crowd of 20,000 in the Hollywood Bowl by saying, "This administration does not look upon the Communist menace as a red herring."

As election day grew closer, both the campaign and the

weather took some odd turns. In Ohio, when George Bender, a House member running against Tom Burke, who had been appointed by a Democratic governor to fill the vacancy left by Taft's death, started a curbside television interview in Cleveland, a passer-by paused to jeer. A Bender fan took offense, and a moment later a fist fight was being televised. Hurricane Hazel, cutting in from South Carolina, swept up across ten states into Canada, causing a heavy death toll, injuries to thousands, and millions of dollars in property damage. In New York, Averell Harriman, candidate for governor, called state Republican leaders liars fifteen times in no more than that many minutes. A seven-inch flood hit Chicago. In Pittsburgh, a large framed picture of Eisenhower fell off a wall and clouted a Republican orator. Los Angeles was buried for weeks under choking smog. In New York, Stevenson said Nixon had campaigned with smut, smear, slander. In California, Nixon said Stevenson was "snide and snobbish."

Election day came and the Democrats won. In the new Congress, they would enjoy a majority of 232 to 203 in the House. The Senate again would be nearly equally divided, but this time the Democrats would have forty-nine members and the Republicans forty-seven, Morse having announced that he was now a Democrat.

Rayburn expressed to reporters the hope that there would be no more talk of a cold war. Eisenhower said at a news conference that, after all, "cold war" was probably too strong a term to use even in the heat of a campaign; he would place no obstacles in the way of cooperation with the Democratic Congress.

* * *

Lyndon Johnson was among the Democrats returned to the Senate. His re-election had been assured in the summer when he overwhelmingly defeated his primary opponent without bothering to wage a formal campaign.

On the night of the primary he received telephoned returns from Texas in the company of a few friends in his minority leader's office. Rayburn was there, but he left at midnight, saying crossly to a companion, "Damned if I understand Lyndon. He's winning two to one or better, and yet he stays on the phone to get the results from some little piddling precinct up in the Panhandle." And it was true that Johnson at the moment was yelping over the long-distance wire, "Fifty-seven to forty-three, huh? That's pretty good in a box where I got just six votes in 1948. Are those final returns?" His anxiety about every vote was no laughing matter to him or to those who had shared with him the consuming worry about the terrifyingly narrow margin of his primary victory six years before.

Johnson had never liked the idea of being the leader of a minority. He had even instructed his staff to use the term "Senate Democratic leader" in news releases and correspondence. Now he was going to be majority leader. He could hardly wait.

To be exact, he did not wait. A few days after the election, he went to Washington for the Senate session to consider the resolution condemning Joe McCarthy. Reporters crammed into his office at a news conference to hear him explain what the Democrats would do in the new Congress. He said a meeting would be held in the near future of members of the Senate Democratic Policy Committee and other senators who would take over as committee chairmen. By the time the congressional session convened in January, he told the reporters, details of the legislative program to be proposed by the Democratic majority would have been thoroughly worked out.

"This will be a constructive program, tailor-made to fit

211

the present needs of the nation," he said. "It will deal with issues vital to the continued security and progress of the United States. I mean such issues as an enlightened foreign policy, an adequate defense program, and domestic policies designed to pass the basic test of what is best for Americans generally."

Johnson added that he had stopped off in Bonham on his way to Washington to confer with Rayburn, who would again become Speaker of the House. "The entire leadership will be coordinated through the Senate Democratic Policy Committee and the leadership organization of the House of Representatives," the senator said. "Out of deference to the President, the program will not be presented until we have heard his State of the Union message."

And, rather grandly, he concluded, "We hope there will be few points of difference."

1955

LYNDON JOHNSON'S YEAR

The President's State of the Union message contained little to which the Democratic leadership of the new Congress could object. Eisenhower's recommendations were moderate, even bland; one unrespectful newspaper reporter said the President had come to Congress with an "uh-huh" message. Its approach was bipartisan, giving Lyndon Johnson an opportunity to comment to the press, "The President correctly states a Democratic premise when he says that the general good should be our yardstick on every great issue of our time. We will consider his program in that spirit."

Static came from the Democratic National Committee. At the same time that Johnson was taking over as majority leader in the Senate, Paul Butler, a lawyer from South Bend, Indiana, was settling into the position of Democratic National Chairman. Butler was the personal—and surprising—choice of Adlai Stevenson to succeed Stephen Mitchell. The new chairman had plans to direct party policy along the line of his own thinking, which was militantly partisan. He did not agree with the Johnson concept of consensus politics in a divided government. Under his direction, the National Committee's research division issued a strongly critical analysis of the State of the Union message.

Johnson and Rayburn, who had not been consulted about this statement or even informed that it was coming, were furious. Johnson hotly told the press that the Democratic leadership was not prepared to surrender its authority to anybody. He also instructed George Reedy to let Washington newspaper correspondents know, not for attribution, that senior congressional Democrats were embarrassed and displeased by Butler's presumption.

This war of words marked the beginning of a conflict that was to continue for six years between the Democratic leadership on Capitol Hill and the chairman of the Democratic National Committee. Butler resented the setting of national party policy by two Texans whom he regarded as far too conservative. The ambitious Indianian wanted to fight—although at times he seemed not to know what about or in which party. Once, after trying vainly to smooth over an intraparty conflict in California, he came out with this astounding remark: "The most significant aspect of the whole business is, I believe, that virtually all of the issues have deep roots, and are all the more consequential for that reason." To Johnson and Rayburn, many of the other observations he offered were quite as meaningless.

The congressional leaders had not forgotten that they were Democrats. But they had a deeper understanding of the political realities than Paul Butler would ever have. They knew that, barring some wholly unforeseen development, the Democrats would have virtually no chance of putting up a candidate who could defeat the popular Eisenhower if he stood for re-election. They were fearful, Johnson especially, that their party might even lose its slim congressional majority if they consistently and publicly opposed the President.

The country was growing fast, the economy booming. The population approached 164 million, up 2.8 million in a year. The stock market average reached an all-time high. Per-capita income was greater than ever before, and so was individual spending. Inflation had been halted, consumer prices having risen by less than 1 per cent in the years since Eisenhower had taken office. Johnson shrewdly judged that the people generally were in no mood for bitter political warfare.

He also knew that Eisenhower's control of the government now extended only as far as the Democrats in Congress would permit. The center of effective power was no longer in the White House but on Capitol Hill. More precisely, it was with the Democrats on Capitol Hill, for many Republicans, including Knowland, their floor leader in the Senate, were more fundamentally opposed to presidential policies in some areas than were Johnson-Rayburn and their followers.

Before the year was a month old, Johnson seized an opportunity to dramatize Democratic support of the President in the field of foreign policy.

A mutual-defense treaty with Nationalist China pledged the United States to defend Formosa and the Pescadores. The treaty was supplemented by notes exchanged between Dulles and the Chinese Foreign Minister stating that by joint agreement the United States could act in other islands if events demanded. In mid-January the Communist Chinese, after moving into the Tachens and seizing the island of Yoikang, began a vociferous propaganda campaign calling for the "liberation" of Formosa and the banishment of Chiang Kai-shek. As counter-propaganda, Eisenhower sent Congress a resolution asking the lawmakers to approve in advance the use of U.S. armed forces "if necessary to assure the security of Formosa and the Pescadores."

Rayburn and others pointed out that the resolution would

merely put Congress on record as approving use by the President of power he already had. In that sense, it was not needed. But Eisenhower remembered well enough how the Korean conflict had been transformed into "Truman's war" within a few short months. He had no wish to make himself similarly vulnerable, so he went to Congress. He was accused by Wayne Morse of "passing the buck." Republican Senator Flanders said the resolution would make preventive war possible. Humphrey introduced an amendment to restrict use of the armed forces specifically to the defense of Formosa and the Pescadores, but it was defeated.

Johnson talked to his Democrats in private, and in public defended the resolution against opposing Republicans. "I hope," he intoned piously, "no Democrat will be heard to say that because the President of the United States came to Congress, he is thereby subject to criticism. The President chose a courageous course, a course which would be taken only by a prudent, patient man, who knows the pitfalls along the course and who knows the horrors of war."

He had a powerful ally to take the lead in pushing for approval of the resolution in the Senate. Walter George, the most prestigious of Senate members, was at the peak of his influence in the body. As the new Congress was being organized, he had been urged by the President himself to waive his claim to the chairmanship of the Finance Committee in order to head the Foreign Relations Committee. His active support of the resolution was absolutely essential for its success, but he had some reservations about certain provisions. Johnson worked hard to convince him that the whole government must show a united front in dealing with a grave situation.

Fortunately, the aging senator was one of those southerners who looked fondly on the Texan as "their boy." He listened. Every morning for a week, Johnson stopped by the Mayflower Hotel to have breakfast with George at his apartment

("And guess who pays for the breakfast!" he said with a self-mocking grimace to one of his staff members). Patiently, persuasively, he pressed home to the old gentleman how essential it was for the country to face the world with a foreign policy on which the entire government was united. He flattered, cajoled, appealed to the Georgian's old-fashioned and honest spirit of patriotism.

He was successful. George threw his prestige behind the resolution in committee and later, delivering a speech prepared by the majority leader's man Reedy, on the Senate floor. The resolution was approved overwhelmingly, only three votes being cast against it in each house. The President signed the resolution on January 29, George's seventy-seventh birthday.

(The senator's reward from the people of Georgia was that in 1956, after he had announced for re-election, he was forced to withdraw in the face of apparently certain defeat by Herman Talmadge. His former supporters deserted him. The same thing had happened in Texas to another Senate Foreign Relations Committee chairman, Tom Connally, in 1952.)

The Formosa resolution triumph whetted Johnson's already voracious appetite for the duties of floor leader of the Senate majority. He grabbed the job by the throat and shook it like a terrier playing with a discarded slipper. Forty-six years old, standing six feet three and weighing 200 pounds, he was at the height of his physical vigor. He was inexhaustible, so filled with nervous energy that he smoked three packages of cigarettes a day and walked around even when he was talking on the telephone. This youngest majority floor leader in Senate history could look back on some twenty-two years of experience in government and eighteen years in Congress. His black hair was beginning to turn gray and thin in front, and lines were deepening on each side of the keen face. These outward evidences of maturity were more than matched by the knowledge he had gained of how to get things done in government. He was, for the Democrats, supremely the right man in the right place at the right time.

Day and night he cultivated his slim majority. His most effective work was done in the cloakroom or in his private office. He rarely made formal speeches on the floor of the Senate, although of course he was on his feet often to help move the legislative wheel around. His forte was not oratory but the personal, informal, man-to-man approach. At times he would be seen in a corner of a Capitol corridor lobbying with a not-yet-convinced senator on some bill or another. His tall form would loom over the other man, both arms waving in windmill circles, his prominent nose thrusting itself ever closer, his voice going nonstop as he told why this could not be done or that had to be done. "The full treatment," Mary McGrory wrote in the Washington *Star*, "is an incredibly potent mixture of persuasion, badgering, flattery, threats, reminders of past favors and future advantages."

This summation, while accurate enough, by no means told all the story. When Johnson approached another senator to talk about a legislative measure, he was unfailingly armed with the pertinent facts—not just some of the facts but *all* of them. He always knew what he was talking about. His method of operation was to prepare the way thoroughly before a bill reached the Senate for action. This process began with the committees. He insisted that his committee chairmen and members give the most minute attention to all provisions, major and minor, of every bill they referred for floor action. When the bill came to the floor, he wanted to have available every last relevant fact about it. The famed "Johnson treatment" simply meant that, once he had these facts, he threw the full weight of his overpowering personality into presenting them.

He had help. Earle Clements of Kentucky, the party whip

in the Senate, held the confidence of labor leaders and could often bridge the gap between the Texan and members of the liberal bloc in the Senate. And Johnson had his own lines among the Republicans. When the moment came for voting on a measure, he was able to predict almost without fail what the outcome would be. Time and again he would lean across the aisle toward Knowland when a controversial bill was coming up and say softly, gleefully, "You just don't have the votes, Bill." Knowland, a deadly serious lone wolf wholly incapable of the cynical in-house banter engaged in by most senators, was apt to give a wry grin in reply, knowing that his opposite number was right.

Johnson also was aided materially in predicting how the vote would go on any given bill by the never-ceasing watchfulness of the secretary to the Senate majority, a sharp-featured, quick-thinking young man named Bobby Gene Baker. Having come from Pickens, South Carolina, to be a Senate page when he was in his teens, Bobby Baker had literally grown up in the body. Now twenty-seven, he knew all the senators and, except for a handful of wary liberals, had the full trust of the Democratic members. He was an invaluable pipeline for the flow of information between them and the leadership. He could count votes on an upcoming bill with amazing accuracy.

Like other people who worked for Johnson, Baker was alternately abused and praised by the man he addressed as "Leader." Johnson was capable of lauding Baker in the Senate chamber as "my strong right arm, the first man I talk to in the morning and the last I talk to at night" on one day and on the next remarking casually to a confidant, "Sometimes I think Bobby is just a cheap conversationalist." But Baker's loyalty never wavered. He was close to being the indispensable man in the majority leader's operation.

Both in the floor leader's office in the Capitol and his

Texas office in the Senate Office Building, Johnson had a superbly functioning staff. The key man was Walter Jenkins, a quiet, incredibly hard-working Texan who had been with Johnson since his graduation from the University of Texas in the late 1930s. Jenkins ran the senator's Texas office, overseeing the handling of a huge volume of correspondence, acting as stand-in for his employer in dealing with important Texas personages, and maintaining close contact with members of the state's delegation in the House of Representatives. He enjoyed and deserved Johnson's full confidence. George Reedy, in addition to serving as staff director of the Policy Committee, wrote speeches and press releases and acted as the senator's liaison with the news media. He was also a general "idea man," turning out a heavy volume of memoranda on issues, trends and personalities. Gerald Siegel, native of Iowa and a graduate of the Yale Law School, was general counsel for the Policy Committee. Unassuming, intelligent and unflappable, Siegel made his way through the jungle of Senate politics with a sure instinct for what would and would not work in the legislative area. All three of these men were under forty.

Concerned solely with Texas affairs was Arthur C. Perry, a long-time fixture on Capitol Hill. He had been administrative assistant to two other Texas senators, Morris Sheppard and Tom Connally, before joining Johnson's staff in 1953. A gentle and kindly man, who knew out of his long experience which department or agency could provide information or assistance needed by constituents, Perry was adored by the corps of young stenographers working under his direction.

All members of the staff—the top aides, the clerks, the secretaries and typists—worked hard, worked long hours, and time off was not encouraged. Once a very competent young woman from Texas, newly arrived in Washington, was thinking about going to work for Johnson and asked a friend, who had been administrative assistant to House members for a number of years, if she should take the job. "Sure," said her friend breezily. "Why not? Employees get treated awfully well over there." "How do you mean?" asked the newcomer. "Well, take the case of a man who's been with Senator Johnson since 1937. He had an appendectomy not long ago and is convalescing now. So they're letting him work just half time—from eight to five every day." There was truth in that, but her friend went to work for Johnson. She stayed five months before thankfully resigning.

In the lower echelons, especially, many employees came and went quickly. But those who remained, including several besides the appendicitis victim who had been with Johnson since he first came to Congress as a young representative, were deeply dedicated to the interests of the man they worked for. To some of them he was, without any question or doubt, the greatest and finest man in the world. Such devotion might be hard for sideline observers to comprehend, but it was there.

Over-all, Johnson had more people in his employ than any other senator. He wore a diversity of hats. Not only was he senator from Texas and Democratic floor leader. He also was chairman of the Democratic Policy Committee, the Democratic Conference, the Democratic Steering Committee, the Defense Preparedness Subcommittee, and the Appropriations Subcommittee for the State, Commerce and Justice Departments. He never had trouble finding a place on one payroll or another for anyone he wanted to hire—and to those he hired there was never any misunderstanding about the identity of the boss.

Members of his various staffs, to whom Johnson regularly complained about their inadequacies and about whose high abilities he often boasted to outsiders, did their work so well that he could give nearly his whole attention to the demands of the floor leadership. That was exactly what he wanted to do.

During the first six months of the year, his desk in the

Senate chamber was a focal point. For five minutes every morning before the body went into session at its customary noon hour, he made himself available to reporters and answered their questions about the business of the day. From twelve o'clock until the day officially ended, usually around six o'clock, he was in constant touch, at his desk or in the cloakroom, with men who seemed to have little more in common than the fact that all were members of the United States Senate: Russell, his friend and mentor; Byrd of Virginia, whose inborn conservatism truly represented the squirearchy of his state; sharp-tongued Wayne Morse, who only a year before had said in a speech in Texas, "Johnson has the most reactionary record in the Senate," but who now said (after the majority leader had given him a longed-for seat on the Foreign Relations Committee), "I consider him not only a great statesman but a good man"; Price Daniel of Texas, who had been elected in 1952 as a Democrat who supported Eisenhower for President; Bill Knowland, arm's length across the aisle separating the Democrats and the Republicans; Hubert Humphrey, with an opinion on everything and a superb facility for expressing all his opinions; Leverett Saltonstall, whose appearance spoke in modulated tones of his New England background; all these and many others.

In the early years of Congress, floor leaders were known officially as managers. The man holding the majority post in the Senate had the responsibility of managing procedures there and keeping the legislative process flowing as smoothly as possible. Now Johnson was the manager and he managed— not, he was quick to say, in the sense of bossing ("Who would be fool enough to try to boss the Senate of the United States?"), but in the sense of coordinating, of deciding who would take the lead on a specific bill, of bringing men and their ideas together.

He managed. If he was accused of compromising in order to reach agreement, he retorted that history showed American democracy was born in compromise and depended, for its effective functioning, on the give-and-take of reasonable men who respected one another's integrity. If newspaper writers, who thrived on controversy, complained that the Senate machinery was working *too* smoothly, his response was that the American people wanted their government to operate quietly and efficiently. "I don't think they want anybody to rock the boat just for the fun of it," he snapped.

Americans for Democratic Action accused Johnson of acquiescing in a Republican "assault on liberalism." Humphrey, an ADA founder, made a speech in the Senate defending the integrity of Johnson's own liberalism and praising the majority leader as "a genius in the art of the legislative process." Neuberger of Oregon, a new member of the Senate's liberal bloc and one for whom Johnson had campaigned in 1954, said bluntly, "I think Johnson is as liberal as he can be and still continue as the effective leader of the senators who sit on the Democratic side of the Senate."

The occasional mumbles of rebellion against the way Johnson was running the Senate—and he *was* running it—never came to anything more than talk. His methods worked, that was the thing.

Besides, when the liberals fumed that Johnson had no interest in a specific measure dear to their hearts, he was as likely as not to prove them wrong. This happened after the Banking and Currency Committee threw out an administration proposal to build 35,000 public-housing units a year for two years and substituted a four-year program to build 100,000 units a year. Proponents of the latter measure wondered forebodingly if Johnson would really do his best—his very best—to get it through the Senate. He did, beating down an effort led by Homer Capehart of Indiana to restore the administration program. Significantly, while losing six Democratic votes in the showdown, he picked up nine Republicans.

A small witticism had long gone around Washington to the

effect that the Senate was called the upper house because it consistently upped appropriations made by the House. Now the Senate was upping White House proposals again and again.

The President asked for an increase in the minimum wage rate from seventy-five to ninety cents an hour; the Democrats insisted on and obtained a dollar. The President asked for a 6 per cent increase in pay for government workers; the Democrats voted a raise of 8 per cent after Eisenhower vetoed a slightly higher increase, and the President signed the bill. The reciprocal trade program, a Democratic undertaking from its inception, was expanded and extended for three years; this had seemed a remote possibility at the beginning of the session. Foreign aid was continued, Johnson leading the Senate to restore a substantial part of the cut voted by the House. Treaties were approved for German rearmament, the end of the Austrian occupation, and mutual defense with Southeast Asia and Nationalist China.

Some political commentators said the theme song the Democrats tauntingly rendered to the administration had the refrain, "Anything you can do, I can do better."

Walter Lippmann, an outspoken admirer of the President, wrote: "I do not think it is any exaggeration to say that Mr. Eisenhower's success as President began when the Republicans lost control of Congress and the standing committees. In his first two years he had suffered an almost unbroken record of frustration and of domination by the senior Republicans, and particularly the Republican committee chairmen in the Senate."

Johnson himself, when asked by a reporter how he could so consistently carry along with him a majority composed of such wondrously dissimilar elements, bowed to the Democratic committee chairmen. "I don't carry them along," he said. "When the Democrats vote together, they do so because each man has become convinced he should vote that way. Most of the credit for this convincing belongs to our committee chairmen. This Senate has the master craftsmen of all time in charge of the committees. That's where the most important work is done, and there has never been a Senate that has had men who were more experienced in the subject matters they deal with than this one."

The committee chairmen, he pointed out, were "old pros." They knew their subjects, whether defense or finance, housing or agriculture or foreign policy, world trade or labor. When problems came up in any governmental field, they understood how to find out the answers.

That answer was by no means calculated to irritate the committee chairmen on whom he depended so heavily. Its accuracy was borne out by the results. And, of course, Johnson himself was an "old pro." And one who liked to win.

He had one experience with failure early in the session and was not pleased. Rayburn rammed through the House a bill cutting every individual's income tax by a flat twenty dollars. The Speaker's simple political motivation was to get the Democrats on record as supporting a tax reduction in order to take a possible issue away from the Republicans in the 1956 campaign. Johnson, not forewarned, was privately dismayed, for he knew he could not muster the necessary votes in the Senate to approve the reduction. He stalled and maneuvered by having the bill amended to provide a cut of twenty dollars from the tax of a family head and ten dollars for each additional member of the family. But it was no use. With Byrd and George denouncing the measure as unsound and the President castigating it as irresponsible, the Senate voted it down.

Johnson naturally regarded this outcome as a personal defeat. He had long paid heavy court to Rayburn, writing him on his birthday, sending little presents, taking the Speaker on fishing trips. A flowery letter he wrote in 1939 to wish Rayburn a happy fifty-seventh birthday, in which he spoke effusively of his great respect and personal affection, was typical. So was Rayburn's three-sentence reply, ending, "I am always glad to be of service to you—you are an apt pupil." Now, after so many years, the pupil had out-distanced the master in legislative acumen. It was a fact of which both became aware and of which neither ever spoke openly. Their personal relationship remained close and unmarred, but thereafter the older man increasingly followed the signals called by the younger.

Both men consulted with the President to an extent known to few Democrats and perhaps no Republicans. Johnson and Rayburn were frequently at the White House in unheralded meetings to discuss legislation with Eisenhower. As the three of them talked informally over drinks, the President's forehead corrugated like a washboard as he worried over the behavior of some of "those monkeys" in his party or his great smile broke forth when Johnson related some tidbit of congressional gossip. These easy sessions smoothed the way for passage of more than one important legislative measure.

Johnson, whose public utterances were likely to come out sounding pompous, had a lighter side which was manifested in badinage with other politicians and in private jokes with his staff. Possessed of a small boy's gift for mimicry, he could convulse trusted intimates with his wicked imitations of some of his fellow senators. Sliding his thick-lensed glasses down his nose and assuming a pedantic, slightly condescending air, he became Fulbright of Arkansas. He puffed out his cheeks and walked across the room with a slow, ponderous stride to show how Knowland approached a legislative problem. He could give a letter-perfect rendition of the venerable Walter George saying, as he so often did say, "We must take the *rrr*easonable view." He once observed of the loquacious

Humphrey, "Hubert prepares for a thoughtful address on a major issue by taking a deep breath." Discussing Saltonstall with a staff member, he said, "He's a fine senator, a real New England gentleman, his word is his bond—but he's so *unaware*. Why, you," he cried, pointing a finger, "could be sleeping with every stenographer in his office and he wouldn't have any idea anything was going on."

As the session wore on, Johnson's fun making became rare. He was driving himself furiously. His usual day began at seven-thirty and ended at eleven or eleven-thirty at night, when he would go home and gobble down a heavy meal before falling into bed. His staff, always stepping lively, stepped livelier in efforts to avoid irritated outbursts from the boss. One day a group of eight Houston "Minute Women," an organization of the extreme right, called on him in his office to exhort the senator to help "get the U.S. out of the U.N. and the U.N. out of the U.S." In about six minutes the little old ladies scurried out of his private room, from which could be heard Johnson's tired, enraged roar, "Just get the hell out of my office!" The outburst was a measure of his nervous exhaustion.

An additional problem—which he turned into an opportunity—arose when Joe McCarthy introduced a resolution to put the Senate on record as opposed to the forthcoming Big Four conference at Geneva unless it was agreed in advance that the status of the Soviet satellite nations would be a topic of discussion.

When this blunt proposal to limit the President's freedom of action reached the Senate Foreign Relations Committee, it was unanimously opposed by Democrats and Republicans. Knowland proposed that the committee kill the resolution by tabling it, a course of which he said Eisenhower approved. But that did not suit Johnson's purpose. He said he also had conferred with the President. The majority leader wanted the resolution to come before the Senate so the body could make its position unmistakably clear. If Republicans were embarrassed as a result, that would be all to the good. He accordingly influenced the Democratic majority of the committee to vote down Knowland's motion to table.

The committee then gave a unanimously unfavorable report, the resolution went to the Senate and was heavily defeated after bitter debate, most of it between Republicans. Only four Republicans voted for McCarthy's resolution, but Johnson had again demonstrated that the Democrats stood solidly behind the President in foreign policy while the Republicans remained divided. He was gratified.

By this time, the press and radio and television representatives on Capitol Hill were telling the country that the Senate had the hardest working and most effective majority leader in the body's history. Gould Lincoln, veteran political writer for the Washington *Star*, headed one of his columns, "Lyndon Johnson Moves Mountains." Doris Fleeson, a liberal-oriented columnist who more often than not criticized Johnson severely, wrote after one exhibition of his leadership that the only thing left to him was to set his next triumph in the Senate to music. Late in June, Sam Shaffer of *Newsweek's* Washington bureau reported: "One day last week the U.S. Senate passed ninety bills, confirmed an ambassador and a Federal Trade Commissioner and then knocked off because it had temporarily run out of business. The elapsed time: Four hours and forty-three minutes."

Johnson was exceedingly fond of this kind of box score. In comparing the session with the first session of the Republican Eighty-third Congress, he let his pride show: "This session passed about thirty per cent more bills in about fifty per cent less time; it left fewer measures hanging on the calendar and fewer measures lost in committee files. . . . Furthermore, this Senate session tackled important and highly controversial legislation—minimum wage, public housing, upper Colorado River project, long-range trade program. No one of these bills took longer than three days to pass."

All these things were being done, Johnson told a friend one evening near the end of June, without the necessity of exhausting night sessions and "without killing any of the old men on my side."

But he almost killed himself.

On July 2, Johnson suffered a heart attack described by his doctors as "moderately severe." He was placed in Bethesda Naval Hospital. His leadership duties were taken over for the remaining month of the session by his deputy, Earle Clements.

Even after he was considered out of danger, Johnson suffered the deep depression characteristic of heart patients. One day his younger brother, Sam Houston, came into his room and found the big man actually crying. "I'll never have a chance to be President now," he mumbled.

Sam Houston, depressed himself, went back to the Capitol and told Grace Tully, Roosevelt's secretary, who had been placed by Johnson on the Policy Committee staff. Miss Tully thought there was a marked similarity between Roosevelt's polio attack in 1921 and Johnson's heart attack in 1955. She pointed out that FDR's illness had proved to be not the finish of his career but a new beginning. So why, she asked, shouldn't her present employer's heart attack also signal a fresh start?

Sam Houston persuaded Holmes Alexander, a syndicated columnist in Washington, to write a column with a first sentence reading, "Senator Lyndon B. Johnson's career, far from ended by his illness, has been given a new beginning." When the column appeared, Sam Houston took a newspaper carrying it to his brother's room. Johnson smiled for the first time since his attack. He started getting well then.

Soon he had his recovery effort organized like one of his

229

political campaigns and was giving it all he had. As he improved, two secretaries were moved out to the hospital from the senatorial office, bringing along their typewriters and their ability to remain unruffled by telephones that never stopped ringing. Walter Jenkins showed up two or three times daily with mail from the office and news of Senate activities. The entire seventeenth floor of the hospital was occupied by the Johnson entourage. Hospital attachés had never seen anything like it: people coming and going, telephones clanging, typewriters rattling, and a general air of productive confusion reigning.

All this activity was sufficiently removed from Johnson's own room not to disturb him. But he was fully aware of it, and was, in fact, pretty much in control. This was a campaign and he was running it.

Eisenhower paid a call before leaving for the Geneva Conference and touched Johnson deeply by saying to him and Lady Bird, his wife, "My heart will be here with you." Vice-President Nixon also came out for a visit. Rayburn, having sternly waited the two weeks the doctors originally had said should elapse before the senator had visitors from outside his family, showed up to urge with fond irascibility that the patient keep in mind that he was supposed to take things easy. Senators visited from both parties, as did Supreme Court Justices and Cabinet members and old friends from Texas. "Get well" messages poured in by the thousands, and each received a personal acknowledgment over the signature of Lady Bird Johnson.

Johnson claimed he was a changed man. He quit smoking for good. He adhered strictly to the rigid diet prescribed by his doctors. He took long naps in the afternoon. He even permitted Reedy to put out stories that his reading was no longer confined exclusively to the *Congressional Record* and newspapers, that he was immersing himself in early American history and Plato. When he received a group of Texas reporters near the end of his stay in the hospital, he told them he had "thrown away the whip" and would never again drive himself and others as he had in the past. He talked at times of retiring from politics at the end of his term in 1960.

He was not talking that way, however, when he left Washington in the early autumn to complete recuperation at his Texas ranch. He told friends he would be back at the majority leader's desk in January. The leopard's spots were the same as ever.

* * *

Throughout the year the Republicans were bedeviled by a multitude of pesky little problems in addition to those deftly created for them by Lyndon Johnson.

One cause for concern was dissension in the party's House leadership. When the Republicans lost control, Joe Martin, necessarily relinquishing the speakership, took back his old job of floor leader. Charlie Halleck was not at all happy about being ousted from the job and made no secret of his dissatisfaction. He complained to Eisenhower that Martin was not a fighting leader and was too friendly by far with Rayburn. The President tried to mollify him by insisting that, even though he held no official leadership position, he must continue to attend the White House meetings for legislative leaders. This was not enough for Halleck. He wanted to start a campaign in the House to replace Martin as minority leader and asked the President's approval.

Eisenhower urged against any such campaign on the sound ground that it would split the House Republicans from top to bottom. He asked Halleck not to engage in a divisive effort but instead to work to help get the administration's legislative program through Congress. "At the same time," Eisenhower wrote in recalling this period, "I asked Martin to find some official role for Halleck in the leadership group that would ease the growing tension between the two. Martin refused, and the situation grew worse rather than better." Nor did relations between the two men ever improve. They and their respective groups of followers carried on a backbiting vendetta all through the session.

In the Senate, the Permanent Investigating Subcommittee, now headed by McClellan of Arkansas, ordered hearings on evidence that since coming into government a high figure in the administration had made use of his public position for private gain.

When Harold Talbott, a businessman in the aeronautics field since its pioneering days, came to Washington as Secretary of the Air Force, he retained a partnership in a New York engineering firm. The New York *Times* obtained and published business-promoting letters Talbott had written on Air Force stationery to clients and prospective clients of the firm. Digging into the evidence, the subcommittee's youthful counsel, Robert F. Kennedy, four years out of Virginia Law School, found that Talbott had indeed been active in working for the interests of his firm. Some of the recipients of his letters and telephone calls had substantial contracts with the Air Force. And during his first two years as Air Force Secretary, Talbott had been paid $132,032 as his share of the engineering organization's profits.

Despite Democratic cries of conflict of interest, Talbott stoutly refused to concede that there was anything improper about his activities. He was not accused of violating any law, and the subcommittee report went only so far as to say he had "acted indiscreetly." Nevertheless, he resigned his post. It was not much of a scandal as scandals went in the Nation's Capital, but it at least gave the Democrats reason to hope that the Republicans would become less eager to talk about "the mess in Washington."

Less serious was a small matter involving Ezra Taft Benson, the Mormon Secretary of Agriculture. No one would ever suspect the upright Benson, no matter how unpopular his policies might be in the farm belt, of being involved in anything even faintly scandalous, and he never was. What happened to him was only embarrassing.

Harper's Magazine published an article in which the American farmer was called "a pampered tyrant," with the suggestion offered that he was a thief picking the pockets of other Americans via farm-crop subsidies. A copy of the magazine was sent to Benson. He did not read the article, but an overeager assistant in the department, who obviously had not read it either, wrote a letter over the Secretary's signature expressing approval of the sentiments set forth in it. Naturally, *Harper's* published the letter, and then there were denials all over the place accompanied by loud Democratic guffaws and the shedding of crocodile tears over the Republican administration's hard-hearted attitude toward worthy agriculturists.

Such minor contretemps did not disturb the complacent certainty of the Republicans that matters were going very well indeed for the Grand Old Party. When the congressional session ended in early August, a substantial part of the President's requests had been met in one form or another. Times were good and the people generally were satisfied. A public-opinion survey showed that eight out of ten Americans approved Eisenhower's performance in the presidency. This happy situation was not adversely affected by the embarrassment of a Benson, the indiscretion of a Talbott, or the stubborn anger of a Halleck.

Then, suddenly, all Republican troubles and triumphs, major and puny, executive and legislative, were thrust out of sight by the year's second famous heart attack. On the night of September 23, Dwight Eisenhower suffered a coronary thrombosis.

He was vacationing in his well-loved city of Denver, with the summer White House established at Lowry Field. He had returned on the morning of September 23 from a four-day fishing trip in the mountains with several companions. During the day he spent a couple of hours in his office, played twenty-seven holes of golf, lost his temper when he was called off the course to answer an unnecessary telephone call, and had a slight case of heartburn after eating a large hamburger with two slices of Bermuda onion for lunch. In the evening he returned to the home of his mother-in-law, Mrs. John Doud, where he and Mamie were staying. The three of them entertained the George Allens, as usual in the vicinity of the President, at dinner. The guests left early and the President was in bed around ten o'clock.

When he awoke in the night feeling ill, Mrs. Eisenhower telephoned General Howard Snyder, the White House physician, who was staying at Lowry Field. Snyder came at once and diagnosed the illness for what it was. This diagnosis was not released to the press, however, until the middle of the next day, by which time the President was in the hospital. The news was given out by Murray Snyder, assistant press secretary, while his superior, Jim Hagerty, was flying from Washington to take charge.

The shock of Eisenhower's heart attack was felt around the world. Heads of state spoke grave words of sympathy and concern. Plain Americans by the tens of thousands expressed their affection for the President in messages pouring into Denver. On Wall Street, corporate stocks suffered the heaviest one-day loss in history. In Washington, key officials met urgently to set the tone for carrying on the government's business. Fortunately, no crisis impended. It was agreed that no delegation of powers was required. The normal affairs of government would be conducted by each official as usual, it was decided, with matters requiring presidential action to be deferred as long as possible. The vice-president would continue to coordinate the work of the executive departments, as he had done before in the President's absence. The Cabinet and National Security Council agreed to send Sherman Adams to Denver. He and Hagerty would keep the lines open to Washington.

Even as these necessary decisions were being made, a massive, although tentative, regrouping and reappraisal began among the politicians of both major parties. The Republicans had assumed that Eisenhower would be their candidate again in 1956 and would again be the winner. The Democrats had gloomily, if privately, conceded both likelihoods. Now terror struck the hearts of the Republicans and hope stirred in Democratic breasts. Republican National Chairman Leonard Hall, when he had been asked what he would do if Eisenhower refused to run for a second term, replied, "When I get to that bridge I'll jump off it." He and many others fearfully wondered if the bridge had been reached.

The uncertainty continued after the President left Denver on November 11 and went to Gettysburg. By the end of the year it seemed that he *might* run but not at all certain that he *would* run. His doctors reported nothing but cheerful news. He himself remained noncommittal about his intentions. Politicians seeking to keep their options open sent out cautious feelers. Associates of Knowland passed along the word that if Eisenhower did not announce for re-election by February 1, the Republican floor leader would become an active candidate for the nomination and would enter state primaries. In Ohio, Bricker accepted the favorite-son endorsement of Republican leaders. In Massachusetts, letters were circulated advocating the nomination of Governor Christian

Herter if Eisenhower was not a candidate. In California, Governor Goodwin Knight indicated that he wanted to be his state's favorite son so he would be in a position to turn over the votes to Eisenhower if the President ran again. And if he did not run? Governor Knight had no comment about that possibility.

Thus the Republicans, while the President, idol of the voters and savior of the party professionals, kept his own counsel in Gettysburg.

* * *

On a December day in the quiet little town of Whitney in Central Texas, a lean and tanned Lyndon Johnson, fully recovered, made a speech on which he and his aides had been working for weeks at the ranch in between visits from a host of leading Democratic politicians. In this speech he set forth what he called, with an element of self-consciousness, "a program with a heart"—a legislative program which he vowed to push in the coming session of Congress. He proposed a social-security bill reducing the age limit for women and extending coverage to most self-employed groups; tax revision to benefit low-income groups; a health plan to aid medical research and to include grants for hospital construction; a school reconstruction program; an ambitious public roads program; restoration of 90 per cent of parity farm subsidies and extension of subsidies to additional products; an expanded housing program; water resources development; aid for depressed areas; liberalization of immigration and naturalization laws; a constitutional amendment to eliminate the poll tax as a voting requirement; and legislation to establish an insurance program for people hit by natural disasters. He also offered a proposal, one not wholly congruent with the others in his program with a heart, to remove federal legislation of the natural-gas industry. This was the only concession he made to his Texas constituency as such.

In this speech, so carefully prepared and polished, so painstakingly hand-carried by messenger to leading columnists and political writers in Washington, D.C., far from the site of its delivery, Johnson with deliberate intent served notice to Democrats in Congress and elsewhere that he intended to be the key congressional figure in 1956. And, possibly, more than that.

1956

ENCORE, MORE OR LESS

The President continued not to say whether he would be a candidate for a second term. Significantly, however, his first-of-the-session message to Congress laid down the basis for a platform which could be comfortably mounted only by an Eisenhower type of candidate. The long address, not delivered in person but read by the reading clerks in both houses, pointed up the President's departure from the Republican tradition of coolness toward welfare programs. Of his sixty-seven specific proposals, many placed heavy stress on the federal government's responsibility in the areas of security for the individual, education, health and housing. Eisenhower proclaimed that under his administration the United States for the first time in many years had achieved both peace and prosperity. He declared that the budget would be balanced without cutting expenditures for defense and without damage to foreign aid and welfare programs. A tax reduction was promised for the future.

Nobody missed the political implications. Lyndon Johnson remarked sourly, "This isn't a speech for January 1956 but a speech for November 1956." In a formal statement, he commented, "To those of us who have attempted to cooperate with the administration in matters affecting the national interest, the political overtones of this message are the subject of deep disappointment and great regret."

The majority leader's disappointment and regret were real enough, but they grew less out of the content of the message than from his knowledge that Eisenhower's lieutenants were carefully laying plans for his renomination and that the President knew of their activities. Harry Truman put on a bold face and sounded off: "We're going to give the American people a chance to vote for a President and not a regency or a part-time chairman of the board. The Republicans, on the other hand, are desperate. They know they don't have a chance with anyone but Ike, and the pressure they're putting on him to run is positively indecent."

Pressure or not, the President bided his time until early March. Then he went on radio and television to say, "I have decided that if the Republican party chooses to nominate me, I shall accept that nomination. Thereafter, if the people of this country should elect me, I shall continue to serve them in the office I now hold." The stilted and self-conscious parody of Sherman's famous antinomination, antielection statement instantly placed a heavy discount on the value of the Democratic nomination. But there would be no scarcity of contenders for it.

Adlai Stevenson, reluctant no longer, had announced in November that he would try again. Kefauver also had formally placed himself in the race. Both men were prepared to try the primary route to the nomination. Averell Harriman, now serving as governor of New York, planned to enter no primaries, but he was definitely a candidate and would go to the national convention with his state's big bloc of votes securely in hand. Stuart Symington, Missouri's favorite son, was seen by many politicians as the probable leader among the dark-horse candidates in case Stevenson and Kefauver canceled each other out.

Such an eventuality seemed wholly possible as these two waged bitter, even vicious, primary fights in Minnesota, Florida, California and half a dozen other states. Kefauver assailed Stevenson as the candidate of the party bosses. His rival retorted, "There may be such a thing as wanting to be President too badly. And that may be one of the reasons why none of Kefauver's colleagues and few of the party leaders around the country have endorsed him." In speech after speech, he accused the Tennessee senator of missing vital votes in the Senate, of having the worst absentee record of any senator. Stung, Kefauver cried that this was mud slinging and character assassination. But, he added self-righteously, "I'm not going to engage in personalities. I will simply turn the other cheek." He did not exactly do that. With no issues of great importance to separate them, each man devoted himself largely to claiming the other was unfit to be President.

Surprisingly, after a stunning defeat in the Minnesota primary, the once aloof Stevenson undertook to adopt Kefauver's folksy campaign style. He rode in a parade dressed as a cowboy, allowed himself to be photographed wearing a false beard, kissed babies, joked with customers in grocery stores. In Los Angeles, he walked four blocks along a busy downtown street, stopping strangers to identify himself and reaching up to shake hands with truck drivers waiting at traffic lights. In San Francisco the next day, he was campaigning along the sidewalk when someone pushed a four-year-old girl into his arms and told him to kiss her. Stevenson looked embarrassed, but he followed instructions. The photographers, in their never-ending zeal for "just one more," asked him to replay the scene. "No!" shouted the distraught candidate. "I'm not really in this kind of competition."

The California primary was the big one and, due in no small part to last-minute efforts exerted on his behalf by Eleanor Roosevelt, Stevenson won it. But Harriman was now an active contender, bearing no primary scars as he swung through a number of states on fast speech-making tours. He countered Stevenson's appeal for a "moderate" approach to government problems with outspoken liberalism and, for whatever it might be worth, he had Truman's backing.

As a party, the Democrats were sorely divided. The liberal wing's distrust of the Johnson-Rayburn leadership deepened with its continued success. Joe Rauh, national chairman of the Americans for Democratic Action, howled, "Under the banner of Senate Majority Leader Lyndon Johnson, the congressional Democrats have become practically indistinguishable from the party they allegedly oppose." National Chairman Paul Butler continued to shoot arrows at the congressional leadership. The civil-rights issue was bitterly divisive. Eisenhower proposed mild civil-rights legislation, not pushing it hard, but Congress took no action. Almost daily, congressmen from the South made speeches expressing defiance of efforts to force integration.

Some party members tried to find a road to unity by at last attacking Eisenhower. Truman, singing once again a familiar melody, told a Democratic gathering in Des Moines that the President "deserves to be rejected by the people just as the Eightieth Congress was, because he is a do-nothing President as that Eightieth Congress was a do-nothing Congress." In New York, Harriman accused the administration of lack of understanding in dealing with Communism. "That fellow," said the governor, meaning Eisenhower, "has been as naïve as any person in history about the true nature of the Communist conspiracy." Harriman's right-hand man, Tammany Boss Carmine DeSapio, attacked the men around the President: "A country club quartet—a small clique of self-appointed and self-anointed men who have never exposed themselves to the mandate of a national election—now rules the White House and runs the nation. These men—Sherman Adams, Charles Wilson, George Humphrey and John Foster Dulles—are the Richelieus and Rasputins of twentieth-century America." Stevenson noted that Eisenhower had said at the time of his second-term announcement that some of the presidential work "can now be done by some of my close associates as well as myself." The Democrat commented, not notably enhancing his reputation as a wit, "I could not help but think of the little rhyme, 'This would not be sinister if we had a Prime Minister.'" Kefauver charged that the administration "has no faith in peace and no hope of achieving it in its time." Bob Kerr bellowed, after Eisenhower voted a monstrosity of a farm bill, "The President has again acted on the advice of little men who made the decision for him."

One Democrat who did not join in the assaults on the President was Lyndon Johnson. Instead, he announced that he hoped to be named as his state's favorite-son candidate for President and chairman of the Texas delegation to the Democratic National Convention.

He was pushed into this decision by Sam Rayburn. The development represented a tactic in Rayburn's continuing war with Texas Governor Allan Shivers for control of the state's party organization. The fight had gone on since Shivers' defection to the Republicans in 1952. In that year, Rayburn had seen to it that the governor's delegation rather than a contesting liberal group was seated at the Chicago convention. He regarded Shivers' subsequent support of Eisenhower as a personal betrayal. His resentment was deep and enduring.

Shivers was willing for Johnson to go to the 1956 convention as the state's favorite son, but he wanted the delegation chairmanship for himself. In that position he could expect to be able to keep the Texans from voting for Stevenson at the convention. As Rayburn saw the picture, it was absolutely necessary for himself and Johnson to be in control of the delegation. It would never do for delegates from the home state of the Speaker of the House and the Democratic leader of the Senate to walk out of a Democratic convention because they were dissatisfied with the nominee, no matter who he might be.

For weeks Johnson agonized, Hamletlike, about whether he should follow the course laid out for him by Rayburn. It would mean, he knew, a bruising contest with Shivers in the precinct conventions, which would choose delegates to the county conventions, from whose ranks Democrats would be named to represent Texas at the National Convention. He might alienate the conservative support he had cultivated so painstakingly in Texas. And, conceivably, he could even lose! He blew hot, blew cold, as he considered these possibilities.

Finally, disgusted with the delay in doing what he considered had to be done, Rayburn took matters into his own hands. While on a visit to his home in Bonham, the Speaker issued a statement to the press that he and other loyal Texas Democrats were going to run Johnson for both favorite son and delegation chairman. In Washington, reporters besieged Johnson. He parried their questions for a time, still hesitant to take the irrevocable step. Then, muttering in an aside, "Well, sometimes a man has to be a damn fool," he read a prepared statement that he would accept the double candidacy thrust upon him.

The campaign in Texas that spring was as hard fought as any the state had ever witnessed. In the end the Shivers forces were badly beaten. Johnson was set to go to the August convention in Chicago as chairman of the big—fifty-six votes—Texas delegation and its favorite-son candidate for President.

At some point he began to entertain, fleetingly and inter-mittently, the thought that he might be more than just a favorite-son candidate. His ego was fed by a triumphant arrival at Washington National Airport on his return from Texas. Walter Jenkins and Bobby Baker, aided by faithful members of the Texas State Society in Washington, organized a large crowd to meet him. He and Rayburn were greeted with boisterous enthusiasm.

Johnson lapped up every press mention of his candidacy, while continuing to insist that he would go to the convention only as the favorite son of Texas. He held to his promise not to go out after delegates in other states. He confided to Jenkins, with whom he talked more freely than anyone else, that he would never permit himself to become a sectional candidate as Russell had been in 1952. Yet he had Reedy and James Rowe, a friend from New Deal days now serving temporarily on the Democratic Policy Committee staff, keep-ing him closely advised about all aspects of the preconvention activities of openly announced candidates. He encouraged a writer on his staff to publish a book about him. And he did not endorse Stevenson, now clearly in the lead, or anyone else, although reporters gave him ample opportunity to do so.

No one knew exactly what he had in mind as he went off to Texas when Congress adjourned late in July.

Then, shortly before the convention opened on August 13, Johnson replied to a reporter who again put the question as to whether he was a serious candidate, "I'm always serious about everything I do." If the Democratic delegates should decide, he said, that "they would like me to be their standard bearer, I will do my duty." And when he was asked whether he considered Stevenson or Harriman the better candidate, he answered, "The best candidate at the moment is Lyndon Johnson."

His statement set off columns of speculation by the political writers assembl. d in Chicago. Kefauver having withdrawn and with Harriman's candidacy faltering despite Truman's endorsement, the reporters were avidly looking for new possibilities to write about.

The anticipated Truman announcement of support for Harriman came at a news conference held by the ex-President two days before the convention officially got under way. Truman arrived in Chicago as beaming and perky as in his best days, reveling in the attention paid him. He was determined to play a key role in proceedings just as he had in 1952. His conviction that he could do so was strengthened by his reception at the press conference. Some eight hundred reporters packed the room and waited there two hours for Truman to appear. When he came, they jumped to their feet and applauded.

Truman was in high spirits. He thought everything was working out just right. On his arrival in Chicago, Sam Rosenman, his old speech writer, assured him that Harriman had a good chance for the nomination. Now, as the newsmen hung on his words, the former President quickly got down to business. Harriman, he declared, was the man who could be nominated. His experience could best serve the Democratic party and the nation. He dismissed Stevenson almost contemptuously, saying it was no time for trial-and-error leadership.

One matter Truman did not bring up was that just before meeting with the reporters, he had summoned Lyndon Johnson to his hotel suite and told him, "I'm opening this thing up so anybody can win—including you."

Johnson had an opportunity the next day for a long talk with Rayburn when the two of them joined other congressional leaders in responding to a summons from Eisenhower to fly to Washington for a briefing on problems springing from Egypt's seizure of the Suez Canal. The senator was by now excited by the thought that his favorite-son candidacy could be transformed into a meaningful drive to get the nomination. It might be done, he urged anxiously, if the Speaker would take the lead. If Truman was able to deadlock the convention and stop Stevenson, who would be in a more advantageous position than Lyndon Johnson? No one, said Johnson objectively.

Rayburn listened, but mostly in silence. He knew, as the other man should have known, that it was too late for the kind of effort Johnson proposed.

After the conference with the President in Washington, the presidential plane transported the congressional leaders back to Chicago in the afternoon. As they alighted at the airport, a number of television and press reporters descended on them. One told Rayburn he was quoted in a dispatch on the news ticker as having "passed the word" for Stevenson. "I haven't said I was for anybody but Lyndon, dammit," the Speaker growled. He kept walking with a companion toward a waiting automobile, and the reporter fell back to join the group clustered around Johnson.

"I don't see why Lyndon lets those buzzards trap him like that," Rayburn said to his friend. He looked around to see if any of the newsmen were in earshot, then muttered, "I hate to see Lyndon get bit so hard by the presidential bug at this stage of the game. Stevenson's got it sewed up."

That proved an accurate diagnosis. Truman's endorsement did nothing for Harriman, evidence of the correctness of the ex-President's frequently expressed opinion that an elder statesman was a dead politician. Johnson was placed in nomination by John Connally and had the pleasure of witnessing an extended delegate demonstration for his candidacy. This show was organized by several Texas congressmen who went around to other delegations and reminded their leaders that Sam Rayburn would keep right on being Speaker and no doubt would be watching with interest to see what states participated in the demonstration for his friend.

But that was all. When the balloting was over, only eighty votes could be counted for Johnson—all but two of them from Texas and Mississippi. Stevenson was the overwhelming victor on the first and only ballot.

All the excitement up to now had either been artificial or only in the minds of men who were unable to bring themselves to believe that the choice of Stevenson was inevitable. Now came genuine suspense. The victor announced that, departing from custom, he would not designate a vice-presidential nominee but would leave the selection up to the convention delegates.

Four members of the U.S. Senate and the son of a former senator were placed in nomination. Two were Tennesseeans: Kefauver and Albert Gore. The others were Hubert Humphrey of Minnesota, John F. Kennedy of Massachusetts, and Robert Wagner of New York. The Texas delegates were led in caucus by Johnson and Rayburn to support Gore on the first ballot. Neither of them really liked the choice, but they considered him infinitely preferable to the other senator from Tennessee. Nevertheless, on the initial roll call, Kefauver with 483½ votes ran far ahead of Gore—and everybody except Kennedy, who, generally regarded in the Senate as an outsider, polled a surprising 304 votes. Wagner and Humphrey trailed Gore.

Much of Kennedy's strength came from southern states, where the Democratic leaders were in general violently opposed to Kefauver. Now the Texas leaders joined them. Johnson sent his emissaries fanning out over the convention hall with the word that Kefauver had polled his peak strength. Kennedy was the man. On the second roll call, when Texas was reached, Johnson jumped to his feet and roared into the microphone, "Texas proudly casts its fifty-six votes for the fighting sailor who wears the scars of battle, Jack Kennedy!"

As the balloting neared its end, Kennedy seemed a certain winner. But Minnesota announced a switch in its votes from Kennedy to Kefauver. Gore released his delegates and they went to the junior senator from Tennessee. Other vote switching followed and Kennedy was left behind.

So, for the time being, was Lyndon Johnson. He had nothing to show for all the noise and frenzy of the convention in which he had hoped to wield decisive influence if not to emerge as its nominee for President. His first serious attempt at playing the national political game had to be accounted a failure.

* * *

It was easier for the Republicans.

They did experience a bad fright in June when the President fell ill with an attack of ileitis, followed by surgery to remove an intestinal obstruction. But he recovered quickly and in mid-July told a meeting of party congressional leaders that he still planned, of course, to be a candidate. Knowland came out of the White House meeting to announce the news to the press, and the Republicans went forward with arrangements for their national convention to be held in San Francisco in August.

Before that event, however, Harold Stassen tried to have Nixon dumped as Eisenhower's running mate. Stassen was still in the administration as Eisenhower's special assistant for disarmament. Other members of the Executive Branch held him in low regard, but after all it was his state that had switched its vote in time to have the distinction of nailing down the nomination for Eisenhower in 1952. So Stassen stayed, with not much to do and with few to take him seriously.

248

In July, he visited the President in his office and said portentously that his own personal political surveys showed considerable popular dissatisfaction with Nixon. It would be a bad political mistake for the convention to nominate him for another term. Nixon would weaken the ticket.

Stassen may have thought that the President would be receptive to this thought because Eisenhower himself had earlier suggested to Nixon that he might better prepare himself for the presidency if he served in a Cabinet position. Nixon said no, thanks, he would rather continue as vicepresident. Some of Nixon's nonadmirers believed the President had been seriously interested in keeping him off the ticket in 1956. But Eisenhower gave Stassen no encouragement. He confined himself to saying, "You are an American citizen, Harold, and free to follow your own judgment in such matters."

Soon after, Eisenhower went to Panama for a meeting of the Presidents of the Americas. While he was away from Washington, his special assistant for disarmament announced that he was opposed to Nixon's renomination. Furthermore, he had a candidate to replace him in the person of Massachusetts Governor Christian Herter.

Hagerty promptly issued a statement that, when the President told Stassen he had a right to exercise his own judgment, he did not mean that a member of the administration was free to undertake independent political activity. When Eisenhower returned, he granted Stassen a leave of absence without pay until after the convention. The hapless Herter said he was not interested in being nominated for vice-president. But Stassen continued to talk about an "open convention."

His mutterings received more attention in the press than they deserved, simply because the political writers were finding it hard to dig up much of interest about preparations for the Republican convention. Everything was proceeding according to plan. National Chairman Hall, in San Francisco a few days in advance of the convention, strolled into a press conference to be greeted by a reporter's question about what was on his mind. "Nothing," said Hall amiably. "What's on yours?"

A minor and quickly passing flurry blew up over the convention program. Its front cover carried a photograph of a sculpture by Auguste Rodin, showing three stalwart men, their lowered heads together, their arms and legs touching. They were without clothing. Republican ladies in San Francisco, where the program was being printed, complained that the photograph was obscene. But that was not all. Once they started probing, they and party officials learned with horror that Rodin had entitled his sculpture *The Three Shades* and that it was part of a work called *The Gate of Hell!*; his legend for it was from Dante: "All Hope Abandon, Ye Who Enter Here." Happily, there was still time to discard the cover. The new one contained a much more appropriate photograph of a smiling Eisenhower.

The presidential smile was symbolic of the entire convention. About the only time it faded was when the keynote speaker, Governor Arthur Langlie of Washington, shouted that the Democrats "are now addicted to the principle that loyalty to a political party comes ahead of devotion to our beloved country." Eisenhower turned sharply to Sherman Adams, and wondered aloud, "Who let him say that?" He knew how Sam Rayburn, for one, felt about such statements. But convention keynote speeches are little noted nor long remembered, so the smile soon came back.

Stassen eventually gave up hope of keeping Nixon off the ticket and in fact made one of the seconding speeches after the vice-president was nominated by none other than Christian Herter. A disgruntled or mischievous delegate from Nebraska tried to get recognition from Joe Martin, the permanent convention chairman, to nominate a mythical Joe Smith for vice-president. But Martin, forewarned, shouted amidst the general uproar, "Take your Joe Smith and get out of here!"

The proceedings in San Francisco offered a vast contrast to the riotous carryings-on of the Democrats in Chicago. Political writers and commentators covering the Republican convention were offended by its blandness, but that very quality reflected the party leaders' complacent certainty. The Democrats would no doubt make more noise; but on election day, the Republicans were confident, a majority of the voters would again demonstrate their faith in Eisenhower.

Only two nagging possibilities disturbed the minds of the Republican hierarchy. *If* the President should again be struck by serious illness, the people, out of fear of the unknown, might turn to Adlai Stevenson. *If* the Middle East crisis should explode into spreading armed conflict, the administration's foreign-policy maneuverings could become a crushing liability.

Hope is an essential ingredient of any political stew, and the Republicans could only hope that neither of these contingencies would come to pass.

* * *

Both candidates for President were in some significant ways different from the men they had been in 1952. Four years ago, Eisenhower had been sure of his ground only in the field of foreign affairs. Now he had a comprehensive understanding of domestic affairs as well. In the early months of his presidency he had been nervous and uncertain. But now he was relaxed and confident. He was no longer the bewildered amateur surrounded by professionals. Now Dwight Eisenhower was the President. The presidency had changed him, giving weight to the contention of Eliot Janeway, the economist and author, that "Presidential personalities do not make presidential politics but, on the contrary, presidential politics make and remold presidential personalities."

Stevenson had changed, during the four years since his defeat, even more radically than Eisenhower. His metamorphosis was summed up shrewdly by Jake Arvey: "In 1952 he went to the American Legion convention and pointed out their faults. He did the same with labor. He thought he had to do this as part of his integrity. He'd never do it again. Now he is a politician."

The trouble was that Stevenson had not become a good politician. He had been transformed, it seemed as the campaign progressed, into merely a desperate politician who wanted desperately to be President.

He had tried the high-level approach in 1952, and it failed. This year he would take a different course.

Soon after his nomination he incredibly chose a meeting of the American Legion to suggest that the military draft should be sharply cut back. He continued to press this proposal in other speeches, and he soon added to it a suggestion that the United States should seek an agreement with Soviet Russia to end H-bomb tests because of the fallout of radioactive strontium-90. Stevenson was ahead of his time. He disregarded or did not choose to believe that in these two matters, affecting as they did the national security, the people would prefer to accept the judgment of Eisenhower as a man with a lifetime of military experience.

The Stevenson campaign went on frenziedly from one mistake to another. The negative quality of his draft and nuclear-weapons test proposals came to color almost everything the candidate said. He offered little to make people want to vote *for* him. In the face of the President's manifest popularity over the country, Stevenson persisted in a dogged effort to cause people to vote *against* Eisenhower. To this end he

252

flailed out in all directions, listening to conflicting advice, racing about the country from one city to another, bedeviled constantly by logistic and technical problems, talking longer than his scheduled time on television and being cut off before he had finished, contradicting himself from one week to the next. He appeared guilty of the sin of which he had accused Kefauver, "wanting to be President too badly."

By the time Eisenhower made his first campaign speech late in September, Stevenson already had covered 12,000 hectic miles and was mapping out a schedule that would add another 6,000 miles to his travel log. But he was not getting anywhere with all this physical movement. He was unable to make a dent in the protective wall of popularity that surrounded the President.

Eisenhower was given credit by most Americans for getting the United States out of Korea and keeping the nation out of war. He was President at a time of record high employment, rising wages and general prosperity. He was thought to stand for not too much government regulation of the people's affairs but for enough to keep the country in balance. He was a middle-of-the-road man, and the people wanted to walk in the middle with him.

Besides, despite the two major illnesses he had suffered, Eisenhower *looked* good. Stevenson tried to make the presidential health an issue in the campaign, but when the President appeared on television, smiling his cheery smile and talking crisply about the record of his administration, he was seen by the people to be vigorous and fit. Most of his campaigning was done on television. He saw no need to put himself through a tough schedule of barnstorming and whistle-stop tours of the country. Toward the end, ired by some of the charges hurled by the Democrats, he expanded his activities somewhat and found that, after all, he thrived on campaigning. He too had become something of a politician.

Events as well as personality favored him. A few days before the election, the British, French and Israelis simultaneously attacked Egypt with the intention of regaining control of the Suez Canal. Israel occupied most of the Sinai Peninsula and all the Gaza Strip. British oil pipelines in Syria were blown up. Soviet Russia brutally crushed a revolt in Hungary. Everything was going to pieces internationally.

Some hopeful Democrats pointed out that these developments should turn millions of votes to Stevenson. Not so, said more realistic observers. "The people have liked Ike because we've had peace," Lyndon Johnson told Earle Clements, who was waging a losing fight for re-election as senator from Kentucky. "Now, if there's going to be fighting, the people would rather have an experienced soldier as President."

In a Boston speech on the eve of the election, Stevenson, looking tired and pudgy and sounding desperate, said Eisenhower's medical history warned that he might not live long enough to serve another term. There was every indication, he declared, that "a Republican victory tomorrow would mean that Richard Nixon would probably be President of this country within the next four years."

This statement, like so many Stevenson uttered during the campaign, harmed rather than helped the Democrats.

Eisenhower's victory was of landslide proportions. He carried all but seven states and amassed 457 electoral votes, leaving only 74 to Stevenson. Congress remained in the hands of the Democrats.

1957

BATTLES, PHONY AND REAL

Old Guard Republicans stirred uneasily as they listened to one passage in Eisenhower's victory speech on election night. "As we look ahead to the problems in front," the President said, "let us remember that a political party deserves the approbation of America only as it represents the inspirations and the hopes of Americans. If it is anything less, it is merely a conspiracy to seize power, and the Republican party is not that. Modern Republicanism looks to the future." Members of the Old Guard, whose lives were devoted to efforts to seize power, wondered just what the President had in mind.

They found out in January when the administration's budget for the fiscal year 1958 was submitted to Congress.

Proposed expenditures totaled approximately $72 billion, some $3 billion above the budget for fiscal 1957 and a rousing $12 billion higher than the annual spending figure promised by Eisenhower in his first campaign. Not merely the total amount but also the purposes of contemplated spending infuriated the conservatives. More money was asked for foreign aid, more for resource development, more for welfare, even an appropriation requested for school construction.

The budget set off political gyrations comparable to the contortions undergone that year by Americans of all ages who succumbed to the lure of twirling hula hoops around their torsos in a fashion some onlookers found sexy and others regarded as only bewildering. The President was stunned, then angered, by the storm that broke in Congress and in the nation's press. He was rocked by the first widespread and sustained criticism he had ever encountered.

Barry Goldwater, standing on the extreme edge of the Republican right wing, passed formal judgment on the budget: "It subverts the American economy because it is based on high taxes, the largest deficit in history, and the consequent dissipation of the freedom and initiative and genius of our productive people, upon whom the whole structure of our economic system depends for survival." Byrd observed curtly, "This budget is the worst yet." The president of the National Association of Manufacturers denounced it as extravagant and inflationary. The *Wall Street Journal* wailed that the budget presented "solid testimony to a failure."

Defending the budget first fell ironically to the lot of George Humphrey, the likeable, hardheaded businessman who four years before had been in the front ranks of those who spoke out strongly for substantial cuts in spending by the federal government. He still felt the same way, but his code of loyalty compelled him as long as he was in the Cabinet to try to stand up for the President's program. Furthermore, he had come to know the pressure for more, not less, spending. So, as Secretary of the Treasury, he was prepared to offer what defense he could of what was called with monotonous frequency "the biggest peacetime budget in history."

When Humphrey was first invited to enter the Eisenhower

Cabinet, he was reluctant, saying, "Almost every time a businessman gets mixed up in politics, he falls flat on his face." He now proceeded to demonstrate how to do it.

The Treasury Secretary was thoroughly briefed by budget experts for a news conference. The reporters were eager to have at him. One immediately inquired who was to blame for this kind of budget, after all the Republican talk about economy. "Everybody," Humphrey replied. "Congress enacts laws. Various groups of the public keep turning to the federal government for everything in the world to be taken care of. It is just everybody."

Another reporter tried to pin him down: "Do you support those parts of the current budget which propose increased expenditures?"

"We ought to improve," Humphrey said uncomfortably. Where would he cut the budget?

"I think there are a lot of places in this budget that can be cut," responded the beleaguered Secretary. "If Congress can find ways to cut and still do a proper job, I would be very glad to see it. We have to be very selective. You can't do everything."

Later in this meeting with the reporters, Humphrey observed thoughtfully, "I would certainly deplore the day that we couldn't reduce expenditures of this terrific amount. If we don't reduce them over a long period of time, I predict that you will have a depression that will curl your hair, because we are just taking too much money out of this economy that we need to make the jobs."

The Secretary had given the newsmen the phrase they needed to create headlines. Within hours the word was everywhere that the Secretary of the Treasury had predicted a "hair-curling depression" as a result of the administration's fiscal policies. Sight was lost entirely of the "long period of time" part of his statement. Some columnists drew a lurid picture of cutthroat internal conflict over the budget in Eisenhower's official family. Democrats, for so long the target of extravagant spending charges, hailed Humphrey's warning with unbounded joy.

In the beginning the President himself seemed little inclined to insist that all the proposed expenditures were really necessary. When he was asked about Humphrey's suggestion that Congress reduce the budget by lowering appropriations, he replied that if the lawmakers could take such action, "It is their duty to do so." He said plaintively that he had already instructed members of the administration to find every place where it might be possible to save money, adding that studies along this line were still going on.

Humphrey was invited by the Joint Congressional Committee on the President's Economic Report to point out places where appropriations might be trimmed, but he turned down the opportunity. "If I knew," he sighed, "I would have done so long ago." Byrd announced that he was working on his own annual "Byrd budget" and would show Congress how to save at least $6.5 billion. Knowland heavily expressed the hope that reductions of at least $2 billion could be made, and Johnson stated with unconcealed pleasure that he would be glad to help the Republicans realize that hope.

Letters and telegrams by the sackful poured into congressional offices. Clarence Cannon, veteran chairman of the House Appropriations Committee, reported that he had received personal letters about the budget from nearly every state in the Union, "and every one of them urged a reduction." Cannon had seen thirty-four administrative budgets in his career; he said he could not recall a similar outcry of public opinion. The man technically responsible for the spending proposals, Budget Director Percival Brundage, was inundated with packages of clean and dirty laundry from all over the country after businessmen started telling one another, "Brundage wants the shirt off your back."

The President's older brother Edgar, a Tacoma lawyer, visited Washington and unburdened himself to a reporter. "I can't for the life of me understand what persuaded Dwight to go for that big budget this year," he told Ruth Montgomery of International News Service. "All his campaign speeches were for decreased government spending. I'd sure like to discover whose influence is at work on my brother." He took a few swipes at these influences, Sherman Adams in particular, before going back to Tacoma.

Eisenhower was able to laugh off his brother's remarks by wryly commenting at a press conference, "Edgar has been criticizing me ever since I was five years old." But he could not dismiss so lightly a resolution passed by the House of Representatives asking the administration to point out where cuts could be made in the budget. By golly, he fumed, he would give them some suggestions.

He did, calling on White House staff and Cabinet members to get up a list of possibilities for economy. The suggestions included raising postal rates to eliminate the chronic deficit in the Post Office Department, changing government interest rates to encourage private capital to participate in federal loan programs, levying fees on users of public facilities such as airports, making it mandatory for states to participate in the disaster assistance program, eliminating rivers and harbors projects not firmly approved by the Corps of Engineers and requiring more substantial local participation in their financing, selling surplus federal land not essential for future use, and giving the President veto power over specific items in appropriations bills.

None of these suggestions was new. Hardly any of them were in the slightest degree politically practical or even possible. And they had no effect at all on Congress.

The House of Representatives, traditional starting point for appropriations bills, evinced determination to cut everything in sight. Money voted for the Department of Defense was reduced sharply from the sum requested by the President. The State Department appropriation was slashed 21 per cent below the budget figure, the Commerce Department 25 per cent. The foreign-aid program, never popular in Congress, was hit especially hard. Eisenhower asked Rayburn's support for his recommendation in this area and denounced cuts made by the House as "the poorest kind of economy we can find." As it happened, this statement was made the day after House Republicans had passed a unanimous resolution demanding even deeper budget cuts. Rayburn growled in the House that the President's words were "a pretty good answer to what his own folks did up here yesterday," but neither of them could sway the majority of the members from their determination to get themselves on record for economy.

At times it looked as if there might not be much government left. After his defensive start the President was late in making a case for his budget. At last he went on radio and television to take the fight to the people. While reiterating his belief in sound fiscal policies, he declared the administration had sent to Congress the best budget it could formulate in the light of the government's responsibilities as established by law, the demands of national security, and the needs of the people as represented by Congress.

This was all very reasonable, but Congress was not in a mood to listen to reason.

Most Washington observers were confident that the Senate, following the custom of the past, would restore most of the budget cuts voted by the House. But suddenly it appeared that things might be different this year.

Lyndon Johnson, from his power seat, approached the Battle of the Budget with characteristic caution. His mail on the subject was heavy, and like Cannon in the House, he noted that nearly all of his correspondents were saying, "Cut the budget!" Still he did not have to commit himself at once to action. Through the early months of the year he gave somewhat evasive replies to constituents who wrote him, emphasizing that the budget was the President's own and speaking of "divided counsel within the administration." He sent out a budget questionnaire to some 40,000 Texans on his mailing list. The questions were slanted slightly to make it easier than not for those replying to advocate budget cutting. As the returns poured in, Johnson made up his mind that at last an opportunity had been presented to take on the Republican President without danger to himself.

"I've never in my career seen such a strong demand for economy in government," he told the Senate after he and other members returned to Washington from the Easter recess.

He laid down a rule that the House-trimmed total on each appropriation bill would be regarded in the Senate as a ceiling, not a floor. There were exceptions. One day the President jabbed at his congressional critics: "I must say it is a very great satisfaction to me to find out there are so many economy-minded people in Washington. They didn't use to be here." He suggested Congress cut down on public-works spending. The next day the Senate increased the appropriations for rivers and harbors projects from $1.52 to $1.54 billion. Mostly, however, in matters less dear to the hearts of congressmen, substantial reductions were ordered. When Eisenhower criticized Congress for the cuts, Johnson retorted, "What we need is not a Republican Congress but a Democratic President." To the fullest extent possible he was exploiting Republican troubles about the budget as a way of diverting attention from the Democrats' deep division over more basic issues, and he met with a large measure of success.

After the House made a deep reduction in the sum requested for the U.S. Information Agency, the President wrote the Senate Appropriations Committee to plead for the sum in

261

his budget. Johnson was chairman of the subcommittee handling this bill. He promptly called the director of the USIA to explain in detail the needs of the agency, which operated the Voice of America and overseas libraries. Johnson had never shown antagonism toward the USIA, so Eisenhower had reason to hope that his plea would receive a favorable response. He was wrong.

Arthur Larson, a lawyer and professor, was director of the agency, having been named to the post after service as undersecretary of Labor. Larson had written some speeches for Eisenhower, particularly on the subject of the "modern Republicanism" advocated by the President, but he had scant knowledge of the practicalities of politics. He was utterly unfitted by temperament and training to deal with a hostile Lyndon Johnson—and hostile Johnson certainly was.

So far as the majority leader was concerned, Larson had made two glaring errors in judgment. One was the publication during the 1956 campaign of a book entitled *A Republican Looks at His Party*, a defense of the Eisenhower brand of Republicanism which succeeded in infuriating both Democrats and Old Guard Republicans. The second mistake was a speech delivered in the spring of 1957 in which Larson tossed off the remark, "Throughout the New and Fair Deals, this country was in the grip of a somewhat alien philosophy, imported from Europe." This statement, viewed by liberals and even moderates as a sort of literate McCarthyism, angered almost everybody who had not been enraged by the book. Johnson felt, correctly, that Larson would have few defenders.

The President had asked $144 million to operate the USIA in fiscal 1958, an increase of $31 million over the appropriation for the preceding year. The House voted $105 million. Larson went before Johnson's subcommittee to argue the inadequacy of this sum. He could not have come to a worse place at a worse time.

From the moment the hearing opened Johnson went for the witness with broad sarcasm. "You appear before us under conditions which guarantee a considerable amount of distinction," he intoned. Of all the agency heads, he went on, "you are asking for the most money to be restored to the funds cut by the House." Johnson professed great interest in how Larson could justify this plea: "We look to you as the distinguished author and spokesman for your party to enlighten us."

The hearings went on for days. Larson writhed on the witness stand as Johnson, with an exaggerated pretense of unending patience and many a smirk at other subcommittee members, openly ridiculed the hapless lawyer-turned-bureaucrat.

Johnson privately told a staff aide, "I guess this'll show Paul Butler whether I go easy on Republicans." To the extent revealed by this remark Larson was an unwitting victim of the continuing feud between the Democratic congressional leadership and the National Chairman.

It was not one of the majority leader's most shining hours. Whatever effectiveness Larson might have had as director of the USIA was destroyed. The agency finally received an appropriation of $96 million, which was $6 million more than the recommendation of the Johnson subcommittee—but not enough to enable the USIA to meet the responsibilities with which it was charged. Its work was hampered for years not only by insufficient funds but also by the scorn with which Johnson had held up to the world its operating personnel from top to bottom. The price seemed high to pay for the Texas senator's desire to appear simultaneously in the roles of an outspoken proponent of economy in government and a stalwart foe of Republicanism.

He appeared to better advantage in working to increase the House-approved appropriation for the foreign-aid program, although for a time he was inclined not to do so. "I'm sick of the way this works year after year," he told Dick Russell. "The administration asks for so much money, the House cuts it, and then the people downtown [in the Executive Branch] expect me to get the money back. I've a good mind just to let it go this year." Russell, himself a foe of foreign aid, regarded the younger man thoughtfully. "No, Lyndon," he said, "you can't do that. You've made a record on support of foreign aid—I wish the record was different, but there it is—and you have to be consistent." Johnson then helped to restore part of the cut made by the House.

The Post Office Department had a special budgetary problem. Back in the first year of the Eisenhower administration, Arthur Summerfield, the Michigan car dealer serving as Postmaster General, called a press conference to announce with considerable self-satisfaction that he was returning to the Treasury $51.7 million of the money appropriated to his department for the fiscal year. His implication was that the Budget Bureau and the appropriations committees of the 1952 Democratic Congress had been careless with public funds. He would show them how to save. He also turned back large sums in 1954 and 1955. These gestures were less meaningful than they seemed, because most of Summerfield's boasted "savings" were the result of getting such items as airline subsidies and free mail for government agencies transferred out of the Post Office Department appropriation. Less than grateful for the Postmaster General's implied lectures on extravagance, Congress eventually cut his budget request to the bone, and in 1957 he simply ran out of money. Summerfield said he would have to close down all mail service on Saturdays. Some members of Congress yelled that this was a threat of blackmail. But it was no threat, it was blackmail in fact, and it worked. After one Saturday closing, Congress hastily voted funds to keep the postal service operating and thus silence the howls of constituents.

George Humphrey left the Treasury post in July, but not

as a casualty of the budget war. He had told the President months before that he wanted his resignation to become effective as soon as he saw the budget through Congress. He was succeeded by Robert B. Anderson, a quiet, level-headed administrator of a large ranching and oil estate in Texas. Anderson was a close personal and political friend of Johnson and Rayburn.

Late in August, following enactment of the last appropriations bills, Johnson announced in the Senate that Congress had reduced the President's budget requests by $5.6 billion or 9.1 per cent. "I hope this is enough," he said caustically, "to avoid having our hair curled by former Secretary Humphrey."

Other estimates of the total reduction varied. Byrd declared, "We've cut $6.5 billion." The House Appropriations Committee estimate was $4.9 billion. The Budget Bureau claimed cuts aggregated only between $900 million and $1 billion, the President having reduced his own budget requests by $2 billion, with shifting of funds and bookkeeping legerdemain accounting for other purported reductions.

These conflicting estimates mattered little. Before the fiscal year was over, Congress passed supplemental appropriations measures and all the loudly acclaimed savings were wiped out and another $4.5 billion added to the spending authority first requested by the President.

Despite all the pyrotechnics, the Battle of the Budget was sham warfare.

Eisenhower, somewhat disillusioned by events in the first year of his second term, observed tartly that "The 1957 session marked the low point in effective cooperation between the administration and the Congress."

* * *

Lyndon Johnson was never a racist, although at times he talked like one and more frequently voted like one. After all, he was a politician in a state of the old Confederacy. During all the time of his House service Johnson consistently voted against such civil-rights measures as an antilynching bill, proposals to eliminate the poll tax as a prerequisite to voting, even a bill to eliminate segregation in the armed forces. (He once told his wife, "I get so sick and tired of having to vote *safe* on everything.") After he was defeated in his 1941 Senate race by the heavy majority given his demagogic opponent in the white-supremacy section of East Texas, he became even more open in paying lip service to the racial bias casually accepted as an unchanging fact of life by most of his fellow Texans. Thus, when he was campaigning for the Senate in 1948, again against a conservative opponent, he did not hesitate to attack Truman's civil-rights program as "an effort to set up a police state in the guise of liberty." He specifically expressed unyielding opposition to an antilynching bill—"because the federal government has no more business enacting a law against one kind of murder than another"—and the Fair Employment Practices Commission, "because if a man can tell you whom to hire, he can tell you whom you cannot employ." In his drive to shake the New Deal label that still clung to him, he told Texans, "Harry Truman knows I am against him on this program. I just don't think Congress should try to cram his program down the throats of southern states."

Once he was in the Senate, he climbed to power from a base of support by senior senators from the Deep South. As floor leader, he successfully led resistance to any significant change in the Senate rules to make it difficult or impossible for southern members to filibuster civil-rights bills to death. When the Supreme Court ruled school segregation unconstitutional in 1954, a Johnson staff aide prepared and proposed that the senator issue a somewhat innocuous statement that, in view of the decision by the highest court in the land, "men of good will" should work together in planning to abide by the law. "I don't see why I have to say anything," Johnson told the aide in the high-pitched note that his voice assumed when he was disturbed or uncertain, and he made no public statement.

Yet during all these years the knowledge was growing that the traditional southern attitude toward the Negro could no longer, or not much longer, be maintained. As early as 1949, only a few weeks after he entered the Senate, he said in a speech from the floor: "For those who would seek to keep any group in our nation in bondage I have no sympathy or tolerance. Some may feel moved to deny this group or that the homes, the education, the employment which every American has a right to expect, but I am not one of those." That cautious testing of the waters was not followed by any immediate action, but it accurately reflected his inmost feeling about racial discrimination. As a practical matter, he sensed that the Negro had passed beyond the stage of humbly requesting his rights and was prepared to demand them. Johnson knew the demand had to be met and he felt that it should be met. At the same time he believed that trying to go too far too fast would almost certainly bring about a reaction in the South that would deepen the division in the nation and probably would result in grave civil disorder.

The civil-rights bill submitted to Congress by the President in 1957 contained provisions which, in Johnson's considered opinion, simply would not be accepted by southern senators. The heart of the measure gave the federal government power to intervene on behalf of any individual, with or without his consent, whose civil rights had been denied or threatened. It proposed to authorize the Attorney General to seek federal injunctions against actual or threatened violations. The bill also created a special civil-rights division in the Department of Justice and established a federal civil-rights commission with subpoena power.

Months before the President's bill passed the House in June, the majority leader had started a determined and complicated struggle to transform the Eisenhower bill into the Johnson bill.

His natural first step was to confer with Russell as the leader of the southern bloc. He began with the certainty that the Georgian would not take the bill as it stood. He had to find out what Russell—and the other southerners—*would* take. Under Senate rules the southerners could long delay, and most likely prevent, action on any measure completely unacceptable to them. A filibuster could be broken only by a two-thirds vote, and even many of those senators who favored civil-rights legislation would hesitate to take a stand against the Senate tradition of unlimited debate.

The two friends talked realities, not abstractions. As their private discussions proceeded in a series of meetings, Russell made it clear, as Johnson had anticipated, that the South would fight to the last against any proposal to impose unlimited federal injunctive power with respect to school segregation. Well, Johnson wanted to know, feeling his way with extreme caution, what if the bill were amended to restrict enforcement only to voting cases? It would then be a voting-rights bill. As such it logically could be tolerated, if not actually supported, by any person who was in office by reason of votes.

Russell listened carefully. He listened also as Johnson warned of the double danger of a filibuster. Sooner or later, he pointed out, there would be civil-rights legislation. If the southerners talked a bill to death this year, the ensuing uproar might well result in a change in the filibuster rule that would greatly and permanently lessen the power of the southern bloc. If, on the other hand, a filibuster should be tried and broken, the advocates of stringent civil-rights legislation would never be content to accept the kind of voting-rights bill Johnson was proposing. They would no doubt amend the Eisenhower bill to make it even more drastic from the standpoint of the South.

The Georgia senator considered these points with grave attentiveness. He could not deny their validity. In the end he told Johnson that if the injunction provision were removed and the bill amended to extend the right of jury trial to all phases of criminal contempt of court, he would undertake to prevent a filibuster. But, he asked, would Johnson be able to gain the support of a sufficient number of the civil-rights proponents to get such amendments approved? They would argue, as they had argued in the past, that southern juries would never convict a person charged with contempt of court in a civil-rights case. And they correctly regarded the provision empowering the Attorney General to intervene in such cases as a key feature of the bill. Russell wondered if they would ever consent to its removal.

"It'll take some doing," Johnson conceded.

It took a great deal of doing. The wheeling-and-dealing Texan had never been busier in his life than during the late spring and early summer months of 1957. He worked quietly, almost in secret, approaching "moderate" Democrats among the civil-rights supporters one by one to urge that the legislation he proposed was better than nothing, to warn that he would be utterly unable to hold off the southerners from conducting a ruinous filibuster against the Eisenhower bill. He knew which senators needed his help on legislation important to their states and which ones would be sufficiently grateful for his help to come to his aid on the civil-rights bill. He collected political I.O.U.s that he had been carefully hoarding against the time of greatest need. He sought out liberals to present his case to other liberals.

During all this activity he refrained from making any public statement of his intentions. Earlier in the year most ob-

269

servers of the Senate scene had taken for granted the majority leader's opposition to any civil-rights legislation. Now there was increasing speculation in the press about what course he would follow.

Just as he had never been busier, so had Johnson never been more effective. Gradually he collected the votes he would need. As the days wore on and he grew increasingly confident, he predicted to reporters that there would be no filibuster and that a "reasonable" civil-rights bill would be enacted during the session.

He was able to get Clinton Anderson, New Mexico Democrat known as a supporter of civil-rights legislation, and George Aiken, liberal Republican from Vermont, to sponsor the amendment removing the provision that would permit the Attorney General to bring suits to enforce school integration. Eisenhower somewhat belatedly expressed opposition to the amendment, but the Senate adopted it anyway by a vote of 52 to 38. O'Mahoney of Wyoming, Kefauver and young Frank Church of Idaho officially put their names on the jury-trial amendment, strongly opposed by the President. The going was harder this time, but when voting time came, the Senate approved it 52 to 42.

The bill itself as amended was passed by the Senate on August 7 after extended debate. Only eighteen members voted against it. Two Texans—Johnson and Ralph Yarborough, who had been chosen in a special election in 1957 to fill the vacancy left when Price Daniel resigned to run for governor—and two Tennesseeans, Gore and Kefauver, voted for it; so did one Floridian, George Smathers. Johnson, in for him an unusually eloquent speech, praised the bill: "Political ambition which feeds off hatred of the North or hatred of the South is doomed to frustration. There is a compelling need for a solution that will enable Americans to live in dignity and unity. This bill is the greatest step toward that objective that has ever been made." The Senate amendments were accepted by the House and the President signed the bill.

Offensive mail did come from Texas, but not in as great quantities as Johnson and his staff had feared. He replied to most of the letters by extolling the jury-trial amendment as a strong blow struck for liberty and explaining how vastly the Eisenhower bill had been improved by his efforts. He was concerned about Texas sentiment, of course, but not quite to the extent that it had concerned him in the past. He had been a Texas politician and a Senate politician. Now he was becoming, indeed had become, a national politician. If opposition to him in Texas mounted too high, he philosophically told a few friends, he could simply retire from public office at the end of his term in 1960 and go home to stay. The civil-rights law would be his political monument.

Those who could see no good in anything bearing the Johnson brand complained that the new law shamefully thwarted its original purpose, choosing to ignore the fact that they themselves had never been able to place any civil-rights legislation on the statute books. It was true that the Johnson bill added nothing to the federal government's power to enforce the school integration decreed by the Supreme Court. But it did provide a strong weapon against denying Negroes their right to vote. It opened the way for future advances. As Johnson pointed out, often and jubilantly, it was the first civil-rights legislation passed by Congress in more than eighty years. Its enactment without a southern filibuster was the greatest political miracle yet brought to pass by the Texan.

* * *

Most key figures in the Eisenhower administration had a tendency to ignore or belittle unfavorable developments which were beyond their control. This attitude came from the top down, the President having made it clear more than once that he wanted the men around him to show him and the world optimistic countenances. They were not able to do so at all times, although most of them tried.

They made a valiant effort when Soviet Russia put a satellite into orbit around the globe in early October. The official White House line was that the launching came as no great surprise. Eisenhower told reporters that the Soviet and U.S. space programs had never been regarded as a race, and added that the Russian satellite "does not raise my apprehensions, not one iota." Sherman Adams loyally said the administration was not "intent on attaining a high score in any outer-space baseball game." Charlie Wilson, just retiring as Secretary of Defense, acknowledged that the Russian accomplishment was a "nice technical trick," but Clarence Randall, a former steel-company executive serving as White House adviser for foreign economic policy, dismissed the satellite as "a silly bauble."

The facts about the first man-made earth satellite hardly justified such complacency. To be sure, the Sputnik—Russian for "traveling companion"—was small: a polished metal sphere about the size of a beach ball and weighing only 184 pounds. But it was circling the globe at 18,000 miles per hour and sending out continuous radio signals. Scientists involved in the U.S. space program calculated that to put Sputnik into orbit the Russians must have an operational ballistic missile driven by a rocket engine at least as big as the biggest and most efficient developed in this country. It was evident that American policy makers had seriously underestimated Russia's scientific capacity. Moreover, U.S. intelligence had no advance warning of the launching.

Soviet Russia had won a substantial victory not alone in scientific accomplishment but in the field of propaganda as well. The best efforts of the professional nonalarmists in the administration could not obscure the significance of the Russian announcement: "The present generation will witness how the free and conscious labor of the people of the new socialist society turns even the most daring of men's dreams into reality." Reading this sentence, many an American shivered at the thought of Communist missiles carrying nuclear warheads hurtling down from space onto the North American continent.

One politician who immediately grasped the significance of Russia's feat was Lyndon Johnson. This was a matter involving the national defense. He was still chairman of the Defense Preparedness Subcommittee of the Senate Armed Services Committee. Except for a few staff investigations and studies, the subcommittee had been largely inactive since the Korean war. But it was available and Johnson proposed to use it.

Within hours after the announcement of Sputnik's launching, he was on the phone from his Texas base to Dick Russell, chairman of the parent committee, urging an immediate investigation of the state of missile development in the United States. Russell agreed that it was necessary. Four days after the bombshell from Russia burst upon the world, Russell announced the investigation.

Johnson returned to Washington and went to work. He said the subcommittee's probe would be strictly nonpartisan. No attempt would be made to pinpoint blame for the nation's lagging behind Russia in the space race. The purpose of the investigation would be "to determine what steps can be taken to strengthen our position and restore the leadership we should have in technology." Nevertheless, Johnson said, "We've got to admit frankly and without evasion that the Soviets have beaten us at our own game—daring scientific adventures in the space age."

He was able to persuade a long-time friend and adviser, Edwin Weisl, to take leave of absence from his prestigious Wall Street law firm to act as general counsel for the subcommittee. Weisl brought along as his assistant Cyrus Vance, a brilliant and painstaking young lawyer from his firm. George Reedy was on hand to deal with the clamoring representatives of the news media. During the two months of the investigation, these men, aided by Gerald Siegel and a corps of researchers from the majority leader's various offices, worked long hours every day to find out, in Johnson's words, what was to be done to meet Russia's challenge to "our supremacy and even our equality."

The committee investigation had little more than started when, a month after Russia's first satellite soared aloft, the Soviet Union sent Sputnik II into orbit. This one was larger than the first, weighing 1,200 pounds, and boasted an air-conditioned compartment containing a live dog. The Russians announced that they were working their way toward manned space flight.

Near panic swept the United States. Members of the Senate Armed Services Committee returned to Washington from their home states for two full days of briefing at the Pentagon. After the meeting Russell, who never spoke recklessly, expressed shock at what they had learned. He said the Russian achievement marked so great a leap forward that nothing comparable was even in the planning stage in the United States.

Such an assessment by the sober-minded Georgian shocked the country as much as Communist Boss Khrushchev's boast that the next war would be "fought on the American continent, which can be reached by our rockets." Congressmen who earlier in the year talked every day about the need for economy in government now inveighed against the poor planning that had caused the Department of Defense to run out of money with a consequent freeze on disbursements to contractors. Newspaper columnists and editorial writers urged immediate government action to meet the threat posed by

Russia's technological superiority. Some hysterical pundits went so far as to suggest a negotiated peace with Russia before it was too late.

At last, in mid-November, the Eisenhower administration admitted that the age of space had arrived. Its spokesmen stopped saying no speed-up was needed in missile and satellite development. The President ordered Neil McElroy, the soap-company executive who had become Secretary of Defense, to begin an urgent review of the U.S. space program. Eisenhower also named James Rhyne Killian, Jr., as a special assistant for space and technology. He conceded that more money would be necessary for the missile program.

The administration was banking heavily on a rocket "shoot" scheduled to take place at Cape Canaveral, Florida, in early December. A satellite test vehicle was scheduled to send a space satellite the size of a grapefruit into orbit three hundred miles above the earth. But even this effort, barely comparable to what Russia had done, failed. The rocket exploded three feet after take-off. Newspaper headlines around the world jeered at the failure. Johnson, in an unaccustomed emotional outburst, cried, "How long, how long, O God, how long will it take us to catch up with Russia's two satellites?"

Meanwhile, the Preparedness Subcommittee hearings proceeded. A starring cast of witnesses paraded before the panel. They included men of science such as Edward Teller, famous University of California physicist, and Dr. Vannevar Bush, wartime director of the Office of Scientific Research and Development; military men like Lieutenant General James Doolittle and Lieutenant General James H. Gavin, recently resigned as chief of research and development for the Army because he believed not enough was being done to modernize the military forces for conventional warfare; the new Defense Secretary; Allen Dulles, director of the Central Intelligence

Agency; William M. Holaday, the Pentagon's guided missiles director.

The testimony of these and many other witnesses made it all too clear that the United States was indeed dangerously behind Russia in its space program. A need was shown for revamping the Armed Services Unification Act to enable the Defense Department to get over-all control of military planning and to soften the effect of incessant interservice rivalries. Some witnesses advocated a sweeping overhaul of the nation's educational system to put greater emphasis on science.

Such findings inevitably had political implications, but Johnson was firm in his refusal to conduct a political investigation. The stakes involved were far too high for that. Efforts to turn the hearings into a broad attack on the Eisenhower administration were made by some subcommittee members, notably Stuart Symington, who never forgot that he had been the first man to serve as Secretary of the Air Force and considered himself an authority on defense preparedness. Symington hammered at the administration for its alleged stinginess with funds for intercontinental missiles and other items of military hardware. Republicans retorted that the lag in missile development could actually be traced back to the Truman administration. This was precisely the kind of political infighting that Johnson was determined to avoid in this particular investigation. He held it down to a minimum, and in the end crustily refused to accede to Symington's demand for a report bitterly chastising the administration.

Johnson wanted the report to be of such a nature that it would be signed by all members, Democratic and Republican, of the Preparedness Subcommittee. Every one of its previous reports had been unanimous. This one was no exception. When it was issued early in 1958, it contained a series of succinct recommendations unanimously approved by the panel. The report recommended that the Strategic Air Force, and

ground and naval forces as well, be modernized and strengthened, that production of ballistic missiles be accelerated, and
that work be started at once on development of a motor
rocket with a thrust of one million pounds.

Johnson reaped more front-page headlines from this investigation than he had ever known before. In the accompanying stories he appeared as the sober, concerned searcher
for the truth about administration failures without seeking to
gain partisan advantage from them. He was hailed as the Senate leader who had led the nation into the space age.

1958

IKE'S DECLINE AND
ADAMS' FALL

As he prepared to depart for Washington for the opening of the second session of the Eighty-fifth Congress, Bruce Alger, a second-term Republican member of the House of Representatives from Dallas, talked to the press. In keeping with his position as Texas' sole Republican representative, and an extremely conservative one, Alger was far from optimistic about what lay ahead. "I foresee bitterness and hatefulness," he said. "We are going to squabble and fight and make the world think we hate each other and that we can't solve our problems. We are going to have bigger budgets, higher taxes, more government spending at home and abroad, and more inflation accompanied by deficit financing."

This unpleasant forecast came from one of the least effectual and most talkative members of the House, a man who had sealed his fate in that body on his first day in Congress by asserting that Sam Rayburn placed the interests of the Democratic party above those of the nation. Alger's prediction of things to come reflected no knowledge that, while the Congress was still the Eighty-fifth, the attitude of most of its

278

members was vastly different from what it had been four months before when the first session was adjourned.

The change was most marked in the feeling of the membership toward the President and his programs. In their time at home many members became convinced that popular faith in Eisenhower as the dependable protector of national security had at last been shaken by Russia in the space race. The President's influence in domestic matters was lessened by his apparent uncertainty about his objectives. He changed courses too often. His series of illnesses, many congressional observers believed, had reduced his ability to function with top effectiveness. Furthermore, an end to his administration could be seen, since the Twenty-second Amendment barred him from running for a third term.

All these factors made open opposition to the President less politically dangerous and, to some extent, added to the risk of supporting him blindly and without question. Congress was in a temper to challenge the policy-making leadership of the White House.

Lyndon Johnson showed his awareness of the new mood on the first day of the session. He opened the caucus of Senate Democrats by saying that, as a courtesy to the President, no speeches would be made in the Senate until after delivery of the State of the Union message. Even as the majority leader addressed the caucus, aides were distributing among senators copies of what amounted to Johnson's own view of the state of the nation. The main thrust of his address dealt critically with the flaws of the national defense system and proposed an action program to correct them—a clear effort to put the administration on the defensive before the President delivered his first message to Congress. Johnson urged that the United States take the initiative in gaining control of outer space. In this and subsequent speeches he presented a comprehensive Democratic platform for the year, which contained such voter-appeal planks as an aid-to-education bill, a liberalized farm program, a housing bill, and an extension of public works.

After Johnson's performance the presidential State of the Union message was awaited with more than usual interest. Rayburn, sensing the changed feeling in the House, commented, "The President's going to have to fish or cut bait in that speech."

The President undertook to fish. Moving to restore confidence in his administration's capability, he forcefully echoed the Senate majority leader's call for a stepped-up missile program. He declared that there must be better organization and integration of the Defense Department. He attacked the idea that foreign aid was a "giveaway," and asked for a five-year extension of the Reciprocal Trade Act.

This incisive address heartened the "new Republicans" in Congress, but most of them were dismayed a few days later when the President sent up his budget message for fiscal 1959. While putting forward a suggestion to spend a billion dollars over the next four years for encouraging "improved teaching quality and student opportunities," he abandoned the effort to get money appropriated for school construction. He said no new starts should be made on new reclamation and water projects, traditional vote getters for congressmen. He proposed to place new limitations on spending for welfare, urban development, and hospital construction. And he called for lower farm price supports.

The budget proposed higher expenditures than in any year since the Korean war, but the general reaction in Congress was that actual spending would rise substantially above the $73.9 billion requested. Hardly anybody was talking about cutting the budget this year.

It was a congressional election year and a spirit of "every man for himself" prevailed in Washington. Republican candidates would have no Eisenhower coattails to which they could cling. They accordingly felt the pressure to make records of their own on which to base their candidacies. Being in a position to oppose the President's program without fear of future political punishment, they did not hesitate to express their opposition to some parts of it. Among Republican senators, such a strong Eisenhower supporter as George Aiken of Vermont publicly turned on the administration's plan to reduce farm subsidies. Reclamation-minded senators like Knowland and Ed Thye of Minnesota balked at the President's ban on new water-conservation projects. The Republican leadership in both houses was wary of proposals for continued foreign aid on a massive scale. The idea of a five-year extension of the trade program appalled many protectionist members.

Wily old Sam Rayburn took note of the squabbling in the "other party," as he consistently referred to the opposition, and began to wonder not whether Democrats would win in November but how big their victory would be. The Republicans, he said, did not know where they were going and would never get there anyway because they persisted in running off in different directions. He observed also that, while congressional members of the President's party were attacking his administration, some members of the administration were attacking the Democratic party. After Sherman Adams made an uncharacteristically partisan assault on the Democrats in a Minnesota speech, Rayburn growled, "Does the White House think it can pass its program without Democratic votes?"

Over on the Senate side of the Capitol, Johnson was still proclaiming nonpartisanship in his approach to legislation. "There simply won't be time for partisanship," he said. "This is a Congress that must take care of the country and let the next election take care of itself." But ample evidence supported the view that he was thinking not merely of the "next election," that of 1958, but also of the one after that, the presidential election of 1960.

When the possibility of his own candidacy for the presidential nomination was raised, Johnson denied that he would be a candidate. He was from the wrong part of the country, he said, and anyway he wanted no job higher than the one he held in the Senate. But such denials by potential presidential candidates were traditional. In Washington at least, the majority leader was regarded as in the running.

One Democrat more open in his intentions was John F. Kennedy, the young senator from Massachusetts. Since Kennedy's surprising showing at the 1956 convention, Johnson had at times allowed the idea of a Johnson-Kennedy ticket in 1960 to flit across his mind. He was instrumental in placing Kennedy on the Foreign Relations Committee in 1957—although Kefauver wanted the post and was, by seniority, entitled to it. This assignment gave the young senator a veneer of special knowledge in foreign affairs, an asset to any ambitious national politician. Johnson also turned over to Kennedy the chairmanship, which he had held, of a select committee authorized to choose the five "greatest senators of all time" and cause their portraits to be hung in the Capitol. The author of *Profiles in Courage* thus added to his stature as an expert on the Senate and its members. He had no objection; neither at the time did the Senate majority leader.

The Texan, despite his political astuteness, did not realize for some while that the young senator had no thought of taking second place on any ticket. Kennedy's near miss for the vice-presidential nomination at the 1956 convention had caused him to step up his timetable. He was determined to go for the presidential nomination in 1960. To some political observers it may have seemed that he had no particular qualifications except for the money and the ambitions for him of his father, rich and hardheaded Joseph P. Kennedy. However, the son considered himself as well qualified as anyone else looked upon as a possibility "except," as he said, "Lyndon." And he believed that Johnson, being from the South, would stand no chance of getting the nomination. A Gallup poll early in the year showed that Kennedy would be a stronger candidate than either Adlai Stevenson or Estes Kefauver against Nixon, the probable Republican candidate.

But it was too early for overt presidential politicking.

* * *

On the night of January 31, the Army successfully launched the first U.S. earth-orbiting satellite. Within the next eight weeks, two more rocket shots, one by the Navy and another by the Army, worked without a hitch. A resolution by Johnson established a special Senate Committee on Aeronautical and Space Exploration. The only senator to vote against it was Louisiana's Allen Ellender, who made a hobby of opposing the formation of any new committee or subcommittee. Johnson later in the year brought about the establishment of a standing Committee on Aeronautical and Space Sciences and became its chairman, which gave him another power base. He won a victory when Eisenhower, who at first favored control of space functions by the military establishment, sent a message to Congress requesting the creation of a civilian space agency, the National Aeronautics and Space Administration. This move represented a sharp departure from the President's earlier attitude. "I don't rule out that eventually there might be a Department of Space," he had said, "but I want to go on record as not being at all interested in volunteering to be the first man to land on the moon."

Johnson had expected control of space to last as an issue through the session, but it did not. So much had been accomplished so fast, with Congress leading the way for the administration, that public anxiety was soothed.

Another issue presented itself to the Democrats. For several months an economic recession, almost unnoticed at first, had been creeping over the country. By February unemployment figures were the highest since 1941. Manufacturers' sales and orders were declining precipitously. Retail sales were down. The "newsletters" sent by many members of Congress to newspapers back home fell silent on missiles and the space race. New subjects for concerned discussion were farm distress, unemployment, small-business failures. Regardless of whether the people generally were fearful that the recession would turn into something worse, the politicians were.

The Democrats talked often and loudly of this danger, charging the Republicans with "betting on a depression." Rayburn rumbled about the economic catastrophe that had fallen on the nation under another Republican President, Herbert Hoover. His second in command, John McCormack, went so far as to say, "This recession was deliberately planned and put into operation by the Republican party." At a Washington dinner which the depression-fearing Democrats paid a hundred dollars a plate to attend, Truman observed, "The present administration has acted like an overbearing banker with a glass eye." Mike Mansfield, the Montana senator who succeeded Earle Clements as deputy majority leader after the latter's upset defeat by Republican Thruston Morton in 1956, said the burning issue before the country was "just as much spuds as Sputniks." The Democratic National Committee voted unanimously to take the official view that the country was in a depression, not just a recession.

The administration, running true to form, attempted at first to meet the situation with reassuring statements. Eisenhower predicted that business would soon be on the upgrade and unemployment would decline. "Let's try to be reasonable," he implored. "Let's use some common sense and not just get a Sputnik attitude about everything." Nixon declared in an Arizona speech, "There is nothing wrong with the economy that a good dose of confidence won't cure." But the vice-president felt more concern than his words indicated. Along with Labor Secretary Mitchell, he was moving behind the scenes to try to convince the President that an immediate tax cut offered the best means of combating the recession and was necessary from both an economic and a political standpoint.

Backed up by Robert Anderson, Humphrey's successor as Secretary of the Treasury, Eisenhower resisted this advice. Nixon and Mitchell might have persuaded the President if Anderson had not forestalled them by convincing Rayburn and Johnson that tax reduction in the existing situation would hold a high element of risk. It was already evident that there would be a tremendous gap between the government's income and its outgo during the coming fiscal year. A tax cut would increase the deficit, Anderson argued, without bringing an end to the recession. The two congressional leaders and the Treasury Secretary reached an agreement that neither the administration nor Congress would spring any surprises on tax policy. If a tax cut clearly became necessary to stimulate the economy, the necessary legislation would be handled on a cooperative basis with political credit divided between Democrats and Republicans.

Nixon tried to torpedo this cozy arrangement by stating publicly that he thought a tax cut was likely. Anderson promptly called a press conference and denied that the administration would present any tax-cutting proposal. He also telephoned Rayburn to assure the Speaker that Nixon was not the administration's fiscal spokesman. The vice-president definitely lost the round to the Treasury head, who was greatly admired by Eisenhower.

Rayburn and Johnson were severely criticized by some liberal Democrats in Congress and by National Chairman Paul Butler for not pressing for a tax reduction, but their agreement with Anderson held firm. One of the senatorial critics, Paul Douglas, tried to attach a tax-cutting proposal to a Senate bill, but his amendment was badly defeated.

Johnson appeared to be giving further ammunition to his liberal scolders when he said it was a mistake to predict depression and hard times. Actually, he had gone into motion to grab the recession issue as his own in the same way that he had made off with the space-control issue. While the more abrasively partisan Democrats were busily accusing the administration of complacency in the face of the economic threat, Johnson's excellent intelligence network brought him word that the President was planning to release a set of specific proposals for dealing with the recession. They would include a sharp acceleration of the highway program, a step-up in public and military housing construction, increased aid for hospital construction, and an extension of the period of unemployment compensation from twenty-six to thirty-nine weeks.

While Eisenhower was still discussing this program with his Cabinet, Johnson came out with the announcement that half a dozen bills to combat the recession were being drafted for presentation in the Senate. He boasted that an expert was in charge of each bill: Albert Gore, roads; John Sparkman, housing; Lister Hill, hospitals; Clinton Anderson, reclamation; Bob Kerr, flood control; William Fulbright, small business.

"As majority leader of the Senate," Johnson said, "I am aided by a Cabinet made up of committee chairmen. I have conferred with them. I think they will expedite action."

Some political writers commented, more admiringly than not, that the Senate majority leader was acting more and more like a President of the United States. He had started the session by delivering his own State of the Union message. Now he was talking about his Cabinet. Would he next name a Secretary of State?

In any case, Johnson had again beaten the administration to the punch.

As it happened, that fight was less prolonged than had been generally anticipated. When members of Congress went home for the Easter recess, they discovered that there was surprisingly little talk about the recession among their constituents. Unemployment was still high, but it was spotty and most people did have jobs. There was no indication of anything approaching panic.

Just after the recess, a Johnson staff member approached him with a draft of the weekly report signed by the senator and sent to Texas newspapers and thousands of citizens on the office mailing list. The report deplored the recession and told of steps being taken by the Democrats to overcome it. Johnson flung the typed pages back at his aide. "Recession!" he yelped. "I'm so sick of hearing about the recession I could puke!"

The complaints reported by congressmen as they returned to Washington had to do more with the President than with economic conditions. People still "liked Ike," but many of them thought that he spent too much time out of the White House and was overly protected by the "palace guard." Farmers, true to form, were restless and dissatisfied; Eisenhower's Agriculture Secretary, Ezra Taft Benson, was anathema to the great majority. Oil producers in the Southwest were angry because the administration had not cut oil imports to keep up domestic production and domestic prices. Republican congressmen were particularly disturbed by freely expressed opinions among their constituents that there was a lack of leadership in the administration.

Eisenhower was experiencing the gradual slide downhill frequently undergone by U.S. Presidents in their second term. The power of the office remained, but seasoned politicians understood that on a given day in the not-distant future it would be abruptly gone. If they were to survive, they must look beyond that day.

But the power was not yet gone and, with the cooperation of the Rayburn-Johnson axis, the President was able to get a good part of his program through Congress. His strong stand on sending troops into Lebanon during another Middle East crisis helped restore popular faith in his ability to act decisively and strongly. He got about what he had asked for foreign aid, and the Reciprocal Trade Act was extended for a four-year period. The Alaska statehood bill was approved. Congress appropriated a total of approximately $5 billion more than had been requested in the President's budget.

Best of all, by the time the session ended on August 27, there was general agreement that the recession also had ended.

* * *

It was a hard year for moral standards.

The television industry discovered the box-office value of the quiz show. Millions of Americans gaped in fascinated wonder as preachers, child prodigies, literary figures, race-horse jockeys, artists, and just plain housewives sweated and strained to answer "The $64,000 Question" or to "Double Your Money." Vast stores of knowledge about the most abstruse subjects were shown to be resting within the most unlikely heads.

That was not quite the case. A misstep here, a disgruntled contestant there, and finally confessions everywhere brought the horrid truth to light. The quiz shows were "fixed," crooked, phony, with answers provided in advance to the performers who had suffered so intensely and so visibly in giving them. The shock to the public psyche was massive.

No less shocking to the political world were disclosures, beginning in June, which raised serious questions about the immaculateness of Sherman Adams, the President's chief of staff, who was generally regarded in Washington as an indestructible symbol of integrity in government.

The Adams episode began with an investigation by the House Commerce Subcommittee on Legislative Oversight into the business affairs of an odd New England industrialist named Bernard Goldfine. The quaintly titled subcommittee had the function of overseeing activities of the federal regulatory agencies to determine whether they were carrying out their responsibilities as intended by Congress. It was looking into Goldfine's relations with the Federal Trade Commission and the Securities Exchange Commission. In the course of their query, staff investigators stumbled upon a number of hotel bills from the Sheraton-Plaza in Boston, incurred by Adams and his wife but paid for by Goldfine.

The bills totaled approximately $3,000. They dated from 1955 right up to May of the present year. And the subcommittee found evidence giving rise to at least the suspicion that Adams had intervened from the White House to seek preferential treatment for Goldfine from the FTC and SEC.

This evidence was not overpowering. Early in 1954 Goldfine had requested Adams, an old friend from the days when the latter was Speaker of the New Hampshire House of Representatives, to get for him additional information about a complaint by the FTC that one of his textile companies was violating a wool-labeling regulation. Adams asked the chairman of the commission to give him a factual memorandum about the case, which he then sent along to Goldfine. A year later the presidential assistant, at Goldfine's request, made an appointment for him with the chairman of the Federal Trade Commission to discuss still another problem regarding the labeling regulation. Adams made the appointment and it was kept. However, the commission nevertheless issued a cease-and-desist order against Goldfine's company because of improper labeling. On another occasion Goldfine complained that the SEC was giving him trouble because one of his numerous companies had not filed reports on its financing practices, and asked Adams for help. This time Adams asked Gerald Morgan, the President's special counsel, to find out if the complaint was justified. No new information having been brought to light, Adams dropped the matter.

Even though these activities could hardly be said to represent determined efforts to influence the actions of regulatory agencies, why did Adams, busy man that he was, bother at all?

John Fox, a Boston financial operator and sometime newspaper publisher whose fortunes had turned downward, claimed to know the answer. Fox bitterly hated Goldfine, blaming him in part for his business troubles. He appeared as a witness before the Legislative Oversight Subcommittee to cry down his enemy. In so doing, he sorely besmirched Adams' good name. Fox said Goldfine had told him Adams would "take care" of his difficulty with the FTC over mislabeling of fabrics and also would resolve the industrialist's problem with the SEC. He told the subcommittee Goldfine boasted that he had bought a house in Washington for Adams, regularly sent him checks, bought corporate stocks for him, and had helped put his children through school. This was second-hand evidence against Adams, and Fox was not a particularly convincing witness; but his testimony made sensational headlines just the same. Adams categorically denied every charge made by the Bostonian.

He could not, however, deny the existence of the bills for hotel accommodations enjoyed by him and Mrs. Adams and paid for by Goldfine. Adams was on a fishing trip in Maine when the subcommittee made this information public. Jerry Persons called him by phone from Washington with the bad news. Adams immediately returned to the capital, prepared to appear before the investigating group in his own defense.

He told Eisenhower he wanted to answer the charges against him and to make it clear, as he said, that he had "nothing to hide." The President, concerned for his friend as well as worried about the political implications of the affair, expressed sympathy and wished him luck.

Adams' prepared statement, which he read before the subcommittee and the newsmen and spectators packing the House Caucus Room, was forthright and explicit. He explained that his association with Goldfine dated back to the early 1940s and continued through his terms as governor and his years in the White House. Adams admired the industrialist as a businessman whose textile mills were an important economic asset to New Hampshire at a time when many New England manufacturers were moving South to take advantage of cheaper labor. The Adams and Goldfine families became friends. They entertained each other and exchanged presents from time to time. The gifts received by Adams included an inexpensive and rather ugly vicuña coat, several suits, and a few blankets made at one of Goldfine's mills. The rug on the living-room floor of the Adams home in Washington had come from Goldfine, but it was only on loan and would be returned when the family went back to New Hampshire. As for the hotel accommodations, Goldfine had told Adams he maintained them for the convenience of his friends and relatives. The Adamses were friends and might as well use the suite when they were in Boston.

Adams maintained that he had no interest in Goldfine's business affairs "beyond the desire to see them continue to serve as an economic asset to the people who were dependent on these industries." He sturdily denied that his calls to the regulatory agencies were attempts to influence their decisions. "Of course," he later conceded, "a telephone call or a letter or a person-to-person statement, when made by a White House staff member to an individual in an agency of the government, receives prompt attention. But I would not wish to place myself in the position of insulting either the intelligence or the integrity of those officials by implying that they might allow themselves to be influenced in their decisions by such a telephone call, letter, or statement."

The New Hampshire politician was not as naïve as this observation implied. He admitted that no expression of interest, however slight, would ever be completely disregarded when it came from the desk where he sat. This was a political fact of life well understood by members of the congressional subcommittee. They themselves were accustomed to forwarding requests from their constituents to agencies in the Executive Branch, as Adams had done when serving in the House of Representatives. They would maintain, as would other members of Congress, that these contacts represented nothing more than efforts to get information. But they knew that a subtle hint of pressure was implied simply by their show of interest. How much stronger the hint if it came to an agency from the President's chief of staff!

In replying to questions at the hearing, Adams said at one point that, while he considered the inquiries he had made at Goldfine's request routine and proper, he might have acted with a little more prudence. That was a mistake. His statement was instantly translated by the press into an admission that he had been imprudent. That was the part of his testimony which captured the headlines.

An uproar followed. The Democrats were reasonably content to let the Republicans fight this one out among themselves, although Adlai Stevenson did remark, "I am tired of pious preaching from Sherman Adams. This is not the only example of hypocrisy in the administration." But it was Republicans who clamored for Adams' immediate resignation. His most severe congressional critics included Representative Richard Simpson, who was chairman of the Republican Congressional Campaign Committee, and such senators as Knowland, Arthur Watkins, Roman Hruska, and Charles Potter. They were joined by every congressman who had suffered a slight, real or imagined, at the hands of the President's man and by members of the Old Guard who, like Eisenhower's older brother, believed that Adams was largely responsible for presidential policies which they disliked as being too liberal.

Eisenhower himself was deeply troubled, but he did not want Adams to resign. In a prepared statement at a news conference the day after his chief of staff appeared before the Legislative Oversight Subcommittee, the President expressed incredulity that anyone could doubt Adams' personal honesty and integrity. Even though he had been "imprudent," Eisenhower continued, "I personally like Governor Adams. I admire his abilities. I respect him because of his personal and official integrity. I need him."

Eisenhower apparently felt that his strong defense of Adams would quiet the storm. If he, the President, trusted his assistant and needed him, that should be the end of the matter. Far from it. The statement "I need him" was interpreted in many quarters as a confession of weakness.

Criticism continued to be hurled against Adams by frightened Republicans, interested Democrats, and a headline-hungry press. Even so restrained a writer as Arthur Krock noted that the testimony before the subcommittee had created "a crisis in public confidence in the official ethics of the administration."

Worse was in store. The subcommittee staff came up with the information that in his federal income-tax returns Goldfine had charged off the hotel bills and the cost of the rug in the Adams living room as business expenses. The industrialist was summoned before the panel. He read a long statement defending himself and his business operations. He testified that he had indeed paid hotel bills for Adams—and for several U.S. senators as well. He said he had given presents of varying value to twenty-three governors and contributed about $100,000 to both political parties. He presented himself as a compulsive giver of presents, testifying that he had sent Christmas gift baskets costing as much as $800 to as many as three hundred persons a year.

It might have been thought that this testimony showing how widely Goldfine had spread his favors would take some of the spotlight off Adams, but that did not happen. Every time Goldfine's name was mentioned in the papers—and it was on the front pages day after day, he made good copy, he "talked funny," he was in a way picturesque—it was linked with the name of Sherman Adams. Nor was the presidential assistant aided by the antics of the flamboyant press agent Tex McCrary, the same who had staged the pro-Eisenhower rally at Madison Square Garden early in 1952. On the day Goldfine appeared as a witness, McCrary preceded him to the committee hearing room, passing out advance copies of the industrialist's statement, briefing television cameramen, and finally serving drinks to the press from a portable bar. Goldfine denied having employed him and McCrary did not say he had. He said he was simply trying to help "my friend Sherman Adams."

The affair had other farcical aspects, but it was no joke to Adams, going about his duties at the White House, wondering dismally if he should resign, watching with growing embarrassment as his former friend was shown up not just as a clown who strove to curry favor and buy friendship with important people but as a quick-dollar operator given to questionable business practices. Goldfine got himself into ever deeper trouble, first by talking and then by refusing to talk. In mid-August, the House of Representatives cited him for contempt of Congress for refusing to answer twenty-two questions which he dismissed as not being pertinent to the investigation. He eventually went to jail on being convicted of contempt.

Eisenhower, still balking at Adams' resignation, asked Nixon to keep an eye on developments affecting the situation. After conferring with key congressional Republicans, the vice-president reported that most party members in both houses thought it imperative that Adams resign. His retention in the White House would be a hurtful issue in the November elections. In fact, the Republican candidates said Adams was ruining them. But still the President hesitated.

After the Democrats won the early election in Maine, Republican Chairman Alcorn told the President that the Adams-Goldfine case was causing a wave of hopelessness among Republicans all over the country. He reported that contributions to the party were being cut off on an alarming scale unless Adams departed. "As Maine goes," chortled Democrats, "so goes Adams." Knowland, running a hard race for governor of California, demanded that Adams resign at once. Kenneth Keating, a candidate for the Senate in New York, added, "and for the good of the country." Goldwater, seeking a second term as senator from Arizona, pessimistically said, "The harm already has been done."

Much of the criticism of Adams was if not unjustified at least hypocritical. Most members of Congress had their desks piled high every Christmas with gifts from lobbyists and favor-seeking constituents. Many committee chairmen were regularly paid generous fees for making speeches before trade-association groups with interests directly affected by congressional action or refusal to act. Not a few lawmakers were as a matter of course frequent nonpaying passengers on corporate-owned airplanes flying between Washington and their home districts. Few indeed were in a position to cast the first stone at a man who had accepted a cheap vicuña coat and free hotel rooms. But the stones came, thick and heavy.

Adams was as much a victim of his own reputation for righteousness and of his stern demand that others in government observe the highest of standards as he was blameworthy for his admitted lack of prudence in receiving Goldfine's favors. He was a symbol of the clean look that Republicans had pledged in the federal government. His fall from grace, regardless of the fact that no one who knew Adams could seriously suspect him of selling his influence, was thus a matter of understandable uneasiness for Republican candidates.

Still Eisenhower would not ask Adams to resign, saying he would leave the decision up to his assistant. But it was made clear through go-betweens that the President was at last prepared to accept the resignation.

Adams went on national television in a statement approved in advance by Eisenhower to explain that he was resigning because the continuing attacks on him were intended to embarrass the President. He had done no wrong, he repeated. "I believe that I can best serve my President and contribute to the support of his objectives," Adams said, his dry New England voice concealing his emotion, "by the course that I have now undertaken to follow."

He had a letter from the President reluctantly accepting the resignation and praising his service. He also received a large sterling-silver punch bowl suitably inscribed "From his devoted friend, Dwight D. Eisenhower." The President suggested a dinner in Adams' honor at the White House to be followed by a square dance, but the New Englander was not in the mood. The man who had been closest to presidential decisions for nearly six years left Washington for his home in the White Mountains—the fallen target of what his friend

Emmet John Hughes, who sometimes wrote speeches for Eisenhower, labeled "the vultures of the Grand Old Party."

* * *

The Republican doom sayers proved correct in their predictions of party disaster at the polls in November. In the next Congress, Democrats would outnumber Republicans by nearly two to one in both Senate and House. In the gubernatorial races, twenty-six Democrats won, to bring their national total of state governors to thirty-five.

In California, Knowland lost his race for governor despite intensive support of his candidacy by Eisenhower. But Nelson Rockefeller defeated Governor Averell Harriman in New York, and in that state Republican Representative Keating won his way into the Senate. In Ohio, John Bricker of Bricker amendment fame, seeking a third term, lost to Stephen M. Young, sixty-nine, a perennial Democratic candidate. John F. Kennedy gained a second term by a vote of three to one. Another presidential hopeful, Stuart Symington, scored a resounding victory in Missouri.

Surveying the results of the national Democratic landslide, Sam Rayburn wondered soberly if he and Johnson would encounter the tender problem of having too many Democrats in House and Senate. "They'll be hard to handle," he predicted.

1959

SOME SOUNDS AND FURY

Eisenhower was deeply disturbed by the results of the congressional elections. They seemed to prove that, while he could be elected and re-elected President, the Republican party itself could not win at the polls. No sound political organization could be based on a personality cult, especially when the personality involved would not again head the ticket. Eisenhower invited Joe Martin to breakfast with him at the White House to discuss ways and means of breathing new life into the party.

The President spoke to the House leader of the need for getting candidates possessing qualities of "natural leadership" to run under the Republican banner. He wanted the party to follow policies and propose programs that would attract young voters. In line with this aim, Eisenhower suggested, as he had before, that some of the younger Republican members of Congress be invited to participate in the regular leadership meetings at the White House. As in the past, Martin was disinclined to enter into such an arrangement.

This reluctance caused the President to be more receptive

when Halleck came once again to complain about the ineffectiveness of Martin's leadership. The tough, experienced midwestern politician said he could no longer put up with it. The time had come for action. "Twice before I've held off," he reminded Eisenhower, "but now I'm determined to unseat him. And I've got the votes to do it." This time the President gave the go-ahead signal. He said he would not attempt to influence the outcome, but would no longer stand in Halleck's way.

The Indianian's statement that he had the necessary votes to win proved accurate. In the Republican House caucus at the beginning of the session, Halleck beat Martin by a close vote of 74 to 70. Martin, bitter in defeat, charged that several members of the White House staff had actively sought support for Halleck. They were against him, he said, because he had never recognized the importance they attached to themselves. The President denied that any of his staff members had intervened in what was solely the business of House Republicans.

Both Martin and his friend Rayburn felt that the fallen leader was the victim of a conspiracy within an administration that followed a policy of throwing out its generals when a battle went the wrong way. They thought also that their own friendship aroused the anger of some Republicans. "I didn't give the Democrats hell enough," Martin said.

Rayburn was almost as upset over the outcome of the fight as Martin himself. At a birthday reception for the Speaker at the Democratic Women's Club on the evening of the day the House caucus was held, Martin came in alone and late. As he approached the receiving line Rayburn stepped away from his host and hostess and with arms outstretched walked toward his friend. Tears came into Martin's eyes. "I won't have the minority leader's room any more, Sam," he said in a choked voice. "Can you find a little hideaway for me somewhere?" "Joe," Rayburn replied, "you can have any place in the Capitol you want."

He was better than his word. Soon afterward, he gaveled through the House measures permitting Martin, as the only living former Speaker, to keep the Cadillac with chauffeur and most of the extra staff of the leadership office he had lost. In spite of a noisy objection from the floor, Rayburn ruled that the bills were passed by unanimous consent. He, like Martin, was convinced that White House staffers—and probably Nixon, whom Rayburn loathed—had supplied sufficient pressure to swing the votes necessary for Halleck's victory.

If this was indeed the case, the results justified the interveners so far as the administration was concerned. In this session Halleck gave House Republicans the most effective leadership they had known in years. His first move was to reorganize the Policy Committee, which had deteriorated into a conversation club. He named to head the committee John Byrnes of Wisconsin, a leader of the revolt against Martin and one of the ablest Republican members. Eisenhower was pleased when Byrnes was added to the leadership group at the weekly White House legislative meetings. Halleck established his own equivalent of Rayburn's Board of Education by holding irregular and informal sessions of a few members in a small office. Participants called it "the Clinic," but Martin, a teetotaler, scornfully referred to it as "Charlie's drinking room." Party discipline was tightened in the House and also in the Senate, where the mellow-voiced and histrionic Everett Dirksen had succeeded Knowland as Republican floor leader. During the session Eisenhower made repeated use of the veto power, and time and time again Halleck and Dirksen were able to muster the necessary votes to uphold the vetoes.

The unwonted experience of seeing congressional Republicans working together as a team instead of being at one another's throats gave the President new confidence in press-

ing his policies. Shocked by the tremendous deficit anticipated for the current year, he grimly determined that the
budget would be balanced for the coming fiscal period. As he
announced this resolution in his State of the Union message
before a joint session of Senate and House, the roving eye of
a television camera happened to catch Lyndon Johnson in the
act of enjoying a huge, unconcealed yawn.

It was symbolic. The Democrats promptly attacked the
presidential budget as unrealistic, dangerous, based on wishful
thinking, a bookkeeping exercise. Even within the President's
Cabinet there was disagreement. Treasury Secretary Anderson, who wielded enormous influence over the President,
firmly supported the budget, as did Maurice Stans, Budget
Director, Commerce Secretary Lewis Strauss and Postmaster
General Summerfield. James Mitchell, Secretary of Labor,
and Attorney General William Rogers thought the President's insistence on a balanced budget was politically unwise.
Their view was shared to some extent by Arthur Flemming,
Secretary of Health, Education and Welfare, and Fred
Seaton, Secretary of the Interior. But their opposition was
expressed only in Cabinet meetings. Publicly they presented
a united front. Eisenhower was much more definitely in
charge of his Cabinet members than he had been during his
first term.

Johnson and Rayburn came up with a legislative program
which called for heavy increases in spending without regard
for the President's lectures on the need for economy. The
course on which each side was embarked became clear early
in the session. Congress passed bills providing generous funds
for airport construction and extensive housing programs.
Eisenhower, set on convincing the American people, as he
said, that "thrift is not a bad thing," vetoed both measures.
Halleck and Dirksen twisted enough Republican arms to have
the vetoes upheld. The Democrats shot through another hous-

ing bill calling for only slightly lower expenditures than the first, and the President vetoed it also. Giving up, the Johnson-Rayburn majority passed a bill that met the President's specifications. They also trimmed down the airport bill to such an extent that Eisenhower approved it. After these shows of strength from the White House, the Democratic legislative program proudly announced in the early days of the session was considerably modified. The President even vetoed the traditionally sacrosanct public-works bill, against the advice of Halleck and other top Republicans. The measure contained "pork barrel" projects for every state, but an all-out drive by Rayburn to have the veto overriden in the House failed by a single vote. Never before had a President so effectively controlled an opposition Congress.

Johnson made an effort to turn to his own party's advantage the President's readiness to veto legislation in the name of economy. He showed up as the only congressional leader at an A.F. of L.–C.I.O. unemployment rally at Washington's Union Station. Unemployment had been going down, but still some seven thousand persons, about half of them union functionaries, were brought into the city in half a dozen special trains. They whooped and cheered as Johnson, in an impassioned speech, announced a plan for a legislative-executive commission on unemployment. The eleven-member commission would be instructed to hold hearings around the country and report back to Congress within ninety days. Johnson told the labor people he was returning to the Senate chamber to introduce on that very day a bill establishing the commission. Andrew Biemiller, A.F. of L.–C.I.O. lobbyist, went back with Johnson to his office, nodding in approval as the senator told him, winking, "We'll just introduce this and send it down there and let him veto it, and then we'll see."

Within three hours sixty-eight senators, including Republican Leader Dirksen, signed the bill as cosponsors. Within forty-eight hours after its introduction the resolution swept through the Senate by voice vote. Johnson was triumphant. Unfortunately for his plan, after organized labor took a second look, their spokesmen protested that the resolution was meaningless or worse, that the proposed commission would give the administration carte blanche to do nothing about bolstering the economy while waiting for the report. Their strenuous opposition baffled and irritated Johnson. It was so intense, however, that on Rayburn's counsel the resolution was allowed to die in the House without even being sent to committee.

The most important legislative measure enacted during the session affected labor but not in a way that labor liked. This was the Landrum-Griffin Bill, which Johnson and Rayburn initially opposed and which Eisenhower enthusiastically endorsed in a nationwide radio and television broadcast. The bill, originally introduced and floor-managed by John F. Kennedy, passed the Senate in a form acceptable, if only barely so, to organized labor, but the House added a number of severe antiunion provisions. Most of them were retained by the Senate-House conference committee, and Kennedy was pleased enough that his name was no longer attached to the measure. It was another victory for the President.

Eisenhower's new attitude of combativeness toward Congress affected his personal relationship with the Democratic leaders. This was especially the case with Rayburn, who had never been as resigned as Johnson about going along with so much of a Republican President's program. The Speaker believed a President should be—for success had to be—political, but not petty, and sometimes he thought Eisenhower was pettish. He thought so when the President failed to invite the retiring delegate from Hawaii, John A. Burns, to the White House for the signing of the Hawaiian statehood proclamation. Rayburn was invited, of course, but his first reaction was that

303

he would not go. He said no one had done more to achieve statehood for Hawaii than Burns, yet he was being left out of the White House ceremony because he was a Democrat. "If they're counting Burns out, they can count me out too," he declared truculently. Burns persuaded the Speaker to attend, but when Eisenhower offered him a pen with which he had signed the proclamation, Rayburn said, "I don't believe I want that." Daniel Inouye, new congressman from the new state, whispered, "Mr. Speaker, maybe Jack Burns would like that pen." "Maybe he would at that," said Rayburn. He strode back to the President's desk. "I'll take that pen after all," he announced. "I'd like to give it to Jack Burns." The Speaker was always protective of his own flock.

In the Senate, Johnson's inability to control events as effectively as he had over the past four years intensified the drumfire of criticism from liberal Democrats. Paul Butler's Advisory Council, which the National Chairman had established in 1957, was constantly issuing blasts against the Democratic leadership. Most congressional Democrats boycotted the council, although two prominent senators, Humphrey and Kefauver, were members from the beginning, and this year Kennedy and Symington accepted appointment to it. Johnson and Rayburn had refused to serve on the council, although when it was created, they professed willingness to consult with its members. The more they saw of the group in action, however, the less they thought of it. Now Butler was severely critical of them for tailoring legislation in such a way as to avoid a presidential veto. He said tartly in a television interview, "Quite a few Democrats around the country are unhappy about the progress that has been made in the first session."

Quite a few Democrats also were unhappy about Butler. Rayburn said stolidly, "We'll just let Mr. Butler stew." But Theodore Francis Green, the nonagenarian senator from

Rhode Island and a member of the Democratic National Committee, warned the chairman not to use his office "as a gun pit from which to fire on Democratic candidates." Talmadge of Georgia said Butler should resign, and if he did not, the National Committee should fire him. Butler had no intention of resigning. He asserted, "Neither the leadership of the party nor of Congress should be above constructive criticism." Rayburn and Johnson were "soft on Eisenhower," he charged.

Johnson was still king of the Senate, but some of his subjects were restive.

William Proxmire, who had been elected in Wisconsin to succeed Joe McCarthy, went docilely along for a time. Now he joined Butler in attacking control of Congress by the two Texans. Proxmire was angry because Johnson would not accede to his repeated requests for assignment to the Finance Committee. "When you get these two men together," he cried, "with the power of making committee assignments, you see the obsequious, bowing, scraping senators and congressmen around them." He also struck out at what he called Johnson's highhandedness in setting Democratic policy. Proxmire, a young man with a craving for newspaper publicity, enjoyed the headlines he reaped by his criticism of the floor leader. And he reported with self-approval that his attack on Johnson drew more mail than anything else he had ever done. Morse also gained attention from the press with a speech in which he complained that the Texan was a "Charlie McCarthy in a political ventriloquist act." Another senator, Michigan's Pat McNamara, who had no glowing record of accomplishment in the body, came out with a charge that Johnson was blocking attempts to broaden unemployment compensation. Joe Clark of Pennsylvania wrote Johnson a letter, which was leaked to the press, to propose that liberals be given more voice in policy making.

Johnson was accused on the one hand of one-man rule and

on the other of failure to organize his unwieldy majority for an all-out onslaught against Eisenhower's policies. From Texas came a resolution passed by the Young Democrats of that state taking him to task for not being liberal enough. In Washington, newspaper writers slacked up on detailing miracles of Johnson's legislative efforts and instead gave satiric descriptions of the greatly enlarged and splendidly furnished quarters Johnson had established for himself in the Capitol. They irreverently dubbed the new office "Lyndon's Taj Mahal."

Unaccustomed to this kind of treatment from either senators or newsmen, stung by what he regarded as unjust representations of his methods and motives, Johnson suffered in silence for weeks, although he bawled Reedy out because of the unfavorable publicity. Then one day, sore and fed up, he got to his feet in the Senate to protest a new attack from Proxmire. "This one-man rule is a myth," he declared sharply. "It does not take much courage, I may say, to make the leadership a punching bag." When matters in the Senate did not go according to the Wisconsin senator's liking, said Johnson, "He puts the blame on the leadership."

Proxmire, perhaps seeing more headlines in the offing, jumped up to say, "I challenge senators to tell me what our policy is on the budget, what our policy is on taxation, or what our policy is on almost any issue."

Dirksen was so happy with this Democratic squabbling that he yielded five minutes of time that had been allotted to him so the discussion could continue. Johnson scoffed at his critics, inquiring with heavy irony, "Do they expect a fairy godmother or a wet nurse to get a majority to deliver into their hands?" Proxmire finally took his seat. The best living example of a Senate leader's problems, the exasperated Johnson snapped, "has just sat down."

The Texan won the argument, which was not on a very

high plane, but this unedifying scene spotlighted the fact that the majority leader's grasp on the Senate was no longer as sure and firm as it had once been. He was losing some senators, and he lost more as it became increasingly apparent that he and Rayburn had decided little was to be gained by fighting Eisenhower's program.

As for the President, a Gallup poll showed that 59 per cent of the people still approved the way he was handling his job. Only 26 per cent expressed disapproval.

* * *

Neither the President's popularity nor his new strength in dealing with Congress could prevent failure and personal disappointment with respect to two important appointments he made.

The nomination of Clare Booth Luce, wife of the publisher of *Time*, as U.S. ambassador to Brazil seemed almost routine in a political sort of way. Mrs. Luce was not a career diplomat, to be sure, but she had served as ambassador to Italy during the early years of the Eisenhower administration. She was a strongly partisan and often a scathingly outspoken Republican, who had been a member of the House of Representatives from 1943 to 1947. The passing out of political ambassadorships as political plums to those deserving them and able to afford them being common practice in both Republican and Democratic administrations, confirmation of Mrs. Luce's appointment was expected to proceed without a hitch.

This outlook was hardly changed when Wayne Morse voted against confirmation in the Senate Foreign Relations Committee. His was the only negative vote. Still, Morse, not a man who minded being in the minority, announced that he would carry his fight against confirmation to the Senate floor.

He did just that, talking on the subject for three and a half hours. Morse had never been accorded kid-glove treatment from the magazine published by the nominee's husband. His attack on Mrs. Luce was personal in nature and acid in content. He lashed out at her vividly expressed criticism of Roosevelt when she was in Congress. He cited a 1952 speech in which Mrs. Luce said, "If a general loses a division he is shot. When Acheson, as undersecretary of state lost 100 million people a year to Communism, including the friendly 500 million Chinese, he was promoted to Secretary of State." Morse said coldly, "I call that subversion." He accused the nominee of emotional instability and shouted that she was unfit for the role of diplomat. "The role for which I believe she *is* well qualified," the Oregon senator went on, "is that of a political hatchet man. She does very well at making inflammatory and demagogic political speeches. She and her husband contribute heavily to Republican coffers. And for this she is being rewarded with an ambassadorship."

This was just Wayne Morse talking, and he was not the most influential member of the Senate. Nevertheless, the next day Dirksen spoke in defense of Mrs. Luce, arguing in particular that it was not sporting to hold past political utterances against her. "Why thresh old hay or beat an old bag of bones?" he inquired in a sorrow-laden voice. The galleries exploded into laughter. Nimble-witted Hubert Humphrey bounced to his feet to say, straight-faced, "I must rise to the defense of the lady." Taken aback for only a moment, Dirksen stared owlishly at Humphrey. "I am referring," he said, "to the old bag of political bones, these old canards." "I object!" cried Humphrey, still playing the situation for laughs. And laughter did sweep through the Senate.

When the game was over, however, only ten other senators joined Morse in voting against confirmation.

That should have been that. But it was not, because Mrs. Luce was unable to resist the temptation to hold a press conference. During it she remarked, "My difficulties of course go back some years when Senator Wayne Morse was kicked in the head by a horse."

This was an egregious mistake. Clare Booth Luce was sufficiently familiar with Washington ways to have known better. The Institution drew together. One senator after another piously proclaimed that if he had known the nominee was capable of speaking in such a fashion about a fellow senator he would never have voted to confirm her appointment. Johnson telephoned the President to ask if he could get Mrs. Luce to withdraw her remark and apologize to Morse, but Eisenhower replied only that sometimes he did not feel complimented by things the Oregon senator said about him. Johnson said wryly that neither did he.

Henry Luce would not allow the controversy to continue. He knew that Morse, as chairman of the Foreign Relations Latin American Subcommittee, could make life continually miserable for his wife if she took up residence at the U.S. embassy in Brazil. He announced that he had asked her to resign. She did so with a parting shot that she planned to take up skin diving so she could "look an honest shark in the face." Although he had met his match in hurling invective, Morse won the day.

The Luce affair had its comic aspects, but there was nothing laughable about events growing out of Eisenhower's appointment of Lewis L. Strauss as Secretary of Commerce.

Strauss, the son of a Richmond, Virginia, shoe jobber, worked for the family firm after graduation from high school, was a volunteer for Herbert Hoover's Belgian Relief Commission, after the war prospered in a New York investment firm. He did desk duty in World War II, ending up as a rear admiral. Truman appointed Strauss, a conservative Republican, to the Atomic Energy Commission. Eisenhower made him chairman of the AEC in 1953, not caring that Strauss had strongly supported Taft the year before.

The admiral was a man of great ability and was much admired by the President. But he had no sense at all of the importance of getting along with congressmen, including members of the Congressional Joint Committee on Atomic Energy. He was soon in deep conflict with Clinton Anderson of the committee. When his term as AEC chairman expired, he declined reappointment because Anderson would occupy the rotating chairmanship of the Congressional Joint Committee in 1959–1960. Eisenhower did not want to lose his services, so in the fall of 1958 he named Strauss to fill the vacancy in the Commerce Department.

It being a recess appointment, Strauss assumed his duties pending the reconvening of Congress and his confirmation by the Senate. Everybody on Capitol Hill knew about the feud between him and Anderson, and it was generally understood that the New Mexican would vote in the Senate against confirmation. But Anderson was not a member of the Interstate Commerce Committee, which would hold confirmation hearings, so the assumption was that his opposition would amount only to one anti-Strauss vote. After all, the nominee had three times been confirmed by the Senate for different positions: rear admiral in the Navy, AEC member and AEC chairman.

Congress returned to Washington for the new session, but for weeks no announcement came from the Interstate Commerce Committee regarding confirmation hearings for Strauss. This was partly the result of a deliberately planned congressional slowdown in acting on Eisenhower's appointments and partly due to the fact that Clinton Anderson had determined to fight the admiral's confirmation with all the strength at his command. He used the time to marshal his forces and to prepare for his own appearance as a witness before the committee.

When the hearings finally started, they were to continue for two months. Anderson having used his influence to the utmost with committee members, most of the witnesses called were hostile. The New Mexico senator himself came before the committee to launch an attack on Strauss lasting two days. He accused the nominee of being arrogant, suspicious-minded, and evasive in his dealings with Congress. He charged Strauss with failure to cooperate with the Joint Committee and declared he withheld information from Congress. He said the former AEC chairman hindered nuclear-power progress while encouraging the creation of myths about his great accomplishments. At one point he accused Strauss of "unqualified falsehoods." A committee member, Norris Cotton, remarked, "That is a polite word, but where I come from that means a liar." Retorted Anderson: "I didn't intend it to mean anything else." Eisenhower was so angry that he broke off his friendship with Anderson, who at times had been a fourth in White House bridge games.

The hearings went on and on, a parade of scientists who had feuded with Strauss drawing a picture of him as a man ridden by pride and as an excessively rough fighter. At the nominee's request some friendly witnesses, including Edward Teller, were called, but the general tone of most committee meetings was decidedly inimical. Strauss himself bent but little, giving Anderson a chance to say of the long-drawn-out hearings, "I thought that if the committee members saw enough of him, he would begin to irritate them, just as he has me." Strauss did irritate some of them, but in the end the committee approved confirmation by a one-vote margin.

Anderson now carried his fight to the whole Senate. Strauss had become an obsession with him. In private talks with senators he used every method of persuasion open to him, including calls upon personal friendship and pointed reminders of political debts owed him. Lyndon Johnson believed that a President had a right to choose his appointees and also had the uneasy feeling that Anderson might not win this one. His old friend and political ally drew on memories of times when he had gone along with something Johnson wanted just because he wanted it. "Are you for me or for Strauss?" he demanded. Johnson made no announcement until voting day of his position on confirmation. John Kennedy had written a letter endorsing Strauss. Now came Anderson to remind the younger man of many favors extended him and to say that this was the time for repayment. Many others were similarly approached. The tall, shambling New Mexico senator, as set on Strauss' defeat as he had ever been on anything in his life, missed no senator with whom he thought he stood a ghost of a chance.

He triumphed. Strauss was refused confirmation by a vote of forty-nine to forty-six. Two Republicans, Margaret Chase Smith and "Wild Bill" Langer, provided the margin of defeat for the Republican nominee. Fourteen Democrats voted to confirm. Not among them were the four senators regarded as strong contenders for the presidential nomination: Johnson, Kennedy, Humphrey, Symington.

It was the first time the Senate had voted not to confirm a presidential Cabinet nominee since 1925, when Coolidge's choice for Attorney General was rejected.

"We beat him!" exulted Johnson in a convivial session in his office after the postmidnight voting, leaving his listeners to decide for themselves whether he was talking about Strauss or the man who nominated him for Secretary of Commerce.

* * *

There was plenty to talk about in 1959.

Fidel Castro, whose ragged forces had taken over Cuba, visited Washington and denied in a speech before the American Society of Newspaper Editors that any Communist influence existed in his government. Herbert Matthews, who had written admiringly of the bearded young Cuban as a latter-day Robin Hood, described the Castro government's "conservative tinge." John F. Kennedy, seeing Castro as "part of the legacy of Bolivar," thought Washington officialdom might have given "the fiery young rebel a warmer welcome." Two congressmen, Charles O. Porter of Oregon and Adam Clayton Powell of New York, accepted an invitation to visit Havana. In Cuba the number of executions of persons charged with being enemies of the Castro regime mounted.

Illness forced the resignation of John Foster Dulles as Secretary of State. He died soon after, a loss that the President felt deeply. He looked up to Dulles as to no other man in his administration.

The nation endured the longest steel strike in history. It extended through 116 days and was ended only by an injunction brought under the provisions of the Taft-Hartley Act.

Serious-minded elders worried about the upsurge of the Beatnik philosophy among young people.

Collegians played Telephone Squash Box, a game with the object of squeezing as many human bodies as possible into a telephone booth.

Such matters as these, grave or trivial, were submerged in the minds of the professional politicians by thoughts of next year. Democrats were thinking with particular avidity of the biggest political prize of all. In 1960 their candidate for President, whoever he might be, would not have to face Eisenhower. They returned thanks for the Twenty-second Amendment, which ironically had been devised by the Republicans as a means of making sure that no President with the popularity of a Roosevelt could be elected to more than two terms of office. Hardly anyone versed in politics doubted that Eisenhower would win again in 1960 if he could run. But Richard M. Nixon, the presumptive Republican nominee, was beatable, in the opinion of numerous hopeful Democrats.

The hopeful ones were indeed numerous. Some old party hands feared that a wild, free-for-all scramble for the nomination could result in dealing and conniving that would endanger party victory.

On a balmy evening in early May, Harry Truman was honor guest at a prebirthday dinner given for him at Oklahoma Senator Mike Monroney's home in Georgetown. The former President, soon to be seventy-five, enjoyed a comfortable evening in the company of old friends, among them Sam Rayburn. When the party ended, Rayburn offered Truman a ride downtown to the Mayflower Hotel. In the back seat of the Speaker's limousine the two men, not needing to waste words, ran down the list of potential Democratic nominees for the presidency. They quickly agreed that Kennedy at age forty-two was too young, in addition to having the handicap of being a Roman Catholic; but he would be the leading prospect for second place on any ticket. Nor would Humphrey do. He talked so much that the professionals regarded him as not enough of a heavyweight to be a real presidential possibility, and his candidacy would be an unbearable burden to the ticket in the South. Adlai Stevenson? No, the Democrats could not come before the voters with a two-time loser. Truman and Rayburn had a complete meeting of minds on that, since neither felt much personal regard for their party's former candidate.

That left Johnson and Symington. Either would be acceptable to the two party patriarchs, each naturally preferring the one from his home state. But if it came down to that, they would combine their power and prestige to promote the man who appeared to have the better chance to win at the national convention. The two old friends parted with the satisfied feeling that they had done a good night's work.

They had not consulted the men they so casually checked off their mental list. At least one of them, John F. Kennedy, had been sniffing down the presidential trail ever since the 1956 Democratic convention. He was traveling widely over

314

the country, usually with his attractive young wife Jacqueline, and where he could not go, his lieutenants went. Kennedy's strategy was to build up good will in the states which held presidential primaries. Only by entering and winning a number of primaries could he hope to convince the big-city political power brokers that he had the ability to get votes on a massive scale. They liked him well enough, but they still remembered Al Smith's defeat in 1928. It was an article of faith with them—political faith, not religious—that a Catholic could not be elected President of the United States. Only with the support of these urban bosses could Kennedy, or anyone else, hope to gain the nomination. His only possible course was to come out on top in some hard-fought primaries and force the bosses to accept him. Public-opinion polls showed that he would win against Nixon if they were the candidates in the general election. Paul Butler, abandoning the tradition that a National Chairman should remain neutral among seekers for the presidential nomination, told reporters, "I would be less than fair if I did not say Senator Kennedy has substantial support throughout the country—perhaps more than any other potential candidate."

In the early fall Kennedy's brother Robert resigned as counsel to the Senate Committee investigating improper labor-management activities to become campaign manager. Headquarters was established in a building near the Capitol. At an organization meeting at the family home in Hyannisport, the nation was divided into geographical areas for campaign purposes and a professional made responsible for each region. Sober, painstaking consideration began about which primaries the candidate should enter. John Kennedy gave no thought to the possibility that Truman and Rayburn could have been right in counting him out.

Humphrey was no less determined to try for the nomination. He too decided that his only choice was to go the primary route. He had some reputation in liberal circles, largely because of his long fight to make civil rights a reality, but otherwise he was hardly known at all except in his home state of Minnesota and in the Senate. If he could win a few primaries, thus gaining national attention, he might be able to go to the convention with some hope of success. He would have to be highly selective about the states he entered. Unlike Kennedy, he could not command the financial resources to go into all of them. Humphrey rightly regarded himself as an effective campaigner. He believed he could run up a good score by taking his candidacy to the people. To be sure, a similar plan had twice failed for Estes Kefauver, but perhaps it would work for him—especially if he could defeat the glamorous John Kennedy in one or two states. That would make the party leaders sit up and take notice, Humphrey reasoned. The Minnesota senator and his friends had always known that he would run for President some day. Nineteen-sixty seemed the right year.

Although Humphrey was not to announce his candidacy until December 30, a campaign committee was established months earlier under the cochairmanship of Minnesota's Governor Orville Freeman and Eugene McCarthy, the junior senator from the state. This triumvirate had revolutionized Minnesota politics and hoped to do the same on the national scene. Their roles were so nearly interchangeable that McCarthy was asked why he did not run for President instead of Humphrey. "That's not a bad idea," he replied, grinning. "I'm twice as liberal as Humphrey, twice as Catholic as Kennedy, and twice as smart as Symington." But in this year he was for Humphrey for President.

Stuart Symington, who had won a landslide victory for reelection to the Senate in 1958, was another prospective candidate who was not well known outside his home state and government circles in Washington. But he had no intention of entering state presidential primaries. His friend Clark Clifford, after making extensive surveys of sentiment throughout the country, advised that there was a strong possibility of a deadlock at next year's national convention. If a deadlock came—if Kennedy, Humphrey, Johnson, and perhaps Adlai Stevenson stymied one another—then Symington would be available as the perfect compromise choice. Having staying out of the primaries, he would not have offended any of the other candidates. With Truman in his corner to deal with the old party kingmakers, a deadlocked convention could be turned to Symington as one who always stayed with his party on important policy matters but never ran ahead of it. He was safe yet progressive, a man who had been successful in both business and politics, a handsome and personable figure who looked like a President.

Symington reached a definite decision in September that he would try for the nomination, although he made no formal announcement at the time. Clifford laid out travel plans that would take him around the country and make him better known to the state and city bosses.

So went the planning of three members of the United States Senate. Another senator widely regarded as a candidate for the Democratic nomination apparently had no plans at all. In the first month of the year Lyndon Johnson disavowed his candidacy, saying, "I don't have the disposition, the training or the temperament for the presidency." Speaking before a joint session of the Texas legislature in the spring, he declared, "I have no aspirations, no intentions, no ambitions for office other than that I hold." He would not even confide to close friends that he might become a candidate for the nomination. Jim Rowe urged him to run, and when he would not declare himself, went over to line up with Humphrey. Senatorial friends argued that he should announce, stay out of the primaries while letting Kennedy and Humphrey destroy each other in those sanguinary encounters, and quietly build up his strength in the South and West. Johnson listened, but he would not commit himself.

Yet that same legislature before which he had denied ambition for higher office passed a law allowing a person to be a candidate in Texas for both statewide office and the presidency or vice-presidency in the general election. It also enacted a measure moving the Texas Democratic primary from July to May, enabling Johnson to secure the Senate nomination before the Democratic National Convention. State Senator Dorsey Hardeman, who sponsored this legislation, remarked that it "might be referred to as the Lyndon Johnson for President bill."

Rayburn was determined that his fellow Texan should be a candidate. In October he held a press conference in Dallas and announced that he and Governor Price Daniel as co-chairmen had formed a Johnson for President Committee and would open headquarters in Austin, the state capital. Rayburn stressed that the committee was unofficial. No blessing came from Johnson. But he was moving around the country, working on his speaking style and trying to get rid of the southern label. After Congress adjourned he had a heavy speaking schedule, mostly in Texas to get county organizations under assured control. He also went into some other states, speaking not of the coming presidential election year but of the Democratic Senate's vast accomplishments under his leadership. For example, in a speech in Harrisburg, Pennsylvania, he boasted: "Hawaiian statehood had been on the calendar for forty years—and a Democratic Senate passed it in four hours. Limiting debate had been on the calendar for nearly thirty years—and a Democratic Senate acted in three days. And it was a Democratic Senate that gave the nation the first civil-rights bill in eighty-two years."

One of his out-of-state appearances near the end of the

year was in Des Moines. Asked once more at a press conference about the presidential candidacy, Johnson said, "I am not a candidate and I do not intend to be." Then he added coyly, "I do not say that I would not serve my country if the convention should do the unusual and select someone who isn't a candidate."

Adlai Stevenson, spending most of his time with his law practice in Chicago and at his home in Libertyville, said he would not endorse anyone for the Democratic nomination, at least not until after the primaries were over. To friends who visited him he seemed wistfully receptive to the idea that he should be the nominee, but he said he would make no effort in that direction.

Among the Republicans, Nixon waited cautiously as New York Governor Nelson A. Rockefeller set up an elaborate political office in New York City with a big staff and embarked on travels throughout a number of states in an effort to gain support for the presidential nomination. But the governor learned that both party leaders and the big businessmen who would, as usual, finance the Republican campaign favored Nixon. The day before Christmas he issued a statement that "the great majority of those who control the Republican convention stand opposed to any contest for the nomination." He said that, if he entered state primaries in an intensive drive on his own behalf, he would not be able to meet his obligations as governor. So, declared Rockefeller, "I am not, and shall not be, a candidate for the nomination for the presidency. This decision is definite and final."

That was what the governor of New York said in December 1959.

1960

JOHN F. KENNEDY'S YEAR

Congress duly assembled in January, the President soon afterward submitted his State of the Union message, statements were issued, speeches made. These customary events and nonevents created a comforting atmosphere of business as usual in governmental circles. It was an illusory atmosphere.

Certainly the caucus of Senate Democrats at the beginning of the session was not in the pattern that had been accepted since Johnson rose to the leadership. Four liberal senators, Douglas, Proxmire, Clark and McNamara, met beforehand and agreed among themselves to offer a resolution deploring the LBJ custom of calling a perfunctory caucus once each year; they would demand regular and frequent party conferences. Johnson, forewarned of the plan, reacted quickly when Clark placed the resolution before the caucus. Of course, said the majority leader, speaking softly, the senators could have as many caucuses as they wanted. He added, however, that in his experience the main effect of such meetings was to give rise to party disputes. Several other senators, including Humphrey (who carefully noted that he was not among those who were critical of the majority leader), spoke in favor of Clark's resolution. Finally Johnson said he would call conferences when asked to do so, and the resolution was withdrawn. But Gore, who had remained silent during the discussion, now proceeded to prove that Johnson was right about party conferences causing party disputes. He offered a motion to fill vacancies on the nine-man Policy Committee by senatorial election instead of by Johnson appointment. This proposal was directed straight at the heart of the majority leader's strength. He was able to have it shunted aside, but he was not happy that it had been made.

On the other side of the Capitol, Rayburn also had his troubles. A House group of approximately one hundred liberal Democrats got together and drew up a legislative program, then sent Chet Holifield of California, Lee Metcalf of Montana, and Frank Thompson of New Jersey to present it to the Speaker. Holifield, acting as spokesman, told Rayburn, "We want school legislation, housing, civil rights, and we don't care if it's vetoed or not." Rayburn, like Johnson, kept his temper and did not argue. "I don't like splinter groups very much," he said with gentle gravity. The dissenters left the Speaker's office without any feeling that their mission had been successful.

The two leaders consulted together and devised a strategy calculated to choke the liberals into ineffectualness with their own demands. They came up with a legislative program that included a new civil-rights measure, another housing bill, medical care for elderly persons, federal aid to education, and an increase in the minimum-wage bill. All this was simply too much to be swallowed in a political year.

The civil-rights bill, made the first order of business in the Senate, touched off a filibuster by southerners which, this time, Johnson could neither prevent nor break. Under the sagacious leadership of Dick Russell, it dragged on for fifty-three days. Eventually an agreement was reached to delete the really significant sections of the bill, those dealing with desegregation of schools and employment, and the southerners desisted.

By this time the session was more than half over. Little more was accomplished than passage of regular appropriations measures, with the Republicans supporting Eisenhower's in-the-black budget and the Democratic leadership pressing vainly for welfare legislation.

Politicians generally were more interested in what was happening outside Washington, in the states where presidential primaries were held, than they were in the standoff in Congress.

John F. Kennedy, to the surprise of no one, formally announced at a news conference in the Senate Caucus Room the day after New Year's that he was a candidate for the Democratic nomination for President. He challenged others seeking the nomination to enter state primaries. He said he would not accept the vice-presidential nomination under any conditions. Thereafter Kennedy was little seen in the Senate. He missed 80 per cent of the roll-call votes during the session.

Humphrey was trying to raise campaign funds and to decide which primaries he should enter.

Early in the spring Symington telephoned Truman to say that his waiting game was not working out as he had planned. Too many delegates were becoming committed to others. If he was to have a chance, he told Truman, he would have to announce his candidacy now and try to become the second choice of enough delegates to put him over after Kennedy and Humphrey or Kennedy and Johnson deadlocked the July convention. Truman agreed with the new plan and Symington went to the Caucus Room to make his own announcement. He said he would not go into the primaries; they were meaningless, since only four states—Wisconsin, West Virginia, Maryland and Oregon—had contested elections.

Johnson would not say he was a candidate. But his friends were trying—without notable success—to line up delegate support for him in the West and Midwest. Seventy-five Texans attended the Western States Democratic Conference in February, greeting all comers with hearty "Howdys," buying drinks for everybody in sight, and talking of Johnson as "that great westerner." This characterization was not universally accepted. Paul Ziffern, California national committeeman and one of the most influential of western Democrats, said, "I consider him definitely to be a member of the southern bloc, where Texas is."

Johnson felt no certainty that any of this effort was worthwhile. At times he upbraided Rayburn and others for even trying to advance his candidacy. Tied down by the Senate filibuster, trying to hold onto his base of southern support, counting the convention votes he would need from other sections to come close to the nomination, he expressed profane doubts that a Texan could be nominated. Yet by June he was privately telling political figures that he "damned sure" was a candidate.

* * *

In April, Kennedy and Humphrey came face to face in Wisconsin, the state where the presidential primary was invented in 1903.

Their campaigns were in sharp contrast, less on issues than on methods and organization. Both men pushed their liberal views. Both deplored the injection of the religious issue into the race. There the similarities stopped.

Kennedy had his private plane for getting around the state. Humphrey caught commercial flights from drafty airports. Kennedy's tightly knit organization functioned with

323

hardly a hitch. His younger brothers, Robert and Edward, headed a team of efficient and single-minded Kennedy men: Ted Sorenson, on the senator's staff since 1953, speech writer and researcher; Lawrence F. O'Brien, advertising and public-relations man from Massachusetts, top organizer; Kenneth O'Donnell, specialist in precinct organization; Pierre Salinger, press secretary. All had youthful vigor. All were dedicated to the proposition that John F. Kennedy must become President of the United States. Other members of the candidate's family in addition to his brothers campaigned in Wisconsin. His seventy-year-old mother and a bevy of daughters were hostesses at innumerable coffee sessions, smiling with the white teeth of the rich and overpowering Wisconsin *hausfraus*. Humphrey had members of his family on hand too, but there were not nearly so many. His wife Muriel passed out copies of her recipe for beef soup, and the Humphrey daughter and two sons went up and down the main streets of the state distributing buttons and campaign literature. Officeholders from Minnesota came over the state line to campaign when they could leave their duties, which was not as often as Humphrey could have wished. The candidates themselves kept up dawn-to-midnight handshaking and speaking tours. But Kennedy had campaign headquarters offices in eight of the state's ten congressional districts; Humphrey was able to set up headquarters only in the cities of Milwaukee and Madison.

It early became apparent to the experts that this was an uneven contest. Paul Butler said publicly that Kennedy would win the Wisconsin primary and the nomination in July, perhaps on the first ballot. Rayburn castigated the National Chairman for "making himself a partisan, not only for a candidate but also against other candidates." Humphrey and some other Democrats demanded that Butler resign, but he paid no attention. Long before primary day the pollsters were predicting a sweep for Kennedy. Some commentators thought he would carry all ten congressional districts. The returns were not that one-sided. When the votes were counted, Kennedy had 56 per cent of the total, including the Catholic bloc vote that was solidly for him. The outcome held deep significance for both candidates. If Humphrey could not prevail in Wisconsin, next door to his home territory, after a strenuous and not badly financed campaign, the outlook for him was not bright in other states farther removed from his base. On the other hand, Kennedy's victory was not sensational enough to send the big-city bosses rushing to the long-distance telephone and pledging him their support at the national convention.

It all came down to the fact that Humphrey had lost but Kennedy had not won. At the same time, the results gave the Massachusetts senator a new card to play in his game with the predominantly Catholic political kingmakers in the big cities. His brothers and other lieutenants could point to the Catholic turnout for Kennedy in Wisconsin and hint with whatever subtlety they chose to exercise that, if he was not nominated in July, the great Catholic vote over the country would be alienated from the Democratic party.

Nevertheless, Kennedy realized with dismay that he had to follow the rugged primary road all the way. He and Humphrey, the one almost sullenly disappointed in numerical victory, the other euphoric over what he quickly convinced himself was a moral victory, set their sights on the West Virginia primary coming up in the following month.

The Kennedy people were deeply worried about this state. The news of the Catholic bloc vote for Kennedy in Wisconsin had been widely headlined, awakening many voters for the first time to the fact that he *was* a Catholic. Ninety-five. per cent of the people in West Virginia were Protestant—and most of them militant in their preaching, if not always in their practice, of the fundamentalist Protestant faith. The Kennedy leaders were angry with Humphrey for not withdrawing after Wisconsin. They felt, truly felt, that he had no right to keep bothering them—had no right, this talkative common man from Minnesota, to run against John Fitzgerald Kennedy. He no longer had a chance to win the nomination; he could at most only keep Kennedy from winning it. He was a spoiler.

The end result was one of the most bitterly fought political campaigns the highly political-minded state of West Virginia had ever known.

Kennedy was not a young knight dreaming of a future Camelot where he would be king. He was a tough, able, well-financed and somewhat ruthless politician who was determined to be President of the United States and therefore master of those other politicians from whom in this year he had to curry favor. He was convinced that "they" were ganging up on him, all those ambitious men who wanted to "stop Kennedy." He seethed with rage when West Virginia's Senator Robert C. Byrd, known as a strong supporter of Johnson for the nomination, advised his constituents, "If you are for Adlai Stevenson, Senator Stuart Symington, Senator Johnson or John Doe, this primary may be your last chance." And he added, "I'm voting for Humphrey." Johnson's man Walter Jenkins was constantly on the phone to urge key political figures to help Humphrey in every way they could. "If they want to stop me, why don't they run themselves?" Kennedy demanded. He struck out at Humphrey as the "hatchet man" who could not win the nomination himself but was being "used" by Johnson and Symington. "Poor little Jack," retorted Humphrey. "I wish he would grow up and stop acting like a boy. What does he want, all the votes?"

That, or as near as he could come to it, was exactly what Kennedy did want.

The Kennedyites had been organizing for this campaign since early in 1959. They knew the territory. In a rural state like West Virginia, the county sheriff is usually the local political panjandrum. Kennedy's men, scurrying purposefully around the poverty-stricken state with well-filled wallets, hired many a county sheriff to "take care" of things for their candidate. Volunteers were organized to hand out Kennedy literature from door to door. An extensive network of county campaign chairmen received instructions for setting up telephone committees, arranging receptions for the candidate, making plans for transporting voters to the polls on election day—all the thousand and one details that go into a political campaign where victory is the sole objective and all considerations of expense, work, lack of sleep, hurt feelings and everything else go by the board. The candidate himself was limited in the time he could spend in West Virginia, being involved in primaries in other states, but his family and campaign leaders were there all the time and working all the time.

The two most significant facts about West Virginia were its poverty and its revival-meeting Protestantism. Newsmen coming in to cover the campaign quipped that the Kennedy expenditures were going a way toward relieving the poverty. In fact, with 15 per cent of its working force unemployed and with many of its people existing under marginal conditions, West Virginia presented a collective face that startled and appalled Kennedy, the man born to wealth and wholly unfamiliar with this kind of thing. His shock was so real that it communciated itself to his audiences at rallies and on television, and the people reacted favorably to his horror that such things could be. Both he and Humphrey in their speeches harked back to Franklin D. Roosevelt and his efforts to improve the lot of the poor. Each vowed that he would do no less. But Humphrey, no stranger to poverty, had always talked that way, and ironically his empathy now communicated itself less forcibly than Kennedy's outrage. So, on balance, Kennedy had the better of the poverty issue, especially after he had brought in Franklin D. Roosevelt, Jr., looking and sounding like his father, to campaign for him.

As for the religious question, Kennedy decided he had no real choice but to meet it squarely. He did this by setting out to convince the people of West Virginia that the only way they could prove they were not bigots was to vote for him. "I refuse to believe," he told them, "that I was denied the right to be President the day I was baptized." He and his workers made much of the fact that no religious test had been applied to him when he joined the Navy for service in World War II—and had he not, the workers inquired, emerged from the war a genuine hero? "If there is bigotry in this country," Kennedy said with deep solemnity, "then so be it—there is bigotry. If that bigotry is too great to permit the fair consideration of a Catholic who has made clear his complete dedication to separation of church and state, then we ought to know. But," he bore down hard, "I do not believe that this is the case." This was a potent approach to the West Virginians, who had not often, if ever, heard appeals to their religious tolerance. They had to show this well-spoken man from the East who was so worried about them that they were not, they certainly were not, bigots. They could do it only by going to the polls on election day and voting for him.

Humphrey struggled and floundered against this campaign, well organized, more than amply financed, capable of blinding people with flashing illogic. He was still in debt for his Wisconsin effort. He had increasing trouble in raising campaign funds, with Kennedy representatives using blandishments and threats to cut off sources on which he had depended. He traveled about the state in a lumbering bus, exhausted, always short on sleep, alternating between ebullience and depression, knowing that, even if he won this primary, he would be as far as ever from winning the nomination. But he persisted right up through election day.

That night, as the returns came in, he had to stop. The game was over for him. Kennedy swept the state, getting 60 per cent of the vote. Miners in the most deeply depressed areas voted for him. The Protestant hillbillies gave satisfactory evidence that nobody could call them bigot. Negroes comprised only 4 per cent of West Virginia's population, but such as there were, they mostly supported Kennedy. His total vote showed how deeply the handsome candidate had enthralled the women.

Humphrey appeared on television after midnight to say, barely able to control his voice, "I am no longer a candidate for the Democratic presidential nomination."

Kennedy went on to win other primaries, seven in all, including one in Oregon where he gave favorite-son Wayne Morse the beating of his political life. But the combined strength of these states at the national convention would not be nearly enough for victory, not even when added to the delegates his lieutenants had nailed down in other states. Most of the big bosses still remained silent. They had not failed, however, to note that the senator from Massachusetts had proved he could move among the voters and win against odds.

Kennedy's position was strong, but he could not look ahead to the Democratic convention with any feeling of complacency. Unless he received a majority on the first ballot, he would be in trouble. Many state delegations listed for him were committed only for that ballot. He and his organization remained tightly alert and incessantly active.

A Johnson for President headquarters of a sort was opened in Washington's Ambassador Hotel that spring under the general direction of John Connally and another Texan, Marvin Watson, a rising young business executive who knew his way around the political scene—in his home state. Old New Dealers Oscar Chapman, Truman's last Secretary of the Interior, and India Edwards, former vice-chairman of the Democratic National Committee, were named cochairmen of the Citizens for Johnson Committee. They talked with the press and telephoned associates from out of the past. After Humphrey was out of the picture, Jim Rowe returned to the Johnson fold. Activity was not frenzied at the Washington headquarters. The senator himself never set foot in the place or openly acknowledged its existence.

It was not until July 5, after Congress had recessed at his instigation to meet again after the two national political conventions, that the Senate majority leader announced his candidacy. At what was billed as a press conference, although the audience also included several hundred Texans living in Washington, the senator rebuked Democrats who were talking about a first-ballot nomination at Los Angeles. It was not the Democratic way, he said, for the nomination to be regarded as sewed up for anyone before the delegates voted. He hit at Kennedy, not mentioning his name, by observing pointedly that his own duties in the Senate had made it impossible for him to spend the last six months campaigning around the country. Privately he was more explicit: "Jack was out kissing babies while I was passing bills."

Johnson took some comfort from a poll recently conducted among fifty of Washington's leading newspaper correspondents. Forty-one of them voted him the ablest Democrat in the Senate. But there was no comfort to be derived from a charge by his old antagonist, Americans for Democratic Action, that "Senator Johnson, by his record in the field of civil rights and labor legislation, by his faithful representation of monopoly interests in oil and gas and other fields, has become a symbol of compromise and political opportunism, and therefore has no fair claim to be the standard bearer of a liberal Democratic party." Regardless of the justice or injustice of this summation, Johnson realized it would do him no good in the areas where he must gain support if he was to succeed in preventing a first-ballot victory for Kennedy at the convention.

His managers were claiming 502 votes for him on that first ballot. Johnson knew the figure was unrealistic, but he set out for Los Angeles hopeful that he would have sufficient support to keep his name before the convention long enough for the Kennedy strength to be eroded.

Stuart Symington had been traveling during the year on a not very rigorous schedule to see businessmen and some politicians and press his suitability for the nomination. He took special pains to explain that he was not a "one-track-mind candidate," but was concerned with "economic, social, moral and spiritual might" as well as with problems of U.S. military weakness. Clark Clifford, his manager, had been approached by Kennedy with the suggestion that a Kennedy-Symington ticket would hold great appeal both at the convention and later at the polls. Symington would not have minded being vice-president, but he was not ready to trade. His hope for the presidential nomination he recognized to be slim, still resting on the possibility of a deadlocked convention; but the hope remained.

The three men—Kennedy, Johnson, Symington—glanced uneasily from time to time toward Libertyville, Illinois, where Adlai Stevenson was saying over and over that he would not seek the nomination again nor would he refuse to serve if his party called him. He too would be in Los Angeles in July.

* * *

The efforts to stop Kennedy in Los Angeles were fruitless. Johnson restlessly roamed the sprawling city to appear before delegations already committed to the Massachusetts senator. (To the Pennsylvania delegation he related a story of a politician who had gained a deserved reputation as a ladies' man in Washington. Back home for a visit, he was told by local political bosses that he must get married in order to stop the gossip about his carryings-on. "Okay, boys," he agreed. "I'm an organization man. Have you got the girl picked out?" David Lawrence, the potent head of the delegation, almost fell out of his chair laughing—but he was for Kennedy.) Johnson challenged Kennedy to a "debate" before the Texas and Massachusetts delegations, which provided an entertaining television show but changed no votes. (When Jake Jacobsen, a Johnson campaign aide, passed glasses of water along to the men on the platform, Robert Kennedy unsmilingly tasted the water before handing a glass on to his brother. He found it safe.) Texas and southern delegates, talking mostly to one another, excitedly asked if their man could conscientiously run on the strong civil-rights plank that had been placed in the platform. Watching convention proceedings on television on nominating day, Wednesday, Johnson commented, "I don't see how we can beat him."

On that same day a well-organized effort by hopeful Stevenson backers packed the galleries of the convention hall with thousands of raucous, wild-eyed boosters (hired? who could tell?) of the man from Illinois. When Stevenson was placed in nomination by Senator Eugene McCarthy, in an address that was the oratorical triumph of the entire week, these spectators erupted into an out-of-control demonstration designed to stampede the convention. It did not succeed.

The eternal cry at any national political convention is "I don't know what's going on!" This perplexed and often angry confession of ignorance comes from delegates, even from delegation leaders, from honest newspaper people, and not infrequently from men who are seeking the presidential nomination. It did not come at this convention from Kennedy or those close to him. *They* knew what was going on. Jake Arvey, the old-time Chicago political boss, spoke the truth when he said, "Kennedy's got this country laid out like one big switchboard." In Los Angeles the candidate toured the city in a white Cadillac, talking with calm confidence before gatherings of state delegations and fitting each speech to their mood and home state. The members of his dedicated crew were in constant touch with all delegations. Their communications system was superb. Their confidence was unshakable. They left nothing to chance. They worked right up to the moment the balloting started.

That moment came late Wednesday night.

After all the days and sleepless nights of struggle and unceasing rumor—Governor Pat Brown had lost control of his big California delegation. . . . Stevenson himself would place Kennedy in nomination; no, he would not. . . . Governor Robert Meyner, New Jersey's favorite son, refused to release his delegation because most of the delegates were for Kennedy and he favored Johnson. . . . Kennedy would be twenty votes short of victory on the first ballot. . . . Kennedy would win on the first ballot because he had captured delegates in the Rocky Mountain states that Johnson thought were his—after all the demonstrations for favorite sons and serious candidates had died down and the final hurrah shouted, John F. Kennedy was nominated on the first and only ballot. He received 806 delegate votes. His jet-propelled bandwagon had brought him home.

That night the presidential nominee gave hard thought to the question of who would be his running mate.

The problem had its delicate aspects. The vice-presidential nomination had been dangled before a number of influential state politicians to get their support at the convention. Governor Orville Freeman, who had left Humphrey before Los Angeles and made the major nominating speech for Kennedy, considered himself and was considered by others a leading prospect. Two other governors, Herschel Loveless of Iowa and George Docking of Kansas, thought that Robert Kennedy had encouraged them to believe they would be chosen. Two senators, Henry M. Jackson of Washington and Gore of Tennessee, were optimistic. And other names, including Symington and Humphrey, were bandied back and forth among the weary delegates and news correspondents as they waited for the nominee to make up his mind or, if he had already made it up, to announce his decision.

One politician at the convention who had not been promised the vice-presidential nomination, by implication or otherwise, was Lyndon Johnson. There was no evidence that he would be the least bit interested in second place.

On the Sunday preceding Kennedy's nomination the candidate casually wondered aloud to Philip Graham, publisher of the Washington *Post* and a friend of both men, if Johnson would take the vice-presidential place if it were offered to him. Graham passed the query on to Johnson, as he felt he was meant to do, and the Texan replied with a single barnyard word.

One of Johnson's rich Texans who was in attendance at the convention decided early that his man would not be chosen and started talking him up for vice-president. Sargent Shriver, Kennedy's brother-in-law, got wind of this activity. On Tuesday morning he came unannounced to the Johnson supporter's suite in the Biltmore Hotel just as the man was composing a memorandum to Johnson urging that if he was unsuccessful in winning the top spot he consider taking the vice-presidential nomination. After Shriver's visit, he added a postscript. Shriver had asked the Texan if he thought there was any real possibility that Johnson would accept it in case Kennedy was nominated. The Texas supporter simply passed on the question.

This memorandum was delivered to Johnson and presumably read by him. On Tuesday afternoon Bobby Baker, deeply involved in Johnson's convention activities, came to an employee of the Texas supporter and told him he had heard of the efforts to have Johnson considered for the vice-presidential nomination. "I want you to stop," Baker said peremptorily. "We will not trade a vote for a gavel." That statement had the authentic Johnson ring. It was hardly the sentiment of a man prepared to "grab" for the nomination, as Johnson later was charged with doing.

On Wednesday night, the moment after Kennedy's nomination became certain, Johnson turned to his wife, with whom he was watching the convention on television, and said, "That's that. Tomorrow we can take the girls and do something we want to do—go to Disneyland, maybe."

Before he went to bed he received a telephone call from Rayburn. The Speaker said he thought Kennedy would offer the vice-presidential nomination and expressed the strong hope that under no circumstances would Johnson take it. The exhausted senator replied that he did not think he would get the offer. If he did, he promised, he would do nothing about it until he had talked with the Speaker.

Kennedy decided that night he wanted Johnson as his running mate if he could get him. It was his own decision, backed up strongly by Governor Lawrence, Mayor Richard J. Daley of Chicago, and his father, Joe Kennedy. Other advisers, including his brother Robert, preferred someone else, some of them almost *anyone* else, but they naturally were prepared to go along with the top man's wishes.

Awakened the next morning about eight o'clock by his wife with word that Kennedy was on the phone asking for him, Johnson took the call and listened as the nominee said he wanted to see him and would come up shortly. At the end of the brief conversation, Johnson immediately called Rayburn. The older man repeated that he thought his friend would be making a mistake if he accepted. Johnson said he thought that Kennedy probably wanted only to heal the wounds of the campaign and to discuss vice-presidential possibilities but not on the basis of his being one.

Kennedy did not merely offer the nomination, he strongly urged it. Johnson expressed appreciation but said, "I'd rather stay on as majority leader." Kennedy gave him a straight look. "How do you know you'll *be* majority leader?" he asked. Not mentioned by either man was the fact that during the year Kennedy had indicated to liberal senators that, if he was elected President, he would throw the weight of his influence against Johnson's retention in the floor leadership.

Johnson said his wife was against the proposition. Speaker Rayburn was against it. Governor Price Daniel and any number of other southern governors and southern senators would be certain to oppose his taking the nomination. Still, he said, he would think it over. Kennedy left it at that, saying he would talk to both Rayburn and Daniel and would call Johnson in the afternoon.

Kennedy appealed to Rayburn on the basis of party loyalty, touching the old warhorse in his most vulnerable spot. With Johnson on the ticket, said the presidential nominee, the Democrats could carry Texas and all or most of the South. Carrying Texas with its twenty-four of the necessary 269 electoral votes was an absolute must, and only Johnson could swing it in view of the strong anti-Catholic sentiment among the Southern Baptists of that state. Rayburn was persuaded. He shifted his position completely and now urged Johnson to take the nomination.

Other advisers were still opposed. They came in a steady stream to Johnson's suite to give all the reasons why he should refuse: his acceptance would be a betrayal of his state and his region, he would give up a position of great power in the

Senate, the voters would turn against him. At one point Bob Kerr, the big Oklahoma senator, became so angry at Bobby Baker, who was now among those saying Johnson must accept, that he slapped the young man in the face. But then Rayburn talked to Kerr, and the Oklahoman also changed his mind. Others did not, but nevertheless when Kennedy called again, Johnson said he was ready to go on the ticket.

Meanwhile, Kennedy had been running into difficulties of his own. The urban political moguls approved the ticket he proposed, but labor leaders were far from enthusiastic. Governor Mennen Williams of Michigan, an early supporter of Kennedy for the presidential nomination, was so incensed that he told Robert Kennedy he was prepared to lead a floor fight against Johnson.

The floor fight never materialized. The threat was cut off when by prearrangement Representative John McCormack of Massachusetts made a motion, after the roll call of the states had started, that Johnson be nominated by acclamation. Governor LeRoy Collins of Florida, the convention chairman, ended the roll call and asked for the "ayes" and "nays." The "ayes" had it, he announced, despite outraged cries from the Michigan delegation and the galleries. The Kennedy-Johnson ticket of 1960 was a reality.

Late that afternoon a Johnson staff man came upon Senator Mike Mansfield of Montana, assistant floor leader. "Well, Senator," he said cheerfully, "I guess you're going to be the majority leader." The senator, a quiet and studious former professor of history and political science at Montana State University, pulled hard on an unlighted pipe. "I don't *want* to be majority leader," he said mournfully.

But that would be his problem. Kennedy and Johnson faced problems of their own, one of which was the return of Congress to Washington in August. The postconventions session no longer seemed as good an idea to the majority leader as it had earlier, but there it was—or would be soon enough.

After that, the campaign.

* * *

During the early months of the year Nixon was in the enviable position of being able, in effect, to run for the presidency from the White House. Rockefeller having announced that he would not seek the nomination, it appeared to be in the vice-president's lap. As a part of the administration, he had Eisenhower's prestige behind him. The Republican Old Guard thought highly of him. He had a bridge to the younger "new Republicans" in a Committee on Program and Progress named by the President in 1959 to study the philosophy of Republicanism. Eisenhower made Nixon responsible for the work of the committee. The vice-president named to head the group a progressive Republican businessman, Charles E. Percy, the forty-year-old boy-wonder president of Bell & Howell, a Chicago camera-manufacturing concern. Under Percy's competent leadership, the committee was busily developing a program and platform for the Republican presidential campaign. Logically, Percy would serve as chairman of the Platform Committee at the party's Chicago convention late in July.

While enjoying such advantages as these, Nixon also found his inside position placed certain limits on his freedom to speak and act. He had no choice but to support in public the administration's policies—on foreign affairs, on defense preparedness, on civil rights. Whatever reservations he might have had about some aspects of these policies could hardly be voiced. Any open criticism from him would arouse the instant ire of Eisenhower, whose good will and unqualified support Nixon must have in the coming campaign.

These limitations were not unbearable so long as matters

affecting the administration were going well. In the spring, however, they started going not at all well.

After Khrushchev's visit to the United States the year before, there had been some lessening of tension in relations with the Soviet Union. Plans were made for a summit conference of the chiefs of state of the great powers in Paris in mid-May to discuss the armaments race and the vexatious problem of Berlin. The Cold War appeared to be thawing.

Then, on May 1, Russian fighting planes shot down an American spy plane flying at a great height 1,300 miles inside Russia. U.S. denials that the plane was on a spy mission were exposed as lies, for the pilot and much of his equipment were captured by the Russians and he confessed that his assignment was to photograph Russian territory. Eisenhower stubbornly went to Paris, hoping that the summit conference could be salvaged. But Khrushchev, after issuing a statement blasting the United States, boycotted the meeting.

The Communists won another propaganda victory in Japan. Eisenhower planned to go there on a good-will mission, but his advance party, which included Jim Hagerty, was greeted by mobs violently protesting the President's visit. Eisenhower said he would go anyway unless the Japanese government withdrew its invitation. Eventually the government felt it expedient to do so, with a consequent great loss of face by the American President.

Other events in various parts of the world further tarnished the nation's foreign policy. The Castro regime in Cuba, so hastily reorganized by the U.S. government, expropriated American business holdings. In Korea, violent student riots caused the overthrow of the government of Syngman Rhee, the American-backed leader. Other riots in Turkey threatened the existence of a government friendly to the United States.

All these developments vitally affected the American political scene, casting serious doubts on the effectiveness of the Eisenhower administration's foreign policy.

Nixon was worried. The Republican position was being hurt, which meant that he was being hurt.

Once the summit conference had collapsed, unlike Nixon, Nelson Rockefeller was under no inhibitions, for his criticism could no longer be viewed as undercutting the President on the eve of an important international meeting. All through the spring, while occupying himself with his duties as governor, Rockefeller was privately confiding to friends his grave anxiety about the government's direction, or as it appeared to him lack of direction, in foreign policy and national defense. Now, with the position of the United States in the world steadily going downhill, he decided that he would no longer remain silent privately or publicly.

The first indication that he was prepared to go into action and take up where he had left off at the end of 1959 came when New York's Republican chairman, Judson Morhouse, told the press the governor might respond to a draft for the presidential nomination. Rockefeller was not long in making it clear that he was completely available. At a press conference in New York City, he crisply accused Nixon of refusal to state his position on national issues. "I am deeply convinced, and deeply concerned," he said, "that those now assuming control of the Republican party have failed to make clear where this party is heading and where it proposes to lead the nation. I find it unreasonable in these times that the leading Republican candidate for the presidential nomination has firmly insisted upon making known his program and his policies not before but only after nomination by his party."

Having leveled down on the vice-president, Rockefeller then proceeded to offer his own program. It borrowed heavily from Democratic programs, for which the New Yorker offered no apology, dwelling on foreign policy, national defense, civil rights, arms control and disarmament, promotion of Latin-American unity, economic growth, education, government reorganization, and health care for the elderly. Rockefeller revealed his intention of taking the fight for his proposals to the convention floor if necessary. If he could not get the nomination, which to him and his advisers seemed unlikely, he was determined at the least to influence the Republican platform.

The Old Guard was equally determined that he should not. The Republican National Committee passed a resolution unanimously praising Eisenhower's policies and Nixon.

The vice-president, reacting instantly to what he recognized as a dangerous threat to his well-laid plans to get the presidential nomination in an atmosphere of amity, suggested a televised debate on the issues between him and the New York governor. Rockefeller refused. He said he had put forward his own program and now Nixon should offer his.

In the weeks that followed, through June and the first half of July, Rockefeller took to radio and television and made numerous personal appearances in his effort to light a fire among Republicans. His statements, amounting to a repudiation of the Eisenhower administration, drew response from many young people who were, or wanted to be, Republicans but were dismayed by the blandness and drift of the government in recent years. A national Draft Rockefeller headquarters was established in San Francisco, then transferred to Chicago shortly before the Republican convention opened the last week in July. National newspaper advertisements and television spots urged Republicans over the nation to appeal to their convention delegations to turn their support to the Rockefeller program and to Rockefeller himself. A million or more letters and telegrams descended on the delegates.

The Republican platform was being drafted in Chicago. In the governor's office in Albany, Rockefeller inspected the first draft and commented that it was "lacking in strength and specifics." His followers promised a fight at the convention to remedy the deficiencies.

In Washington, Richard M. Nixon followed these developments in a spirit of cool pragmatism. He arranged to go to New York City on the Friday night before the convention opened on Monday for a full-dress discussion with Rockefeller on the basis that no deep divisiveness of opinion existed between them on the principal issues.

At their meeting Nixon first offered, as he had offered before, the vice-presidential nomination. Rockefeller did not want it. By now he realized the hope of his dedicated followers that the convention could be blitzkrieged into nominating him for President was not likely to be realized. He gave his full attention to the platform, sensing that Nixon would concede much to avoid a damaging confrontation at the convention.

The two men spent much of the night together, talking at times by telephone to Percy and members of the Rockefeller staff in Chicago. They reached agreement on platform planks calling for stronger defense measures, government reorganization, and the use of government policies to stimulate economic growth. On civil rights, they agreed on language demanding aggressive action to eliminate segregation or discrimination in all areas of national life, a promise which went far toward matching the language of the Democratic civil-rights platform.

The news of their agreement broke in Chicago the next morning to considerable hubbub. Conservative Republicans denounced the proposals as "the Compact of Fifth Avenue," that street being the location of Rockefeller's apartment where the meeting was held. The Chicago *Tribune* ran a headline, "GRANT SURRENDERS TO LEE." Barry Goldwater, hitting hard at what he called "a surrender," told his Arizona delegation, "Governor Rockefeller is out to destroy the Republican party." Thad Hutcheson, chairman of the Texas delegation, predictably talked of "a damned sellout." Dwight Eisenhower, vacationing at Newport, received the implied criticism of his national defense policies with decided coolness; he said he had not been consulted about the platform changes.

But Senator John Sherman Cooper, who was serving as chairman of a platform subcommittee, said the meeting of minds between Nixon and Rockefeller was "the best thing that could have happened to the Republican party."

Parts of the platform already released to the press had to be recalled for revision. An effort at rebellion in the full 103-member Platform Committee had to be put down. Compromises had to be reached on some proposals in order to soothe Eisenhower. In the main, however, the agreement between Nixon and Rockefeller stood and the New York governor no longer talked of a floor fight.

Some of the die-hards stood pat. Before the end of the convention they had crowned Goldwater king of the nation's conservatives and even talked wildly of making him the nominee. The Arizona senator appealed to them to put such an idea out of their minds for this year, saying he would be unable to get enough votes in the convention to make the conservative cause look good. Nevertheless, Arizona's Governor Paul Fannin nominated him. When Goldwater rose to withdraw his name, he did not play down his differences and those of his adherents with the views of those Republicans who had been brought into the Nixon-Rockefeller alliance. "If we want to take the party back," he admonished sternly, "let's get to work."

Goldwater received ten votes on a final roll call. Nixon got the rest. His choice, Henry Cabot Lodge, became the Republican nominee for vice-president.

343

"Whatever the political consequences," said Nixon in his acceptance speech, "we are not going to try to outpromise our opponents in this campaign."

He had watched Kennedy as the Democratic candidate appeared on television at the conclusion of the Los Angeles convention and felt reasonably confident that he could beat him.

* * *

Three factors exerted a decisive influence on the 1960 presidential campaign. If any one of them had been lacking, the outcome would almost certainly have been different.

The first was the religious issue and the manner in which Kennedy dealt with it.

The candidate was off on the campaign trail as soon as the dreary, futile postconvention session of Congress ended, and almost at once he became painfully aware that he had not succeeded in killing the religious issue once and for all by his victory in West Virginia. Honest fear of the unknown mysteries of Roman Catholicism was endemic among millions of American Protestants. This fear was played upon by bigots and men with their own ends to serve, particularly radio evangelists of a certain type. In midwestern farm areas and throughout the southern Bible Belt, these men cried in the press and on the air waves that all religious liberty would go down the drain if a Catholic should be installed in the White House.

Kennedy decided early that he would have to face the issue candidly and openly. The questions were how and when.

Down in Texas a young third-generation Baptist minister, Luther Holcomb, executive director of the Greater Dallas Council of Churches, suggested answers. He proposed to former Texas Attorney General Gerald Mann, a devout

John F. Kennedy's Year

Methodist layman who was state campaign manager for Kennedy-Johnson, a gathering of ministers of different faiths to hear a statement by the presidential candidate with a question-and-answer session to follow. It should not be a staged affair, Holcomb insisted. There would be no rehearsals. The audience must not be composed entirely or even largely of ministers who served privileged congregations; representatives of minor sects must be included. The candidate should agree to answer any question bearing on the issue.

Holcomb and Mann took the idea to Washington. It was discussed and eventually approved by Kennedy's advisers and by the candidate. An invitation to discuss his religion went to Kennedy from the Greater Houston Ministerial Association. On the evening of September 12 he stood before three hundred ministers in the Rice Hotel ballroom to state his belief "in an America that is officially neither Catholic, Protestant nor Jewish."

"I believe in an America," he said, "where the separation of church and state is absolute—where no Catholic prelate would tell the President (should he be a Catholic) how to act and no Protestant minister would tell his parishioners for whom to vote—where no church or church school is granted any public funds or political preference—and where no man is denied public office merely because his religion differs from the President who might appoint him or the people who might elect him."

His address was short—less than two thousand words—and Kennedy delivered it in his most effective style, crisp and forthright, serious without portentousness. He knew this could well be the make-or-break speech of the campaign, but if the knowledge made him nervous, nothing in his manner indicated it.

When he had finished his statement, questions came. Most

of them were hostile, but he answered all without any attempt at evasion. Yes, as President he would stand for the right of free religious practice anywhere in the world without regard to doctrine or geography. No, he would not ask Cardinal Cushing of Boston to send the Vatican his endorsement of separation of church and state because, just as he refused to accept the right of any ecclesiastical official to tell him what to do as President, he also did not propose to "ask Cardinal Cushing to ask the Vatican to take some action." No, he would not accept Church direction in public life. If he found any conflict between his religion and the responsibility of the presidency, he would resign the office. But he expressed confidence that there would be no conflict, no effort at interference by the Roman Catholic Church.

At times Kennedy was interrupted by applause as he replied to these and other questions. Most members of his audience were favorably impressed by his candor, although one high-ranking member of the Catholic hierarchy told Holcomb the candidate sounded like "a damned good Protestant" and Dr. W. A. Criswell, pastor of the First Baptist Church of Dallas, the largest Southern Baptist congregation in the nation, said, "Senator Kennedy is either a poor Catholic or he is stringing people along." But they were in the minority.

With this one speech, well covered by the press and widely broadcast during the remainder of the campaign, Kennedy effectively disposed of the religious issue. The bigots were still against him, but the market for their vitriol was sharply curtailed.

(After President Kennedy's assassination in November 1963, Steve Smith, his brother-in-law, asked Holcomb to trace down a tape recording of the program for inclusion in the John F. Kennedy Library in Boston. Holcomb was able to do so, although not without much difficulty.)

John F. Kennedy's Year

The second event of profound importance in the campaign was the series of four "great debates" between Kennedy and Nixon.

Their impact was surprising, even startling, in view of the fact that these television programs scarcely deserved to be called great and were not really debates as the word is generally understood. But at times nine out of every ten television sets in the country were turned on to the screened meetings of the two candidates. What the viewers and listeners saw and heard on September 26 and October 7, 13, and 21 massively affected their voting.

Nixon's advisers had urged him not to agree to these meetings with Kennedy, less because they felt their candidate could not hold his own than because they considered it a mistake for the vice-president to upgrade the senator's prestige by accepting him as an equal worthy of engaging in debate. They were right in their advice, if wrong in their reasons for it.

In the first meeting, broadcast from Chicago over the CBS network, the discussion was on domestic issues. Kennedy had prepared himself by hours of brain work with his bright young aides. They tried to find the answer to almost any question that could conceivably be raised either by his adversary or by the panel of television reporters who were permitted to quiz the candidates after their opening statements. Nixon had all too obviously not undertaken such thorough preparation. Again and again he expressed agreement with goals Kennedy put forward and said he disagreed only about the methods used to attain them. Both made speeches that for the most part were already becoming familiar, Kennedy talking about getting "America moving again," Nixon pleading for the American people to choose him as the candidate who could keep peace with honor and maintain Eisenhower's record. Their big differences were in their methods of presentation. The Republican spoke as if he were engaged in a high-school debate with a watchful coach carefully scoring points. He talked to Kennedy and the reporters in the studio. The Democrat talked to the vast audience out there in their living rooms, often sliding away from the direct impact of a question in order to discuss an issue he wanted to impress on his unseen listeners.

The two men might have come out even, or nearly so, if their discussions had been covered only by radio. But the merciless eye of television saw them in glaring contrast: Kennedy poised, cool, occasionally smiling, letting his prep school and Harvard manners show to exactly the right extent; Nixon, haggard from a recent illness, the great black circles of his eyes giving him a glowering expression, the darkness of his beard showing beneath the skin of his earnestly sweating face, his tenseness revealed by nervous gestures. It was an evening of total disaster for the vice-president.

He did somewhat better on the three debates that followed, which were concerned with foreign affairs, monetary policies, organized labor, and other matters. But it was too late. Nixon never was able to gain back what he had lost in the beginning, when tens of millions of Americans saw him looking like a loser and Kennedy like a winner.

The third factor of overriding significance was simply the presence of Lyndon Johnson on the Democratic ticket.

Even after he had received the vice-presidential nomination, the Democrats were worried about the South. In August, Kennedy and Johnson called on Harry Byrd in the hope that this symbol of southern conservatism would give them his blessing. The patriarchal Virginia senator talked with them amiably enough—he was fond of both—but then, to their consternation, said he had not supported a national Democratic ticket since 1936 and, the party having continued to depart from principles sacred to him, he would not change his course this year.

This was a blow, but worse was to come. For a time it seemed that Johnson would hurt rather than help the ticket in the very area he was expected to deliver to the Democrats. Southern conservatism was on the rise. Noisy opponents of any civil-rights measures raised the old cry that Johnson was a traitor to the South. Former supporters said that to them "LBJ" had a new meaning: "Let's Beat Judas." Right-wing newspaper editorialists called for defeat of "the Yankee from Boston and the turncoat from Austin."

Kennedy and Johnson had agreed that the vice-presidential candidate would campaign mainly in the South, although by no means to the exclusion of appearances in other sections. In October the Texan and his wife, along with thirty-five staff people and thirty reporters, got aboard an eleven-car special train and started a swing through the South. Johnson's purpose was twofold: to bring himself before as many southern voters as possible and to prod reluctant southern politicians into open support of the ticket.

Some of the reporters poked good-natured fun at what they called the Cornpone Special, which rumbled through Dixie with the song "The Yellow Rose of Texas" blaring from loudspeakers and Johnson pumping his arms and shouting the perfervid political oratory dear to the hearts of southerners. The newsmen had to concede that the trip was effective. On the whole, the candidate drew good crowds. As the journey continued they grew increasingly responsive. Johnson stressed the Catholic issue, following Kennedy's example of appealing to his listeners to show the world that they were not bigots. On civil rights he pledged a guarantee of "constitutional rights for all Americans, no matter where they live"—the last clause subtly reminding his audiences that he, like they, knew the South was not the only place where racial discrimination existed. He ridiculed Nixon as a man who could have his mind changed overnight on basic issues by the persuasion of a Rockefeller. He said the Republicans under Eisenhower had used the South as a golf course for the last eight years. His speeches were crowd pleasers.

By Johnson's count, 1,247 southern politicians came aboard the train. He lobbied intensely with each of them on behalf of the Democratic slate.

He felt better about the South when the trip came to an end, but he was met with bad news in Texas. Public-opinion polls showed the state almost evenly divided between people who said they would vote Democratic and those who said they would vote Republican. A loss in his home state would be personally disastrous to Johnson even if the Democrats won nationally, which he doubted they could do without Texas.

The candidate's mood was understandably less than frolicsome when he arrived in Dallas on November 4 to speak at a Democratic rally at the Adolphus Hotel. At noon he and Mrs. Johnson came across the street from the Baker Hotel to find several hundred vociferously anti-Johnson Texans packed into the Adolphus lobby. Many were women. Some held aloft placards bearing slogans which ranged in content from the silly to the insulting. They surged around Johnson and his wife, encouraged by Bruce Alger, the Dallas Republican congressman, who kept repeating, "Get in closer, closer. We'll be on television all over the country." The congressman himself, a handsome Galahad to the young wives and daughters of rich Dallas men, carried a sign with the accusation "LBJ Sold out to Yankee Socialists."

Nothing of the casual give and take to which politicians

are accustomed was evident. Most of the people in the hotel lobby were amateurs in politics, engaged in what Alger and others like him assured them was a crusade for better government. Crusaders are quick to anger, and members of the jostling assembly were hot with righteous wrath. They were close to physical violence as the Johnsons, arm in arm, moved slowly and with dignity through their ranks. Women spat at them; men yelled insults. Johnson's face wore a look of rigidly controlled fury. His wife smiled tightly and without mirth. The crowd sullenly made way before them. Finally the couple reached the staircase leading to the second floor and ascended it.

Bruce Alger was right about the television coverage. That night and the next day the whole nation saw what had happened in Dallas. But the result was not what Alger had expected. He was in tune only with the sentiment of Dallas Main Street bankers and merchants and restless women living in the suburbs. Outraged southern chivalry took over. Four days later the Kennedy-Johnson ticket carried all but four states of the South and one of them, Mississippi, was won not by the Republicans but by an independent segregationist ticket of electors who eventually voted for Byrd in the electoral college.

In the country as a whole the margin of Democratic victory was excruciatingly thin. Kennedy-Johnson received 49.7 per cent of the popular vote, Nixon-Lodge 49.6 per cent, the remainder going to minority-party candidates. The Democrats won twenty-three states with 303 electoral votes, the Republicans twenty-six states with 219 electoral votes.

The Democratic victory would almost surely have been impossible without the South. The party could not have taken such states as Alabama, Georgia, Louisiana, North Carolina, South Carolina, and especially Texas if Johnson had not been on the ticket with the Catholic Yankee from Massachusetts. Kennedy's political judgment was completely vindicated.

The Democratic victory in most of the southern states was the final link in a chain of events that made John F. Kennedy the thirty-fifth President of the United States and inaugurated a new era in the political history of the nation.

*

BIBLIOGRAPHY

Abels, Jules, *The Truman Scandals*. Chicago: Regnery, 1956.

Acheson, Dean, *A Democrat Looks at His Party*. New York: Harper & Brothers, 1955.

Adams, Sherman, *Firsthand Report*. New York: Harper & Brothers, 1961.

Allen, George E., *Presidents Who Have Known Me*. New York: Simon & Schuster, 1960.

Allen, Robert S., and Shannon, William V., *The Truman Merry-Go-Round*. New York: Vanguard Press, 1950.

Anderson, Jack, and Blumenthal, Fred, *The Kefauver Story*. New York: Dial Press, 1956.

Barkley, Alben W., *That Reminds Me—*. Garden City, N.Y.: Doubleday & Company, 1954.

Bell, Jack, *The Splendid Misery*. Garden City, N.Y.: Doubleday & Company, 1960.

———— *The Johnson Treatment*. New York: Harper & Row, 1965.

Biographical Directory of the American Congress, 1774–1961. Washington, D.C.: Government Printing Office, 1961.

Bibliography

Bowen, Catherine Drinker, *Miracle at Philadelphia*. Boston: Little Brown and Company, 1966.

Brown, John Mason, *Through These Men*. New York: Harper & Brothers, 1956.

Brown, Stuart Gerry, *Adlai E. Stevenson*. Woodbury, N.Y.: Barron's Woodbury Press, 1964.

Byrnes, James F., *All in One Lifetime*. New York: Harper & Brothers, 1958.

Cater, Douglass, *The Fourth Branch of Government*. Boston: Houghton Mifflin, 1959.

Childs, Marquis, *Eisenhower: Captive Hero*. New York: Harcourt, Brace & Company, 1958.

Congressional Directory, 1945–1960 editions. Washington, D.C.: Government Printing Office.

Congressional Record, 1945–1960 editions Washington, D.C.: Government Printing Office.

Connally, Tom, *My Name Is Tom Connally*. New York: Thomas Y. Crowell Co., 1954.

Cullinan, Gerald, *The Post Office Department*. New York: Frederick A. Praeger, 1968.

Daniels, Jonathan, *The Man of Independence*. Philadelphia and New York: J. B. Lippincott Company, 1950.

Doherty, William C., *Mailman USA*. New York: David McKay Company, 1960.

Donovan, Robert J., *Eisenhower: The Inside Story*. New York: Harper & Brothers, 1956.

Dorough, C. Dwight, *Mr. Sam*. New York: Random House, 1962.

Eisenhower, Dwight D., *Mandate for Change: 1953–1956*. Garden City, N.Y.: Doubleday & Company, 1963.

———— *Waging Peace*. Garden City, N.Y.: Doubleday & Company, 1965.

Encyclopaedia Britannica. Chicago: Encyclopaedia Britannica, Inc., 1961.

Ernst, Margaret S., *In a Word*. New York: Alfred A. Knopf, 1944.

Evans, Rowland, and Novak, Robert, *Lyndon B. Johnson: The Exercise of Power.* New York: New American Library, 1966.

Halsey, Margaret, *The Folks at Home.* New York: Simon & Schuster, 1952.

Hays, Brooks, *A Southern Moderate Speaks.* Chapel Hill, N.C.: University of North Carolina, 1959.

Hillman, William, *Mr. President.* New York: Farrar, Straus & Young, 1952.

Hughes, Emmet John, *The Ordeal of Power.* New York: Atheneum Publishers, 1963.

Ives, Elizabeth Stevenson, and Dolson, Hildegarde, *My Brother Adlai.* New York: William and Co., 1956.

Janeway, Eliot, *The Economics of Crisis.* New York: Weybright and Talley, 1967.

Kevin, McCann, *Man from Abilene.* New York: Doubleday & Company, 1952.

Kilman, Ed, and Wright, Theon, *Hugh Roy Cullen.* New York: Prentice-Hall, 1954.

Krock, Arthur, *In the Nation: 1932–1966.* New York: McGraw-Hill Book Company, 1966.

Larson, Arthur, *A Republican Looks at His Party.* New York: Harper & Brothers, 1956.

————— *Eisenhower.* New York: Charles Scribner's Sons, 1968.

Learned, Henry Barrett, *The President's Cabinet.* New Haven: Yale University Press, 1912.

Longley, Marjoe, Silverstein, Louis, and Tower, Samuel A. (eds.), *America's Taste 1851–1959.* New York: Simon & Schuster, 1960.

Lynes, Russell, *The Domesticated Americans.* New York: Harper & Row, 1962.

MacNeil, Neil, *Forge of Democracy: The House of Representatives.* New York: David McKay Company, 1962.

Muller, Herbert J., *Adlai Stevenson: A Study in Values.* New York: Harper & Row, 1967.

Martin, Joe, as told to Robert J. Donovan, *My Fifty Years in Politics*. New York: McGraw-Hill Book Company, 1960.

Neustadt, Richard E., *Presidential Power: The Politics of Leadership*. New York: John Wiley & Sons, 1960.

Newsweek, 1945–1960 editions.

New York *Times*, 1945–1960 editions.

Nicholson, Harold, *The Later Years: 1945–1962*. New York: Atheneum, 1968.

Phillips, Cabell, *The Truman Presidency*. New York: Macmillan Company, 1966.

Raymond, Jack, *Power at the Pentagon*. New York: Harper & Row, 1964.

Ridgway, Matthew B., *The Korean War*. New York: Doubleday & Company, 1968.

Rovere, Richard H., *The Eisenhower Years*. New York: Farrar, Straus & Cudahy, 1956.

———— *Senator Joe McCarthy*. New York: Harcourt, Brace & Company, 1959.

————, and Schlesinger, Arthur M., Jr., *The General and the President*. New York: Farrar, Straus & Young, 1951.

Sann, Paul, *Fads, Follies and Delusions of the American People*. New York: Crown, 1967.

Scott, Hugh, *Come to the Party*. New York: Prentice-Hall, 1968.

Steinberg, Alfred, *The Man from Missouri*. New York: G. P. Putnam's Sons, 1962.

Stevenson, Adlai, *The New America*. New York: Harper & Brothers, 1957.

———— *Friends and Enemies*. New York: Harper & Brothers, 1959.

Simpson, George. *A Book About American Politics*. New York: Harper & Brothers, 1952.

Time, 1945–1960 editions.

Truman, Harry S., *Memoirs, Vol. 1: Years of Decision*. New York: Doubleday & Company, 1955.

_____ *Memoirs, Vol. II: Years of Trial and Hope.*
New York: Doubleday & Company, 1956.

Washington Post, 1945–1960 editions.

Washington Star, 1945–1960 editions.

Weaver, John D., *The Great Experiment.* Boston: Little, Brown and Company, 1965.

Wheeler, Burton K., with Healy, Paul F., *Yankee from the West.* New York: Doubleday & Company, 1962.

White, Theodore H., *The Making of the President, 1960.* New York: Atheneum House, 1961.

White, William S., *The Taft Story.* New York: Harper & Brothers, 1954.

_____ *The Citadel: The Story of the U.S. Senate.* New York: Harper & Brothers, 1956.

_____ *The Professional: Lyndon B. Johnson.* Boston: Houghton Mifflin Company, 1964.

INDEX

Acheson, Dean G., 98, 103, 104, 116, 117, 118, 121–22, 161, 180, 196, 308

Adams, John (army counsel), 198

Adams, John (vice-president), 6

Adams, Sherman, 132, 164–65, 183, 200, 208, 235, 242, 250, 259, 272, 281, 288–97

Aiken, George D., 46, 270, 281

Albright, Bob, 80

Alcorn, Hugh Meade, Jr., 295

Alexander, Holmes, 229

Alger, Bruce R., 278, 350–51

Allen, George E., 4, 9–10, 13, 25, 32, 56, 132, 164, 234

Allen, Mrs. George E., 234

Alsop, Joe, 76

Anderson, Clinton P., 15, 270, 286, 310–12

Anderson, Robert B., 265, 285–86, 301

Arvey, Jake, 63, 137, 148, 252, 333

Ayer, Frederick, Jr., 79

Bailey, John M., 63

Baker, Bobby Gene, 219, 244, 335, 337

Ball, Joseph H., 90

Barkley, Alben W., 3, 5, 7, 22, 37, 70–71, 72, 84–85, 89, 91, 136–38, 145, 146, 148

Barkley, Mrs. Alben W., 148

Barnes, James M., 5

Baruch, Bernard M., 7, 13

Beauchamp, Emerson, 145

Bender, George, 210

Benson, Ezra Taft, 163, 233, 287

Benton, William, 110

Biddle, Francis, 14

Biemiller, Andrew, 302

Biffle, Leslie L., 34, 70, 145

Black, James C., 164

Index

Blake, Thomas Dawes, 137, 139
Bloom, Sol, 11
Bohlen, Charles E., 180–81
Boyle, Bill, 75, 95, 124
Brewer, Basil, 130–31·
Bricker, John W., 68, 69, 188–90, 235, 297
Bridges, Styles, 166, 180, 205
Brown, Clarence J., 44, 141
Brown, Edmund G. ("Pat"), 333
Brownell, Herbert, 66, 69, 75, 162–63, 189
Browning, Robert, 156
Brundage, Percival F., 258
Bryan, William Jennings, 44
Burgess, W. Randolph, 163
Burke, Thomas A., 210
Burns, John A., 303–4
Bush, Dr. Vannevar, 275
Butler, John Marshall, 107, 119
Butler, Paul M., 213–14, 241, 263, 285, 304, 315, 324
Byrd, Harry F., 176, 222, 225, 256, 258, 265, 348–49, 351
Byrd, Robert C., 326
Byrnes, James F., 2, 5, 7, 13–14, 30–32, 92
Byrnes, John W., 300

Cannon, Clarence, 89, 258, 260
Capehart, Homer E., 223
Carlson, Frank, 204
Carter, Amon, 158
Case, Francis H., 204
Castro, Fidel, 312–13, 339

Chambers, Whittaker, 98
Chapman, Oscar L., 75, 330
Chavez, Dennis, 27
Chiang Kai-shek, 60, 99, 108, 215
Church, Frank, 270
Churchill, Winston, 12, 15, 52, 105, 180, 185
Clark, Joseph S., 305, 320–21
Clark, Tom C., 14, 35, 38
Clay, General Lucius, 132
Clayton, William L., 38
Clements, Earle, 145, 218–19, 229, 254, 284
Clifford, Clark M., 20, 33–34, 36, 38, 48, 57–58, 75, 122, 317, 331
Cochran, Jacqueline, 132
Cohn, Roy, 182, 196, 200–204
Coleman, Thomas E., 141
Collins, LeRoy, 337
Connally, John B., 246, 330
Connally, Tom, 11, 31, 116, 126, 217, 220
Connelly, Marc (quoted), 127
Connelly, Matt, 9, 75
Connelly, Philip, 19
Coolidge, Calvin, 8, 169, 312
Cooper, John Sherman, 81, 343
Costello, Frank, 126
Cotton, Norris, 311
Cox, Gene, 62
Criswell, Dr. W. A., 346
Crump, Ed, 90
Cullen, Hugh Roy, 129, 189
Cullinan, Gerald, 79
Cushing, Richard Cardinal, 346

Daley, Richard J., 335
Daniel, Price, 222, 270, 318, 336
Daniels, Jonathan, 8
Dante, 250
Davidson, C. Girard, 48
Davis, William H., 49
Dawes, Charles G., 8
Dawson, Donald, 123
DeSapio, Carmine, 241–42
Deschler, Lewis, 5
Dewey, Thomas E., 38–39, 44,
    46, 54–55, 60, 61, 66, 67, 68,
    69, 70, 75, 76, 77–82, 129, 130,
    141, 168
Dewey, Mrs. Thomas E., 54
Dirksen, Everett, 198, 205, 300,
    301, 302, 306, 308
Disraeli, Benjamin, 156
Docking, George, 334
Dodge, Joseph M., 178
Doolittle, Lieutenant General
    James, 275
Doud, Mrs. John S., 234
Doughton, Robert, 89
Douglas, Helen Gahagan, 107–8
Douglas, Paul H., 90, 127, 147,
    286, 320
Douglas, William O., 4, 70, 119
Driscoll, Alfred E., 132
Duff, James H., 141
Dulles, Allen, 275–76
Dulles, John Foster, 93, 119,
    160–61, 180, 189, 192–94, 195,
    215, 242, 313
Durkin, Martin P., 162

Early, Stephen, 14, 137

Eastland, James O., 62
Eaton, Charles A., 11
Edwards, India, 330
Eisenhower, Dwight David, 56,
    61–64, 100, 129–32, 141–44,
    150–53, 155–58, 159, 160–70,
    177–79, 183, 184, 185, 186–94,
    196, 199–200, 205, 206–10,
    213–17, 222, 224, 225, 227,
    230, 231–36, 238–39, 241–42,
    245–46, 248–49, 250, 251–54,
    255, 256, 258, 259–62, 265,
    267–72, 275, 276, 279–81, 283,
    284–88, 291, 293, 295, 296,
    297, 298–300, 301–7, 309, 310,
    313, 320, 322, 338, 339, 340,
    341, 343, 347, 350
Eisenhower, Mrs. Dwight D.,
    132, 234
Eisenhower, Edgar M., 259, 293
Ellender, Allen J., 283
Ervin, Samuel J., Jr., 204
Evans, Silliman, 134, 138
Ewing, Oscar R., 48

Falkenberg, Jinx, 131–32
Fannin, Paul J., 343
Farley, James A., 44–45
Fell, James, 149
Fields, Richard, 38
Fisher, Fred, 202–3
Flanders, Ralph E., 106, 204, 216
Fleeson, Doris, 228
Flemming, Arthur S., 301
Flynn, Edwin M., 4
Forrestal, James V., 16, 23, 28,
    52, 115

Fox, John, 290
Freeman, Orville L., 316, 333
Fulbright, J. William, 39–40, 123, 148, 226, 286

Gabrielson, Guy George, 100
Gallup, George, 185
Gardner, Max, 38
Gavin, Lieutenant General James H., 275
George, Walter, 89, 190, 216–17, 225, 226
Gildersleeve, Virginia, 11
Goldfine, Bernard, 289–96
Goldwater, Barry, 171, 256, 295, 342–43
Gore, Albert, 205, 247, 248, 270, 286, 321, 334
Graham, Philip, 334
Green, Dwight, 69
Green, Theodore Francis, 105, 304–5
Gruenther, General Alfred M., 164

Hagerty, James C., 168–69, 200, 208, 234, 235, 249, 339
Hague, Frank, 63
Hall, Leonard W., 208, 235, 250
Halleck, Charles A., 44, 69, 231–32, 233, 299–300, 301
Halsey, Margaret (quoted), 159
Hannegan, Robert E., 3, 4, 5, 14, 38, 48, 58
Hardeman, Dorsey, 318
Harding, Warren G., 169
Hardy, Porter, Jr., 127

Harlow, Bryce, 166
Harriman, Averell, 11, 138, 139, 145, 146, 147, 210, 239, 241, 244, 245, 297
Harrison, George, 18
Hartley, Fred, Jr., 47
Herter, Christian A., 235–36, 249, 250
Hickenlooper, Bourke B., 105, 106
Hill, Lister, 286
Hiss, Alger, 98, 118
Ho Chi Minh, 191
Hobby, Oveta Culp, 163
Hoey, Clyde, 96–98, 124
Holaday, William M., 276
Holcomb, Luther, 344–46
Holifield, Chet, 321
Holmes, Oliver Wendell, 156
Hoover, Herbert, 169, 187, 284, 309
Hopkins, Harry, 7, 16, 32, 33
House, Colonel E. M., 39
Hruska, Roman L., 293
Hughes, Charles Evans, 39
Hughes, Emmet John, 297
Hume, Paul, 121
Humphrey, George M., 160, 161, 162, 164, 178, 189, 242, 256–58, 264–65, 285
Humphrey, Hubert, 62, 71, 90, 172, 173, 176, 216, 222, 223, 227, 247, 304, 308, 312, 314, 315–16, 317, 320–21, 322, 323–29, 330, 333, 334
Hunt, James V., 96, 97
Hutcheson, Thad, 343

Ickes, Harold L., 16, 28–30, 32, 62
Ingalls, David, 141
Inouye, Daniel K., 304
Ives, Irving M., 46

Jackson, Henry M., 334
Jacobsen, Jake, 332
Janeway, Eliot, 251–52
Jenkins, Ray, 201–2
Jenkins, Walter, 220, 244, 326
Jenner, William E., 105, 118, 155
Johnson, Edwin C., 94, 95, 96, 181, 204
Johnson, Louis A., 75, 115
Johnson, Lyndon, 2, 90, 94–96, 127, 148, 158, 171–77, 180, 181, 183, 187–88, 189, 190, 191, 193, 205, 209, 210–12, 213–31, 236–37, 238–39, 241, 242–48, 254, 258, 260–71, 273–77, 279–80, 281–82, 283, 285–87, 288, 297, 301–7, 309, 311–12, 314, 317–19, 320–23, 329–33, 334–38, 348–52
Johnson, Mrs. Lyndon B. (Lady Bird), 230, 335, 349, 350–51
Johnson, Sam Houston, 229
Johnston, Olin D., 63, 89
Jones, Alton, 164
Jones, Jesse, 6
Jonkel, Jon M., 107

Keating, Kenneth B., 295, 297
Kefauver, Estes, 90, 125–27, 133–35, 138, 145, 146, 147–48, 239, 240, 242, 245, 247, 248, 253, 270, 282, 283, 304, 316
Kefauver, Mrs. Estes, 135
Kennedy, Edward M., 324
Kennedy, John F., 99, 131, 205, 247–48, 282–83, 297, 303, 304, 312, 313, 314–15, 316, 317, 322, 323–29, 330, 331–38, 342, 344–52
Kennedy, Mrs. John F. (Jacqueline), 315
Kennedy, Joseph P., 282, 335
Kennedy, Mrs. Joseph P. (Rose), 324
Kennedy, Robert F., 232, 315, 324, 332, 334, 335, 357
Kerr, Robert S., 90, 139, 145, 242, 286, 337
Keyserling, Leon H., 48
Khrushchev, Nikita, 274, 338
Killian, James R., Jr., 275
King, Cecil, 124
King, Mackenzie, 7, 15
Kinsey, Dr. Alfred O. (quoted), 128
Kleberg, Richard M., 173
Knight, Goodwin, 236
Knowland, William F., 185, 190, 205, 215, 219, 222, 226, 227, 228, 235, 248, 258, 281, 293, 295, 297, 300
Krock, Arthur, 22, 87, 109, 293
Krug, Julius A., 32–33, 35

La Follette, Robert M., Jr., 102
Lahey, Edwin A., 151–52

Langer, William ("Wild Bill"), 312
Langlie, Arthur, 250
Larson, Arthur, 262–63
Laski, Harold J. (quoted), 61
Lawrence, David, 332, 335
Leahy, Admiral William D., 7
Lewis, John L., 35–36, 49, 62
Lincoln, Abraham, 112, 121, 149
Lincoln, Gould, 228
Lindley, Ernest K., 64
Lippman, Walter, 27, 64, 224
Littell, Norman M., 29
Lodge, Henry Cabot, Jr., 39, 105, 106, 130–31, 141, 144, 343
Long, Huey P., 90
Long, Russell B., 90
Loveless, Herschel, 334
Lucas, Scott, 89–90, 91, 93, 94, 107, 119, 148
Luce, Clare Booth (Mrs. Henry), 67–68, 307–9
Luce, Henry, 309

MacArthur, General Douglas, 55, 66–67, 111–21, 185
McCardle, Carl, 80
McCarran, Pat, 89, 127, 180, 181
McCarthy, Eugene, 316, 332
McCarthy, Joseph Raymond, 101–111, 118, 156, 180, 181–84, 195–206, 211, 227–28, 305
McClellan, John L., 232
McCormack, John, 37, 91, 284, 337
McCormick, Robert, 69
McCrary, Tex, 131–32, 294

McElroy, Neil H., 275
McFarland, Ernest W., 119, 171
McGrath, J. Howard, 58, 63, 72, 75
McGrory, Mary, 218
McKay, Douglas, 163
McKeller, Kenneth, 89
McKim, Eddie, 10
McKinney, Frank, 138, 148, 153
McMahon, Brien, 105
McNamara, Pat, 305, 320
Mann, Gerald C., 344–45
Mansfield, Mike, 192, 284, 337
Maragon, John, 96, 97
Marshall, George C., 7, 32, 51, 108, 109, 110, 113, 115, 155, 156
Martin, Joseph W., Jr., 22, 44, 55, 67, 79, 116, 117, 167, 171, 177, 185, 231–32, 250–51, 298–300
Matthews, Herbert, 312–13
Matthews, J. B., 182–83
Meade, James M., 39
Mencken, H. L., 182
Mendès-France, Pierre, 195
Metcalf, Lee, 321
Meyner, Robert, 333
Minton, Sherman, 3
Mitchell, James P., 285, 301
Mitchell, Stephen, 153, 213
Monroney, A. S. Mike, 148, 314
Montgomery, Ruth, 259
Morgan, Gerald, 165–66, 290
Morgenthau, Henry, Jr., 15
Morhouse, Judson, 340

Morse, Wayne, 40, 46, 91, 170, 210, 216, 222, 305, 307–9, 329
Morton, Thruston B., 284
Mundt, Karl F., 199, 201
Murphy, Charles S., 48
Murray, James E., 172
Murray, Philip, 49
Myers, Francis J., 71

Neuberger, Richard L., 207, 223
Nicholson, Harold, 118, 119
Nixon, Richard M., 39, 108, 144, 189, 194, 199, 200, 206–7, 208, 209, 210, 230, 248–50, 254, 283, 284–85, 295, 300, 313, 319, 338, 341–44, 347–48, 350

O'Brien, Lawrence F., 324
O'Donnell, Kenneth, 324
O'Dwyer, William, 49, 63, 126
Olds, Leland, 94–96
O'Mahoney, Joseph C., 270

Pappas, Thomas A., 79
Patterson, Robert P., 23
Pauley, Edwin W., 4, 28–30, 32
Pearson, Drew, 86–87
Pendergast, Tom, 2–3
Pepper, Claude D., 62, 63–64
Percy, Charles E., 338, 342
Peress, Dr. Irving, 197–99
Perkins, Frances, 14–15
Perón, Juan, 86–87
Perry, Arthur C., 220
Persons, Major General Wilton B. ("Jerry"), 165, 200, 290
Pew, Joseph N., Jr., 42

Porter, Charles O., 313
Porter, H. J. ("Jack"), 143, 157
Porter, Paul A., 38
Potter, Charles, 199, 204, 293
Powell, Adam Clayton, 313
Proxmire, William, 305–6, 320

Radford, Admiral Arthur W., 192–93, 194
Randall, Clarence B., 272
Rankin, John E., 89
Rauh, Joseph L., Jr., 241
Rayburn, Dick, 16
Rayburn, Sam, 5, 6, 7, 16–18, 31, 37, 44, 48, 61, 71–72, 88, 91, 93, 98, 111, 116, 119, 124–25, 139, 146, 147, 148, 157, 158, 171, 175, 177, 184, 187–88, 196, 207, 208–9, 210, 211, 212, 214, 215, 225–26, 230, 231, 241, 242–43, 244, 245–47, 250, 260, 265, 278, 280, 281, 284, 285, 288, 297, 299–300, 301–7, 314, 315, 318, 321, 323, 324, 335–36
Reece, Carroll, 40, 141
Reed, Daniel A., 178, 185
Reedy, George, 4, 190, 214, 217, 220, 230, 244, 274, 306
Rhee, Syngman, 339
Richardson, Sid, 132
Ridgway, General Matthew B., 117
Roberts, Clifford, 164
Robertson, David, 18
Robinson, William, 164
Rockefeller, Nelson, 297, 319, 338, 340–43, 350

Rodin, Auguste, 250
Rogers, William P., 182, 301
Roosevelt, Eleanor (Mrs. Franklin D.), 5, 7, 10, 16, 49, 241
Roosevelt, Elliott, 62
Roosevelt, Franklin Delano, 1–2, 3, 4, 5, 6, 8, 9, 10, 11, 12, 13, 14, 15, 16, 17, 18, 22, 26, 28, 30, 33, 36, 38, 44, 58, 70, 83, 89, 94, 169–70, 174, 180, 187, 229, 308, 313, 327
Roosevelt, Franklin D., Jr., 328
Roosevelt, James, 62
Roosevelt, Theodore, 42
Roper, Elmo, 78
Rosenman, Samuel I., 18, 20, 25, 33, 245
Ross, Charlie, 9
Rovere, Richard H., 81
Rowe, James H., Jr., 244, 317, 330
Russell, Richard B., 51–52, 72, 121, 137, 138–39, 145, 146, 172, 192–93, 222, 244, 264, 268–69, 273, 274, 322

Salinger, Pierre, 324
Saltonstall, Leverett, 166, 167, 201, 205, 222, 227
Schine, G. David, 182, 196, 200, 202
Schwellenbach, Lewis B., 3, 15, 48
Scott, Hugh, 100
Seaton, Frederick A., 301
Seward, William H., 121
Shaffer, Sam, 228

Shaw, George Bernard, 156
Sheppard, Morris, 174, 220
Shields, Robert, 38
Shivers, Allan, 157, 242–43
Short, Dewey, 118
Shriver, Sargent, 334
Siegel, Gerald, 220, 274
Simpson, Richard, 292–93
Smathers, George A., 205, 270
Smith, Alexander, 106
Smith, Alfred E., 315
Smith, Margaret Chase, 106, 312
Smith, Stephen, 346
Snyder, General Howard, 234
Snyder, John W., 3, 6, 20
Snyder, Murray, 234
Sorenson, Theodore C., 324
Sparkman, John J., 148, 157, 181, 286
Sprague, Russel, 75
Stalin, Joseph, 12, 55, 107, 180
Stans, Maurice H., 301
Stark, Lloyd C., 3
Stassen, Harold E., 11, 55, 61, 66, 67, 68, 129, 133, 144, 162, 248–50
Steelman, John R., 25, 34
Stennis, John C., 204
Stettinius, Edward R., Jr., 10, 13
Stevens, Robert T., 196, 197, 198–200
Stevens, Thaddeus, 77
Stevenson, Adlai, 136–37, 138, 145, 146, 147, 148, 149–50, 151, 153–54, 155, 156, 157, 158, 162, 183–84, 208, 210, 213, 239, 240–41, 242, 244,

245, 246–47, 251–54, 283, 292, 314, 317, 319, 326, 331, 332, 333
Stevenson, Adlai (grandfather), 149
Stewart, Tom, 90
Stimson, Henry L., 16
Stone, Harlan, 6
Strauss, Lewis L., 301, 309–12
Summerfield, Arthur E., 163, 264, 301
Swift, Jonathan (quoted), 156
Symington, Stuart, 124, 239, 276, 297, 304, 312, 314, 316–17, 322–23, 326, 331, 334

Taft, Robert A., 22, 34, 41–43, 44, 45, 46, 47, 50, 51, 52, 53, 54, 55, 57, 58, 61, 66–68, 75, 79–80, 81, 93, 105, 129, 130, 132, 134, 141–44, 151–53, 156, 162, 163, 166–67, 171, 176–77, 178–81, 183, 184, 210, 309
Taft, Mrs. Robert A., 42, 80
Taft, William Howard, 42
Talbott, Harold, 160, 232, 233
Talmadge, Herman E., 85, 217, 305
Taylor, George W., 49
Taylor, Glen H., 74
Teller, Edward, 275, 311
Temple, Shirley, 61
Thompson, Frank, 321
Thurmond, Strom, 73, 82, 85
Thye, Edward J., 144, 281
Tobey, Charles William, 28–29
Tobin, Dan, 38

Truman, Harry S., 2–45, 48–54, 56–60, 63–66, 68, 70–78, 80–94, 96, 98–100, 103, 104, 108, 111–15, 117, 118, 121–27, 129, 130, 133, 135–39, 145–48, 153–57, 161, 167, 170, 172, 178, 179, 186, 193, 195, 207, 216, 239, 241, 245, 246, 266, 284, 309, 314, 315, 317, 322, 330
Truman, Mrs. Harry S. (Bess), 5, 10, 80, 97, 121, 122
Truman, Mrs. John A. (mother), 7, 10, 13, 146
Truman, Margaret, 5, 80, 121
Truman, Mary, 7, 13
Tully, Grace, 229
Tunney, Gene, 45
Tydings, Millard E., 89, 105, 106, 107

Vance, Cyrus, 274
Vandenberg, Arthur S., 11, 31–32, 43, 52, 55, 66, 68, 69, 93
Vanderbilt, William H., 46
Vardaman, Commodore Jake, 9, 33
Vaughan, Harry, 3, 9, 85, 86, 96–98
Vinson, Carl, 89
Vinson, Fred M., 6, 15, 135–36
Voorhis, Jerry, 39

Wagner, Robert F., 45, 93, 247
Walker, Frank C., 14
Wallace, Henry A., 2, 4, 16, 22, 30–32, 49, 50, 57, 74, 82

Index

Walsh, David I., 39

Warren, Earl, 55, 69, 79, 129, 133, 144, 190

Washington, George, 8, 112

Watkins, Arthur V., 204, 293

Watson, Edwin M. (Pa), 4

Watson, Marvin, 330

Weeks, Sinclair, 163, 189

Weisl, Edwin L., Jr., 273–74

Welch, Joseph H., 201–4

Wetherby, Lawrence W., 145

Wheeler, Burton K., 3

Wherry, Kenneth S., 43, 52, 63, 105

White, Wallace H., Jr., 43

White, William S., 5, 50, 80

Whittington, William M., 89

Wickard, Claude R., 14–15

Williams, Mennen, 337

Willkie, Wendell L., 42, 55, 56

Wilson, Charles E., 161–62, 200, 242, 272

Wilson, Woodrow, 39, 161, 169

Woodward, Stanley, 121

Wright, Fielding, 73

Wyatt, Wilson, 150, 153

Yarborough, Ralph W., 270

Young, E. Merl, 123

Young, Stephen M., 297

Ziffern, Paul, 323

Zweifel, Henry, 142–43

Zwicker, General Ralph W., 197–200, 205

DATE DUE

MAY 29			
Dec 20			
APR 12			
APR 9			
APR 24			
GAYLORD			PRINTED IN U.S.A.